John Orlebar Payne

Records of the English Catholics of 1715

Compiled wholly from original documents

John Orlebar Payne

Records of the English Catholics of 1715
Compiled wholly from original documents

ISBN/EAN: 9783741192753

Manufactured in Europe, USA, Canada, Australia, Japa

Cover: Foto ©Lupo / pixelio.de

Manufactured and distributed by brebook publishing software (www.brebook.com)

John Orlebar Payne

Records of the English Catholics of 1715

RECORDS

OF THE

English Catholics of 1715

COMPILED WHOLLY FROM ORIGINAL DOCUMENTS

EDITED BY

JOHN ORLEBAR PAYNE, M.A.

LONDON: BURNS & OATES, Limited
NEW YORK: CATHOLIC PUBLICATION SOCIETY CO.
1889

PREFACE.

LITTLE, perhaps, need be said by way of introduction to this volume of *Records of the English Catholics of 1715*.

Apart from the great interest and importance attaching to a collection in abstract of nearly four hundred wills and letters of administration with which it opens, the genealogical value of such unpublished and authentic documents will be at once apparent, while the Index, of course, will illustrate this in a way which nothing else can.

Of the two dates given at the end of each will, the first is that of *execution*, and the second that of *probate*. Where not otherwise stated, it may be assumed that probate was granted in the Prerogative Court of Canterbury, Somerset House being naturally the chief source of information. I am also under an obligation to H. F. Burke, Esq., *Somerset Herald*, and to Dr. J. J. Howard, for permission to inspect a MS., the property of Sir John Lawson, Bart., now in course of publication, to which occasional reference is made, and which at the present time is deposited at the College of Arms.

The collection of wills from the Probate Court at Lincoln is of some interest, while from the bulk of the others it is difficult to know what to select as the more noteworthy. Charles Eyston of East Hendred, *e.g.*, gives us a pious confession of faith, and the bequest to his eldest son, of "Bishop Fisher's Staff," possesses a peculiar attraction for us who are now rejoicing at the recent beatifications. The mention, however, of relics, works of art, church plate, valued heirlooms, &c., in such wills as those of Elizabeth Lady Dormer, Walter Fowler, Anne Markham, Francis Prujean, John Vaughan, Frances Progers, Lady Dunbar, and of many more, is frequent enough. We note, too, the bequest of Cardinal Pole's cross by John Pole, to his cousin Francis; that of Belle-tree House to Giles Hussey the artist, by his father John, and "the hanging of green velvet, wrought by the hand of Mary, Queen of Scots," named in Lord Stafford's will.

Then we have the eccentric testators, such as William Plowden, Thomas Hawkins, George Kingsley, &c., notably so the first-named. Lady Gerard would like to remain unburied as long as possible; Mary Porter's daughters must not go to their mother's funeral lest it should injure their health; and the unhappy Lord Waldegrave despises his daughter Henrietta, the widow of seventeen, for marrying John Beard the comedian.

The wills of such as Lord Aston, Robert Needham, Richard Bostock, &c., are pleasing, which is certainly more than can be said of that of Henry, Lord Stafford, whose sole bequest to his widow, of "45 brass half pence to buy her a pullet for her supper," is followed by some observations on her character, and on that of her parents, the notorious Count and Countess de Grammont, which it is still less pleasing to repeat.

There are, of course, many bequests for masses, often enough couched in studiously concealed terms, as in the case of Edmund Adys; while the poor are not forgotten by the Minshull family, and many more, or by John Weston, who regards "the miserable condition of the poor Catholics of England as very deplorable"; and, lastly, the disconsolate Lady Derwentwater gives to "all such as were servants to her dear Lord, and were prisoners on account of the *unhappy rising* . . . for their great sufferings, £20 each".

In passing, however, attention might be called to the wills of two apostates—Francis Poole and Dr. John Purcell. Of the latter, it is worthy of notice, that no less than eight members of his family occur in Cosin's "List," so that the fact of his *own* name thus conspicuous by its *absence* from it affords an indirect proof of the Catholicity of the whole. This, however, touches a question on which we shall have more to say presently. A few early Catholic Mission Registers, and other original documents in private hands, such as the Derby MS., the will of Dorothy Thorold, &c., have kindly been placed at my disposal; and my thanks are due to others also, who have generously helped me with information not otherwise accessible.

A different class of interest, however, unhappily attaches to the greater number of the documents selected from the "Forfeited Estates" Papers at the Record Office, which make up the latter half of this volume; for in many cases the "information" which they afford is supplied by those who, either wearied out by the long course of pains and penalties under which for generations they had been crushed, or—what is more unaccountable — dazzled by the temptation of a paltry reward, bartered the faith to which their forefathers had so gloriously and perseveringly adhered. Indeed, it would almost seem that that mysterious apostacy which so darkens the eighteenth century history of the Church in England, dates its commencement from the proceedings of the Forfeited Estates Commissioners. And the unmitigated contempt with which the adherents of the Old Religion regarded such obscure apostates as Hitchmough, Thomas Fletcher, Edward Shaftoe, William Gibson, and others, is but paralleled by the odious clamouring with which some of these unhappy men from time to time besieged the Commissioners for their reward. Still more revolting, for example, is it to find a mother offering in cold blood to sell the souls of her children for a farm! For we read that the widow of Mr. Richard Butler humbly proposes to become farmer of the estate of her uncle Richard Butler of Rawcliffe, on behalf of her two infant sons, "*whom she offers to be educated Protestants*".

The "Rebellion," however, of 1715 was not only followed by a vigorous punishment of all Catholics who directly took part in it, but it also afforded the Commissioners an additional pretext for seizing any Catholic property upon which they could lay their hands, more particularly of any who had died immediately before the outbreak of the "Rebellion," and whose executors had the administration of an estate that was worth the trouble of sequestration. The lengthened statement of the apostate Francis Brooke relative to the will of Catherine Winford, and the almost romantic story of Sir Henry Fletcher, have been recorded somewhat fully in these pages, not merely because of the interest attaching to the narrative itself, but on account of their connection with so many names that occur in Cosin's "List". Indeed, a more suggestive theme for the novelist than that afforded by the circumstances surrounding the life and death of the good convert baronet could not well be desired. Little appears to be known of him beyond what is told us by Dodd, or is briefly recorded in the baronetage. Assigning by deed of gift his Hutton estate to his Catholic relative Thomas Fletcher in 1710, he retires to lead the life of a recluse in a small apartment adjoining the Franciscan Convent at Douay; having first, also, temporarily deposited with Thomas Hickin, a London goldsmith, some rich altar plate, of which an elaborate description is given, but which, alas! failed to reach the destination for which his piety had designed it. Everything he appears to have given to God. "The English Rector at Douay," he says, "is to have my two large silver payles I used to sett my bottles in . . . to make two Holy Water potts." Sir Henry, however, did not long survive; his will is dated 10th May, 1712, and in nine days more he was dead. Next comes the apostacy of Thomas Fletcher, the man on whom he had lavished all his estate. On the 12th September, 1716, this unhappy man informs the Commissioners at Preston of the altar plate that was in the custody of Hickin the banker-goldsmith in Holborn, and in five more days it was seized, the poor goldsmith in his fear escaping meanwhile by a back door, leaving his wife to tell the sheriff where he could find it. The banker's daughter we meet again in Cosin's "List". The plate is sold under the hammer, and even the money that Sir Henry left to the Scotch Jesuits and others to say masses for his soul is seized—all, in fact, but a watch and chain bequeathed to the Bishop of Arras, and £400 to the poor of his diocese, whom the Commissioners tried hard to rob also, and—judging by their printed report—eventually succeeded in accomplishing, despite counsel's opinion as to the propriety of the act which they thought it best to take, but the receipt of which must have made them blush.

The system of bribery, moreover, which the Commissioners worked so well, appears to have inspired some of the "informers" with a like policy. And of this we have a most droll illustration. A servant of Lord Molyneux, who had informed against his master, was evidently anticipating a rich reward. Acccordingly, to intensify their obligation to him, he despatches to one of the Commissioners four bottles of brandy, with a regret that lemons did not accompany the gift, at the same time gently expressing a hope of increased favour! The wounded dignity and consequent perplexity of the Government official is in delightful contrast with the insolent familiarity of the servant. It is to be questioned, however, if the unopened brandy remained long unclaimed.

But if the Commissioners had a velvet paw with which to caress the informer, they had also another with sharp talons in it for any on whom their wrath descended. An aged dame of fourscore is turned out of her home for no other reason than that she was the mother of the Jesuit Father, Thomas Eccleston, who, with just indignation, demands of them some explanation of the outrage; the Ladies Radcliffe, two nuns, "in years and very infirme"—sisters by birth as in religion—appeal for some guarantee that their annuities may always be paid them, "being all their subsistence"; and John Crook is sent to prison for being too stupid to stand the cross-examination of the Commissioners; while the many anxiously-worded petitions, Richard Towneley's urgent letter to his attorney, and the obsequious language of another attorney, Edward Ward, who "hopes he has not incurred the displeasure of the Commissioners" by acting on behalf of his Catholic client, all go to prove the terror in which they were held. Suspicion even on one occasion appears to have attached to their Accountant-General, Chambers Slaughter himself. Altogether, then, this combination of apostasy and bribery, mistrust and cruelty, make up a melancholy picture.

Still, it must be remembered that the sources from which our information has been derived could hardly be expected to afford matter for much satisfaction. We have been examining the proceedings of a government whose avowed object was—as it ever had been from the time of Queen Elizabeth—if possible, to crush out the very existence of the Church in England: indeed, on one occasion, we shall find the Commissioners dissuading the lords of the Treasury from adopting any measures of leniency, on the ground that their "*proposal would set the Roman Catholic interest very near in as good a condition as before the Rebellion, whereas,*" they add, "*if they* (Catholics) *are divested of their estates, and Protestants succeed, the Roman Catholic interest in the Northern Counties must be entirely ruined*".

There is no mistaking the meaning of language such as this. Yet even from these "Forfeited Estates Papers" there every now and then peeps out evidence that the majority of Catholics rejected, as we find the Widdringtons doing, every overture of the Government to buy up their *faith*.

While, however, it was but natural that Catholics should bitterly lament and even resent the dethronement of their lawful and Catholic Sovereign, yet, at the same time, there is ample evidence to show that, in the retrospect, many regretted the active participation of any of their number in the rising of 1715; so that the question is forced upon us, would not the Church in this country have been less harassed, earlier suffered to remain at peace, and have more speedily attracted souls within her fold, had Catholics, where no principle of *faith* was at stake, but passively acquiesced in the political changes of the time. Lady Derwentwater, for example, as we have seen, speaks of the "unhappy rising," and Henry Butler of Rawcliffe characterises the "Rebellion" as "horrid," and the action even of his own son, who was condemned for his part in it, as that of "an inconsiderate, rash young man".

Among the *Add. MSS.* [20310, f. 173] at the British Museum is a remarkable letter bearing on this subject from the pen of the Rev. Dr. John Ingleton, dated " St. Germains, December 15, 1716, and addressed to "Monsr. Nairne, secretaire du cabinet a Monsr. le Chevalier de S. George, a Avignon," the opening passages of which, however, will be enough for our purpose. The writer says : "Since my last by Mr. Kirby, I have another from Bishop Giffard upon a very vexatious subject, dated November $\frac{14}{30}$: he says he has lately received a letter from Mons$^{gr.}$ Santini, internonce at Brussels, brought him by the Duke of Norfolk, wherein Monsr. Santini tells him that he (Santini) is ordered by the Pope to publish that English Catholics may and ought to promise fidelity and entire obedience to the present Government, but to make no mention of the Pope's authority. The words are: Omnibus palam facere Catholicos Anglos fidei quidem atque integra obedientiæ professione præsentem regni formam ita agnoscere posse, atque adeo debere, ut ab eorum consiliis nihil quisquam metuere possit. Sacræ veræ Rom. Pontificum authoritatis nullam omnino injiciendam esse mentionem." . . .

But to revert once more to the evidence afforded by our "Forfeited Estates Papers". William Charlton depriving a poor fellow of his solitary horse at Rothbury, and detaining him for three hours on his way back from business at Alnwick, in October, 1715, reads as rather a paltry item of preparation for a campaign; or again, what stand against regular troops could a motley, undisciplined, and undrilled body of men be expected to make, such as that described by William Baines as meeting at the Mitre Hotel at Preston only a day or two previous to the action there, some of them with a "gun," some with a sword or case of pistols, all of them, without doubt, valiant to a man, and cheerfully willing to sacrifice themselves in their rash enterprise? And while the toast of James III. is going round at the Mitre, we have another auxiliary gathering of a similar character, fourteen miles away, at Stonyhurst. Sir Nicholas Sherburne gave a supper party there on Thursday evening, 10th November, 1715, but it does not transpire that he was actually present at it himself. After supper, a pan is borrowed from a mason at work on the premises and some lead, and the guests set to work bullet-making. The poor mason, evidently a little alarmed, does not appear to have approved of the proceedings, and retired to bed; but next morning tells us he saw the party all ride off at seven o'clock with their guns and blunderbuss, and mounted on the coach horses of Sir Nicholas. All this really savours more of a frolic of the happy boys that were destined less than three-quarters of a century afterwards to celebrate their "Blandyke" within the same precincts rather than of the proceedings of a military outpost. Still more would the boys have enjoyed the excitement, when, six weeks later, a constable and twenty men with him arrived at Stonyhurst to search the house for a "rebel" servant of the good baronet, for whose arrest he had a warrant. Sir Nicholas was at home, and sent down word by his steward that entrance was to be refused. And the boys would certainly have cheered when the constable afterwards retired only to depose that "the house was very strong, having a greate pair of iron gates to the front, and a pair of wooden gates on the back". This was the 27th December, 1715, and Sir Nicholas was after all permitted to sit by his Yule log undisturbed.

There is, however, no need for us to question any further the wisdom or discretion of those Catholics who took an active part in the Rebellion; but a few final observations relative to the title which Cosin prefixed to his "List" may not be out of place, as some slight doubt appears still to exist as to whether it is made up *solely* of Catholics. Now it must surely at the outset occur to anyone as highly improbable that, in the terrible days of the penal laws, anybody *besides* a "Papist" would be so misguided as to think himself called upon to take any step whatever in response to the Act 1 Geo. I., cap. 55, "*obliging Papists* to register their names and real estates". Indeed, the opening passages of the Act (see Appendix II., *Eng. Cath. Nonj.*) are sufficiently explicit as to what class *alone* it had reference. Then, again, this Act is constantly being confused with another (9 Geo. I., cap. 24), which "obliged Papists in *Scotland and* ALL PERSONS *in Great Britain* refusing to take the oaths to register," &c. Here again the language of the Act is unmistakable, for we find that "*all persons* refusing to take the oaths of allegiance had . . . before 25th March, 1724, to register their names . . . *in such and the same manner and form as* PAPISTS *were obliged and directed to register their names . . . in and by an Act passed in the first year of his Majesty's reign*". The distinction between the two Acts is marked. Consequently, we find at the Record Office [*Court of Exchequer, Q. R. Papists' Estates*] that, of those who registered their names under the Act 9 Geo. I., hardly a Catholic is to be found, except for the most part the son or widow of one who had previously registered under the *first* Act, but who had died during the eight intervening years. On the other hand, we find in the latter (the Exchequer) list numbers of *nonjurors*—nonjurors, *i.e.*, in the *ordinary* acceptation of the term, *ministers and their wives*, such, *e.g.*, as Thomas Brett, the nonjuring bishop, and others. Here we might remark in passing that the title of the volume, *English Catholic Nonjurors of 1715*, was not decided upon without much deliberation; for 1*st*, there was a distinct objection to the title as given by Cosin; 2*ndly*, the " List" being that of those who had "*refused to take the oaths* to his Majesty King George," the numbers comprising it became *ipso facto* " Nonjurors," as Burke in his *Dictionary of the Landed Gentry* so designates them [see *Eng. Cath. Nonj.*, p. 33]; 3*rdly*, since the names—though hardly any of them were among the "rebels"—are so interwoven with the events of " 1715," that year was mentioned on the title-page in preference to 1716-18—the date of the "registers," the collection of which by the various clerks of the peace was necessarily a work of time. It is interesting, moreover, to record that the Act 1 Geo. I., c. 55, together with the Act 3 Geo. I., c. 18, "explaining" it, were repealed by Act 31 Geo. III., c. 32, sec. 21, though, singularly enough, *both* were *reprinted* as recently as 1859. The Act 9 Geo. I., c. 24, was not, however, repealed until 1867 by the Statute Law Rev. Act.

But the question returns—Why did *Cosin* describe his " List" as that of "*Roman Catholics, Nonjurors,* and *others*"? Possibly a reason may be found in what follows. In the Public Record Office, among the "State Papers Domestic Anne," is a "bundle" (No. 14) very important for our purpose: one portion of it has reference to "the City of Westminster," and the other to the "County of Middlesex". The first-named bears the following title: "*List of all Papists, Nonjurors, and other Persons* suspected to be disaffected to your Majesty's Government, with such particular distinctions and remarks upon them as have severally appeared before us . . . which is humbly submitted to your Majestie". This is signed by the Justices of the Peace for the City of Westminster. That for the County of Middlesex is a similar document, being a "Return of Papists and reputed Papists," &c., and dated 13th April, 1708. The title, however, is *significant*, and, in all probability, Cosin had seen this very "List," and unreflectingly decided upon a similar title for his own a few years later. These Lists of 1708, which are certainly in perfect harmony with their title, possess great interest, and are well worth our brief examination. The names are classified under the following heads:

(A.) Those who took the oath of allegiance, but refused the oath of supremacy, or to repeat and subscribe the declaration against transubstantiation.

(B.) Persons summoned to appear before the Justices of the Peace, but who did *not* appear.

(C.) Those who took the oaths of allegiance and abjuration.

(D.) Those who refused the oath of abjuration.

(E.) Those who subscribed the declaration against transubstantiation.

Of course, in these lists, we meet with several names familiar to us in Cosin: of these, some occur under *two* headings, but *none* of Cosin's names appear under Class E.

Mrs. Cæcilia Cornwallis, of Kensington, refused all oaths, and is described as "keeping a Popish school":

Francis Bird, of St. Giles', mason, and George Beveridge, "a dancing master," took the oath of allegiance, but gave bail for their personal appearance.

Under Class A we have Nathaniel Pigott, of Boswell Court : Peter Brand, of St. Andrew's, Holborn, gent. : Bernard Tourner, of Brownlow Street : Charles, Lord Baltimore, of Devonshire Street : and Richard Pepper of Gray's Inn, gent. Under both A and D we have Charles Tancred, of Russell Street, woollen draper : Thomas Pendrel, of Bridge Street, distiller : Richard Wright, of Russell Street, goldsmith: Ferdinando Pulton, a hosier at Mr. Turner's, a hatter : Francis Robotham, distiller.

Under Class B we find Sir Charles Ingleby, Basil Fitzherbert "*prope* Turnstile," Henry Tasburgh : Charles Smalbone: Richard Pendrel, in Change Court, apothecary: Stanislaus Bowes, chirurgeon at Hammersmith : Thomas Rouse, of St. Paul's, Covent Garden, milliner : Charles Tempest, "of St. Giles', goldsmith, and Richard Towneley, his lodger".

George Beveridge is further described as a chandler, living in Shorts Gardens, St. Giles' : Ric. Purcell, of King Street, Bloomsbury, gent., and Edward Berington, of Silver Street, printer, also refused the oaths ; while "Benedict Conquest and John Roper, of St. Andrew's, Holborn, gent. : Edward Webb, of Gray's Inn, and Christopher Atwood, of Lyons Inn, all refused the said oaths, and paid the penalty of 20s. each : Henry Curzon, of St. Andrew's, gent., likewise refused, and paid the penalty of 30s.".

Several others could be named here whom Cosin also gives, but more to our purpose is it to notice in this 1708 List the names of many returned as "Nonjuring Parsons" —some of them eminent as Nonjuring Bishops—such as

Archdeacon Fitzgerald, Thomas Stamp, Edward Stacey, of Plumtree Square; Thomas Wagstaff, of Charterhouse Yard; Shadrach Cook, "Mr. Seth Lamb, a nonjuring minister living in the parish of Ealing"; Nathaniel Spinckes, and Henry Gandy, "of Old Street Square," &c. These men we find in the *same* lists with Basil Fitzherbert and others familiar to us as Catholics, yet *none of them figure in Cosin's List*, and we must remember that Spinckes did not die until 1727, nor Gandy until 1733.

Finally, I would record, while on this subject, that the late Canon Estcourt (R.I.P.) was strongly of opinion that Cosin's "List" was exclusively comprised of Catholics. Nor should we forget that the times of which we are treating were unhappily, in too many cases, the commencement of a great falling away from faith, arising from numberless mixed marriages, general laxity of life, and other causes already noted. This may, therefore, in a measure account for occasional inconsistency of language, whether in a will or in the registers themselves.

But while there is much to deplore, there is, on the other hand, abundant matter both for consolation and edification to be gathered from these authentic records of our Catholic ancestors.

JOHN ORLEBAR PAYNE.

HOLLY VILLAGE, HIGHGATE,
July 14, 1888.

RECORDS OF ENGLISH CATHOLICS.

BEDFORD.

MARGARET BRAND, of Turvey, names her four sisters Christian, Susan, Winifred, and Mary B., her nieces Margaret and Petronilla, das. of her brother Peter Brand, and her aunt Mary Waters. [1st February, 1720—23rd June, 1729.] The name of Waters occurs several times in the *Catholic Registers of Weston-Underwood, co. Bucks*, privately printed in 1887.

BENEDICT CONQUEST, of Irnham, co. Lincoln, son of Ben. and Anne Conquest, names his son Benedict and da. Mary, to whom George Markham was guardian, also his three sisters Eliz. and Winifred Conquest and Mary Wright, with his nephews William and Thomas Rayment. Admon. of his estate was granted, 19th April, 1762, to Mary, widow of George Markham, the executor, who died before fully administering, [3rd July, 1753—12th November, 1753.]

BERKS.

FRANCIS PERKINS, of Ufton, son of Francis and Anne P., in his will names his four sons—Francis, who died in 1750; James, who died in 1755; Charles, in 1762; and John, the last of his race, who died in 1769. [6th October, 1734—6th May, 1736.] John Berington was one of the executors. From an interesting paper in *Merry England* for January, 1888, on "Old Berkshire Missions," Ufton appears to afford an unhappy illustration of the way in which, for some mysterious cause, Catholics began to fall away from the Faith about this period. The writer tells us—his authority evidently being the old Catholic Mission Register—that in the year 1750 the Ufton congregation numbered 98, exclusive of any member of the Perkins family; but he adds, alas!—"It is curious to notice how many of the families whose names are there given still exist in the neighbourhood, although *there is not now a single Catholic among them*".

The will of EDWARD WOLLASCOTT, of Sutton Courtney, was proved by his nephew Thomas Betham, 3rd October, 1718, and besides his nephew Thomas Wollascott, the elder, he names also his nephew Martin Wollascott, who had six children—William (the eldest), Martin and Thomas, Anne, Mary, and Frances; his sisters Mrs. Catherine Wollascott and Mrs. Mary Betham, nephew John Betham, and nieces Frances Betham and Mrs. Mary Stanford.

Woolhampton, the old residence of the Wollascotts, although it now boasts of its Diocesan College, seems to have shared very much the fate of the Mission of Ufton.

CHARLES EYSTON, of East Hendred ". . . being by God's grace steadfast and certain in the intregrity of that Faith which his ancestors have received and learned from the 'wholly' [*sic*] Roman Catholic Church, the head of all Churches, in which Faith, and in obedience to the Apostolic See of Rome, he professes to have always lived and desires to dye, and that he may be able to accomplish this his desire by the great goodness and mercy of God through the merits of his Lord and Saviour Jesus Christ, and may persevere to the end in the same Faith and obedience, earnestly begs the assistance of the suffrages and prayers of the ever Blessed Virgin Mary and the universal Church of Christ, triumphant and militant, with fear and trembling beholding himself and his great unworthiness, yet so far confiding in the grace and mercy of God as to have a firm hope and expectation of the salvation of his soul, and everlasting life through Jesus Christ . . ." names his wife Winifred-Dorothy (whose will, afterwards dated 13th December, 1750, was proved 6th November, 1753), brother

Robert, mother Ann, eldest son Charles, to whom he bequeaths " Bishop Fisher's Staff," sons Basil, John, and William, and das. Winifred, Frances, Ann, and Catherine. [26th May, 1718 —20th February, 1722.]

JOHN YATE, of the p. of St. George, Bloomsbury, names his grandfather William Blount, of St. Giles'-in-the-Fields, whose will, dated 22nd December, 1699, was proved 6th February, 1700. This William Blount, desiring burial by his wife and brother in St. Giles', names his brothers Peter and Colonel John Blount; his godson William Yate, who had a brother and sister Thomas and Mary Yate; his nephew —— Perkins, niece Margaret Seagrave, and this his grandson John Yate, who is probably identical with the one in Cosin's List. John Yate names his wife Mary, son John, and brother Thomas, and claims property under the will of Frances, da. of Rob. Brent, whose executor he was 4th August, 1739, she describing him as " of Southampton Street, Bloomsbury ". He was married at the date of his grandfather's will; his wife, —whom he "thanks and praises" for her care of him,—Edward Webb, and Richard Clayton, of Adlington, near Standish, co. Lanc., being his executors. [25th February, 1740—3rd November, 1741.]

ANNE SHERWOOD, of East Hendred, spinster, by her will of 14th June, 1711, left land called " Mason's Close " to Edward Sherwood, of East Hendred, naming her half-brother William Wogan, father-in-law Will. Wogan, sen., and her half-sister Alice Hancock, with her kinsmen Laurence Spicer and Richard Wise; administration of her estate being granted, 18th September, 1744, to her nephew Edward Hancock, passing, 29th March, 1745, at his death to another " nephew by the sister," William Hancock.

ROBERT EYSTON, of ditto, names his wife Elizabeth, eldest son George Hildesley Eyston, and youngest son William. [20th December, 1725—8th March, 1726.]

ROBERT BILLING, of Old Windsor, gent., in his will, dated 11th April, 1719, " in good health," and proved 8th November, 1727, names his wife Sarah and brother Thomas.

Francis Hyde, of Chipping-Faringdon, desires burial near his father at Purley, his brother John being executor of his will. He settled on Elizabeth, his wife, 14th November, 1715, in bar of dower, lands at Balking. Bequests to Charles Coffin, of Buckland, and to Francis C., his son. A further admon. was granted, 13th December, 1750, to Mary, the widow of his brother, John Hyde. [18th August, 1726—25th August, 1746.]

Stonor Crouch, of Wallingford, names his nieces Mrs. Eliz. Crouch, Lucy Bigg, and Dorothy Bigg, her daughter. [12th March, 1722—8th May, 1723.]

Dame Anastatia J. Moore, of Fawley, names her mother Helene Aylward; sons Sir John, Benedict-James, Henry, Thomas, and William; and daughters Mary and Anastatia; her wardrobe and plate going to her "daughters in France and Flanders," with "£30 to poor prisoners to be distributed by her daughter". Some of her daughters had entered Religion. [29th September, 1741—12th August, 1742.]

Edward Mooring, of Chipping-Lamborne, names his sister Mary, the wife of William Collett, and their children Edward and Mary; his brother-in-law William Lovell, of Brambridge, being his executor. [5th July, 1721—25th August, 1721.]

Mary Chadwick, of ditto, widow, names her sister Elizabeth, niece Margaret Smalbone, and nephew Francis, son of Charles Clifton. [11th January, 1723—27th October, 1724.]

John Dancastle, of Binfield, names his friend Charles Young, of Leigh Farm, in Lamborne, and Eliz., widow of his brother Thomas D.; admon. being granted, 6th July, 1749, to her son John on attaining his majority. [8th January, 1740—1st December, 1740.]

Catherine Wollascott, of Sutton Courtney, dating her will 9th September, 1721, names her son Thomas, together with William, Martin, Thomas, Mary, and Frances, the children of dec. son Martin.

HENRY ENGLEFIELD, of Sunning-Erley-Shinfield. Admon. of his estate was granted, 31st March, 1720, to his widow Catherine.

JOHN BATSON, of Great Queen Street, in the p. of St. Giles-in-the-Fields, left his estate to his friends and executors Edward Shaw, living at Blackmore Park, Worcestershire, gent., and Thomas Pickering, of Aspley, co. Notts, gent. [3rd February, 1741—12th January, 1747.]

BUCKS.

ROBERT DORMER, of Peterley, appoints his nephew the Hon. John D. and his "brother" Edward Webb, of Gray's Inn, trustees, and names his father John Webb and nephew Peter Webb, sister (Mary) Havers and godda. Frances, the da. of my "cousin Charles Howse," depriving also of a legacy any of his nephews, the sons of Charles, Lord Dormer, that enter Religion. [21st February, 1726—16th July, 1729.]

CHARLES, Lord DORMER, names his sons John, Robert, Walter, Edmund, James, Joseph, John-Baptist, and Francis; grandson Charles, the son of John D.; das. Mary D. and Frances Plowden; the executors being his brothers Robert D., Francis Biddulph, and his son-in-law William Plowden. [15th September, 1726—6th November, 1728.]

ELIZABETH, Lady DORMER, widow of foregoing, by will dated 18th December, 1749, with three codicils, the last dated 18th July, 1750 (proved in 1752), desires if she die at Plowden to be buried there: her "body to be put in a plain decent coffin, covered only with black cloth, her age, date of death, and initial letters of her name to be in brass nails, surmounted by ✠, and underneath R.I.P.". Among others already noticed, she names also Ann, the wife of her son Robert, da. Elizabeth, nephews Richard Biddulph and Anthony Wright, brother-in-law Edward Webbe, sister-in-law Frances Dormer, granddas. Dorothy-Mary, Eliz., Frances, Ann, and Mary Plowden; to her da. Frances she leaves a picture of Queen Mary, wife of James II.; picture of the

B.V.M. in silver filigree frame, a locket of Lord Derwentwater's hair set in gold, and "my sedan chair, now left with the widow Lady Jernegan in Winchester"; £20 for prayers, 3 guineas to the priest who assists her at death, £5 to poor Roman Catholics of Idsworth congregation where she lived; to Rob. Dormer, her Church stuff . . . little mass book, wooden cross, inlaid with mother-of-pearl, and a brass image of our Saviour upon it: "a picture of our Blessed Saviour on the Cross, now in Mr. Parker's room at Plowden" [this Mr. Parker being evidently the chaplain was a witness to the will]: "a gilt chalice and paten, a silver box to carry the Blessed Sacrament in, and another silver box to carry the Holy Oils".

ANNE WEEDON, of Bierton, co. Bucks, left her estate to her niece Ann Howse, of Bierton, spinster; a witness to her will being Mary Minshull. [19th February, 1751—25th October, 1751.]

ROBERT BURNHAM, of West Wycombe. Admon. of his estate was granted, 10th May, 1732, to his widow Dorcas, who married, secondly, Joseph Gray: on her death a further admon. was granted, 30th July, 1755, to his son Richard B.

ROBERT ROOKE, of Weston-Underwood, names his brother John and wife Elizabeth, the da. of John Fisher. His widow, by her will, proved 10th February, 1730, left her personal estate to her son-in-law John Wright. [20th September, 1694—17th November, 1718.]

URSULA PRICE, of Tusmore, spinster, does not state her relationship to any of her numerous legatees, but names Mary, James, Frances, Robert, and Richard, the children of James Fermor, dec.; the five das. of William Waters, of Ousley Lodge, in Warwickshire; and Dorothy and Winifred Clapcote. [31st August, 1724—14th March, 1734.]

Sir ROBERT THROCKMORTON, of Weston-Underwood. His will, dated 13th August, 1720, was proved 20th June, 1721.

ELIZABETH, Lady LINDSEY, left much of her personal

estate to her servants and dependants, her son, the Hon. Charles Bertie, being executor. [20th June, 1719—26th September, 1719.]

LONGUEVILLE MOSDELL, of Fulmer, names his wife Lucy, eldest son Longueville, second son James, and grandson Christopher M. [4th April, 1737—27th May, 1741.] The will of his widow Lucy, "late of Fulmer, co. Bucks, and now (6th January, 1749) of Uxbridge, co. Middx.," was proved 11th September, 1750.

CARDIGAN.

CATHERINE PALMER, of Willington Cross, names her da. Catherine Chichester, and grandda. Mary C., John Smith, of Acton-Burnall, being her executor. [27th February, 1727—28th July, 1730.]

CHESTER.

FRANCIS POOLE, of Poole Hall, between 1717 and 16th November, 1725, the date of his will, evidently forsook his Religion. He says ". . . estate in trust for my half-brother Rowland, if he shall, at my decease, profess the Protestant religion according to the doctrine of the Church of England as now by law established, or shall, in six lunary months, conform thereto, and qualify himself in such manner as by the law and statutes of the realm persons professing the Roman Catholic Religion are obliged to conform, in order to take lands by descent or devise . . ."; or, "the estate is to pass to James, son of Rowland P., if he conform, within six months of his eighteenth birthday, to Protestant Religion"; or, "to other issue of his brother"; or, ". . . to William, son of my late uncle William Poole . . ."; but, "until they conform, the trustees are to apply the proceeds of my estate to my daughter Harriet"! His wife Frances is named executrix of his will in a codicil dated 13th March, 1740; but she, dying in her husband's lifetime, admon. was granted, 10th March, 1763, to his son Sir Henry, and on his death to Sir Ferdinando P., 3rd June, 1786, afterwards 4th bart.

CORNWALL.

RICHARD ARUNDELL, of Lanherne, names George-Henry, Earl of Lichfield, as trustee of his two daughters Frances, wife of Sir John Giffard, and Mary Arundell, spinster, his will bearing date 5th August, 1723; admon. of his estate being granted, 1st June, 1734, to a creditor, upon the non-appearance of executors.

ANNE COUCHE, late of the p. of St. Sampson, otherwise Golant, co. Cornwall. Admon. of her estate was granted, 22nd December, 1753, to her husband William. The will, also, of Richard C., of Lostwithiell, gent., dated 5th November, 1739, may be that of R. C., named in *Eng. Cath. Nonj.*, p. 23: he names his brother John, sister-in-law Eliz. C., nieces Ann and Martha C., and Anne John, and his nephew John C.

CUMBERLAND.

THOMAS HOWARD, of Corby, desires "to be carried by his tenants to his grave in Wetheral Church if he dye at home," and names his eldest son Charles, younger son Philip, da. Catherine, brother John, and sister Eliz. Sanderson, widow. [17th October, 1733—31st January, 1741.]

HENRY C. HOWARD, of p. of St. Clement Danes, co. Middx., desires burial at Dorking, appoints his wife executrix and Basil Fitzherbert overseer of his will, leaving to Henry, his eldest son, the furniture of Gray Stock and London house. [8th June, 1720—1st July, 1721.] His widow, Mary Howard, of Hammersmith, dates her will 28th March, 1721, but the executors she had appointed—John Dancastle, of Binfield, and Philip Howard—both dying in her lifetime, admon. of her estate was, on 4th August, 1748, granted to her da. Frances H., spinster: her sister Anastatia Jane, wife of Sir Richard Moore, had been named as guardian of her daughters Mary, Catherine, Frances, and Eliz. Howard.

ANNA MARIA RADCLIFFE, Lady DERWENTWATER, dates her will from Brussels, 5th March, 1722, with seven codicils, the last bearing date 3rd April, 1723, but it was not proved in

London until 27th May, 1734, by her father, Sir John Webb. She leaves £200 to her servant Dorothy Busby, and adds: "All such as were servants to my dear Lord, and were prisoners on account of the unhappy Rising, may for their great sufferings have each £20". The *Lawson MS.* says Lady D. died, aged thirty-three, in 1723, and was buried in the Church of the English Nuns at Louvain.

DERBY.

The following extracts are from a MS. in the possession of H. J. Pye, Esq. of Clifton Hall, and entitled "An Account of Papists in Appletree Hundred," in the co. of Derby, dated May, 1706, and whose names were "presented to ye cheife Constable of the Hundred aforesaid". The list is interesting, containing, as it does, several names that we afterwards identify among the English Catholic Nonjurors:

	At
Marston-Montgomery.	Mary, wife of John Wood, shoemaker.
Norbury and Roston.	William Fitzherbert, Esq., of London.
,,	Christopher Adams, of Norbury, sen.
,,	John Mole, of Roston, yeoman.
,,	William Cooper, ,, ,,
,,	Robert Bill, ,, ,,
,,	John Oldacre, ,, ,,
,,	Thomas Cope, sen., ,, ,,
,,	Ignatius Greensmith, ,, ,,
,,	John Bill, ,, ,,
Anthony Greensmith.	Richard Harrison.
Laurence ,,	Thomas Wood, of Norbury.
Bazill Milnhouse.	John Slator.
Nicholas Harrison.	William Cooper.
William Palmer, jun.	Thomas Sherlock.
,, ,, sen.	Thomas Smith.
Nicholas ,,	Gregory Milnhouse.
,, ,, jun.	Bazill Palmer.
Bazil ,,	•

All of whom do live in Roston and are styled Pauperes.

At Snelston.	Richard Milnhouse, yeoman ... his estate about £10, but at present in Derby gaol.
,,	William Cooper, } paupers.
,,	Dorothy, his wife,
Bradley.	Gilbert Whithall, living in London.
,,	Charles Pegg, sen., of Yeardesley.
,,	George ,, ,, ,, yeoman.
,,	Jos. Fretwell, of Pentershane, husb.
,,	Thomas Harston, ,, labourer.
Duffield.	John Lunt, sen., and his wife.
Breileford.	Charles Arton, husb.
,,	Susannah ,, his wife.
,,	Jane ,, his sister, spinster.
,,	,, ,, his daughter.
Sutton.	Peircy Fairebrother, pauper.
Spondon.	Francis Jackson, stocking-weaver.
Longford.	Thomas Brandon, } paupers.
,,	Ann ,, his da.,
Ormoston.	Thomas Oldacre, husb.
Alkmonton.	Ann Hood, pauper, living upon Mr. Browne's charity.

CHARLES LOW, of Oldgrave, names his wife Mary and three das. Mary, Teresa, and Margaret. [6th September, 1709—9th July, 1717.]

GILBERT WHITEHALL [see CATH. BRENT] was one of the banker-goldsmiths "plundered by Charles II. to the amount of £248,866 3s. 5d. by the shutting up of the Exchequer in January, 1672, for which he was awarded 6 per cent. interest, amounting to £14,931 19s. 4d. per annum". The payment of this interest ceased after a time. [Collins, *History of Banking*, p. 43; C. H. Price, *Handbook of London Bankers*.]

JOHN POLE, of Spinkhill, names his wife Ursula, nieces Mary, Eliz., and Catherine Hodgson; niece "formerly Mary Lacon, but now by marriage Littlehells," and his nephew James Morphew. One bequest is "to my cousin Francis Pole,

Esq., my gold cross, commonly called Cardinal Pole's cross".
[15th July, 1718—1st November, 1724.]

JOHN EYRE, of Bury's Hall, co. Norfolk, whose will was proved by his brother James Eyre, doctor of physic, speaks of "the vast business of his brother Henry, and of the large extent of his transactions". [19th May, 1724—8th May, 1739.]

Sir WINDSOR HUNLOKE names his "now living four sons Henry, Thomas, Robert, and James; his five das. Catherine, Charlotte, Ann, Mary, and Marina, by his late wife Charlotte; and his sisters Ann-Teresa and Marina: he left £5 a-year "to Mrs. Catherine Whetnall, of Pontoise". [13th March, 1744—24th April, 1752.]

GERTRUDE BEVERIDGE, of the p. of St. Giles-in-the-Fields, "spinstress," in her will, dated 21st October, 1716, and proved 15th March, 1725, names her brother George and nephew George, her sister Catherine Carter and niece Catherine Carter.

DEVON.

HUGH, Lord CLIFFORD, desires burial at Ugbrooke, if he dye in Devon, at Canington if in Somerset, at Westminster Abbey if in or near London, or in the nearest cathedral if elsewhere: he left to the heir of the family, books, paintings, &c., and a diamond ring given him by the late Queen Catherine, his wife Anne being executrix. [18th October, 1726—24th May, 1731.]

EDWARD CARY, of Tor Abbey. Admon. of his estate was granted, 31st October, 1718, to his son George.

CLEMENT TATTERSHALL, of Dartmouth, bachelor. Admon. of his estate was granted, 9th April, 1750, to his sister Mary T., spinster.

DORSET.

JOHN HUSSEY, of Marnhull, leaves to his son Giles his house at Bath called the "Belltree": he names also his da. Frances, and his brother Edward Burdet, of Thames-Ditton, co. Surrey. The overseers of his will were Hubert Hussey, of Charlton-Horethorne, co. Somerset, and John Knipe, of Semley. Of his wife Mary he says: "She has hitherto behaved so well for the good and benefit of her family ... and will make a proper use of what I leave her". [29th May, 1736—1st September, 1736.]

"Beltre House was," writes Dr. Oliver in his *Western County Collections*, p. 55, "for a long period the missionary residence as well as chapel held under the Corporation of Bath, at a ground rent of £8 per annum."

GEORGE PENNE, of Hewish, in p. of Crewkerne, co. Somerset, names his grandson George, son of his son Edmund P.; his das. Anne P. and Elizabeth Bishop, and his granddas. Dorothy, Susan, and Anne, the das. of Mr. John Mackrell. [18th February, 1723—28th August, 1724.]

REBECCA HUSSEY, of Marnhull, names her son Thomas H. and Eliz. his wife, her cousin Mary H., of Marnhull, widow, and her granddas. Anna Maria and Charlotte O'Hara. She named her cousin John H. executor of her will, dated 12th July, 1751; but he dying in her lifetime, admon. was, 29th November, 1754, granted to his widow Mary.

JOHN ARUNDELL, of Brinsome, in p. of Netherbury. Admon. of his estate was granted, 17th March, 1752, to his da. and only child Frances, the wife of John Hanne.

MARGARET LACY, the elder, of Harmsworth, within the p. of Old Alresford, co. Southton, spinster, by her will dated 19th July, 1740, desires burial at St. James', near Winchester, naming her sister Jane L., nephew Henry L., of Wardour Castle, gent., and her niece Margaret his sister, her nephew William L. and Peggy his da. On 4th December, 1746, admon. was granted to William, brother of Henry Lacy, the latter, her executor, having died before he had administered.

JANE STRODE, "now of Kensington, co. Middx.," by will dated 30th April, 1735, with codicil 9th September, and proved in London 29th October, 1735, left to her cousin George Chafin, of Chettle, co. Dorset, her "three parts and a half" of the Manor of Stoke Abbotts, and to her cousin Rachel Chafin all money and stock in her town house at Paris, in Hotel de Ville.

HUMPHREY WELD, of Lulworth Castle, under his will of 24th July, 1721, proved 27th July, 1722, left one shilling each to his two sons Edward and James, and his two daughters Mary and Elizabeth, and the residue to his wife Margaret. Alluding to his marriage with that lady, the da. of Sir James Simeon, Dr. Oliver, in his *Western County Collections*, p. 48, says: "This union, like that of his father, eventually brought large possessions to the Weld family". The terms of the will certainly hardly favour this conclusion; many and constant, however, were the devices and precautions necessary among Catholics, and Dr. Oliver goes on to tell us of the "smuggled education abroad" which the grandsons of this Humphrey Weld were obliged to obtain.

Lady BARBARA WEBB, wife of Sir John Webb, of Great Canford, in her will of 2nd June, 1738, with two codicils dated 25th February, 1739, and proved 13th June, 1740, names her son John; da. Winifrid, the wife of William Frankland; Ann, the wife of her son Thomas; her da. Montague, and granddas. Lady Petre, "the Miss Brownes," and Lady Henrietta Beard.

DURHAM.

Sir JOHN SMYTHE, of Eshe Hall, in his will, witnessed by Richard Clough and Peter Woodington, dated 14th January, 1736, with codicil of 11th September, 1737, proved 6th December, 1737, names his sons Edward (the eldest) and Walter, and his da. Constantia.

ESSEX.

Sir EDWARD SOUTHCOTT, of Witham Place, names his son Francis, and adds that if none of his sons leave issue, his estate is to pass to Mathias, Earl of Stafford. The furniture, &c., of Witham Place he left to his wife Jane, to be, at her death, the property of his da.-in-law Mary Southcott. [21st September, 1745—2nd March, 1751.]

WILLIAM COLEGRAVE, of St. Giles', co. Middx., desires "to be buried in St. Sepulchre's Church, near his wife, and where so many of his children and grandchildren lie": he names his eldest son Henry, second son William, and his three daughters, Frances, the wife of Edward Simpson; Mary Walmesley, and Barbara Mordaunt; also a nephew John Savery. [9th August, 1712—21st October, 1721.]

MARY, the wife of Joseph Petre, youngest son of Joseph Petre, of Fidlers, made her will 24th February, 1726, her husband thus attesting it: "This is my dear wife's will, which I promise to comply with". This Mary, "a few days only before her death, was delivered of a son, baptised John". She was a sister of Anne Hickin, of Wolverhampton. Her husband married, secondly, Teresa ——, as appears by his will, dated 8th October, and proved 31st October, 1729, leaving her *enceinte.*

JOHN WRIGHT, jun., of Kelvedon. His second wife, Constantia, re-married, in 1756-7, Peter Holford, and died before 1764. [*Lawson MS.*]

WILLIAM PETRE, of Belhouse, desires to be buried "in a plain and handsome coffin, in the chancel of Stanford-Rivers Church, among his ancestors," and names his brother Francis, and his sons William (the eldest), Edward (executor), and Robert, and adds: "My youngest son Thomas, now at school, is to have the interest of £300 only for life if he enter the priesthood". [19th April, 1728—13th June, 1733.]

The Dowager Lady MARY PETRE. Of her husband Thomas, Lord Petre, Dr. Oliver says (*Western County Collections*, p. 202): "King James II. highly esteemed and favoured him, as well on account of his own merits, as for the distinguished virtues of his persecuted brother, the Lord William. At the revolution he was consequently subjected to much vexation, but he lived to a good old age, dying 4th June, 1707."

HENRIETTA, Lady WALDEGRAVE. Admon. of her estate was granted, 10th June, 1734, to her son Lord James W.

Sir THOMAS MANBY, of Southweald, writes: "I would have no strife or contention arise after I am dead". His marriage settlement is dated 5th September, 1694: he names his sons Francis, Robert, and Edward, his nephew —— Cary, cousin Francis Petre, and sister —— Gibbons. [23rd April, 1729—6th September, 1729.]

THOMAS DANCASTLE, "late of Binfield, but in the p. of St. Clement Danes, co. Middx.". His will was proved 2nd January, 1728-9, but on the death of his brother and executor John Dancastle, admon. of his estate was, 10th October, 1766, granted to his own son John, as Charles Young, the executor of his brother, renounced admon., and Eliz., his widow, was then dead.

MARY COFFIN, of Ramsden Heath, names her cousins Martha and Bridget Coffin; Eliz. Poston, of Bloxwich, co. Stafford; Charles Parker, of Flemings, and his brother Robert Parker, of Runwell. [7th January, 1726—3rd July, 1728.]

JOHN WRIGHT, of Kelvedon, names his sons John, Charles, and William; his son and da. —— Strickland, and their son Thomas. He adds: "I desire my eldest son will take care of my brother Lawrence . . . that he be not absolutely destitute of subsistence, and I bequeath also £10 to my good friend Mr. Charles Browne, who lives with me". This was the Jesuit Father Charles le Maitre, a native of Artois, who served the mission of Kelvedon Hall until his death, 7th January, 1737. [21st August, 1721—21st July, 1732.]

EUGENIA WRIGHT, widow of foreg., names her da. Mary, wife of Mannock Strickland, cousin Frances Chapman, nephew Charles Bodenham, and her father —— Trinder; concluding thus: "I give £1 to my brother Lawrence Wright, viz., 5s. a quarter till the £1 is paid". [30th August, 1732—2nd July, 1752.]

ANN, wife of Ralph Eure, of London, names her son Edward, sister Mary Sheldon, nephew William Sheldon, and granddas. Philadelphia and Ann Stapleton, making other disposal of property, "if her grandda. Philadelphia become a Religious". [22nd June, 1724—24th April, 1733.]

THOMAS ROOKWOOD, of Coldham Hall, "desires to be buried among his ancestors in the parish church of Stanningfield," naming his sisters Ann and Margaret R., his wife Dorothy-Marina, and his da. Eliz. Gage, and her children Thomas and John Gage. [17th March, 1725—27th February, 1727.]

BARBARA DANIEL, of Great Waldingfield, co. Suffolk, widow, left Pentlow Hall, &c., in trust to John Bromley, of London, fishmonger, and Eliz. Gage, of Coldham Hall, the following legatees, all of them "cousins," being named in a codicil dated 29th September, 1739 : Catherine Martin, of Long Melford; Margaret Martin; Frances Dormer, widow; Eliz. Jernegan, "who now lives with me"; Thomas Jernegan, of London, house carpenter; Mary, widow of John Low, of Twinstead Hall; Barbara Johnson; Amy, the wife of John Bromley, her executor; and Eliz., da. of my cousin James and Elizabeth Kerington, of Borley Hall. [17th May, 1734—11th March, 1740.]

RICHARD LANGHORNE, of East Ham, made his will when "somewhat infirm". He held lands under the will of Henry Holcroft, of Patcham, co. Sussex, and gave legacies to his brother Charles and his sister Lætitia Langhorne; his cousins Richard L., junior, of St. Martin's-in-the-Fields, gent., and Elizabeth, wife of Roger England, tailor. [14th October, 1719—19th December, 1719.]

JAMES, Lord WALDEGRAVE, whose will, dated "Paris, 29th January, N. S., 1738-9," was proved 21st April, 1741, his eldest son Lord Chewton being sole executor, names also his son John W., Captain of H.M. Foot-guards, and his da. Henrietta, widow of Edward, Lord Herbert. He desires burial at Navestock, and that his son pays his loans, debts, &c., contracted during his (testator's) embassy, and leaves money to send back his servants to France. In a codicil dated 8th March, 1740-1, he names his "worthless daughter, heretofore Herbert, and now Beard". Her husband, John Beard, the comedian and singer, died at

Hampton, co. Middx., 5th February, 1791, æt. 74. Lady Henrietta married him 8th January, 1739-40. She died 31st May, 1753, aged 36, and was buried at St. Pancras—an undoubtedly chequered career!

NATHANIEL PIGOTT, of the Inner Temple, desires burial in the parish in which he shall die, two coaches and six persons only (to be named by his son Edward) to attend his funeral, and his house in Holborn Row, Lincoln's Inn Fields, and that at Whitton to be sold. His wife is to "dispose of plate as she may think fit, if she shall recover her memory". He names his late son Ralph, da.-in-law Alathea Pigott and her children; his sons Charles (eldest), Nathaniel, George, and Francis; eldest da. Catherine, the wife of Edward Caryl, and their da. Eliz. C.; his da. Charlotte P.; grandchildren Rebecca, Nathaniel, and Catherine Pigott; brother Adam P.; brothers-in-law Francis Canning and John Busby; sisters-in-law Hannah Busby and Teresa Phillips; sisters —— Atton and —— Bowen, and cousins Margaret Brent (who had a catalogue of his library) and Mary Binge. [5th February, 1736, with two codicils—11th July, 1737.]

MARY POWTRELL, of London, widow, names her brother Francis Canning, and Francis Canning his eldest son; brother and sister Richard and Victoria Canning; nephews Humphrey, Nathaniel, Edward, and Richard Elliot; and her nieces Anne, Winifrid, Appolonia, Margaret, and Frances Elliot, the children of "my brother and sister Elliot"; nephew —— Betham and "my niece Mary his wife"; cousin Nathaniel Pigott and Rebecca his wife, and cousin Charles Busby and his sister Constantia B. [31st August, 1720—5th February, 1721.]

FLINT.

Sir PYERS MOSTYN mentions his father Sir Edward, his sons Pyers, George, and Thomas, and das. Mary, Frances, and Anne Mostyn; sons-in-law Thomas Culcheth and John Hornyold; also Mary Culcheth, the mother of John C., of Gray's Inn, and his uncle Henry Mostyn, &c. [25th April, 1720—7th December, 1721.]

GLOUCESTER.

Elizabeth Conquest,
Margaret Brent,   } of Larkstoke.   Their mother
Mary Brent,

Catherine Brent, in her will dated 14th October, 1706, and proved 19th July, 1724, eighteen years after her death, leaves £100 "to her very good friend Gilbert Whitehall, of London, goldsmith, as a grateful acknowledgment for the trouble he had in the affairs of her family," and names her sisters Mary Green, of Corescome [?], in Ireland, and —— Bartlet, of Evesham, niece Mrs. Mary Knatchball, and cousins —— Edney, Nath. Pigott, and Mary and Anne Cassey.

The will of Mary Brent, spinster, of the p. of St. Andrew, Holborn, dated 11th September, 1724, when "infirm of body," was proved 15th October following: she names her cousins Thomas Mitchill, Mary Knatchball, and John Green.

Her sister Margaret Brent desires to pay all the just debts of Gilbert Whitehall, bequeaths £200 "to Mr. Richard Challoner," and names her cousins Mary Green, Gilbert Langley, Holdenby Langley, and James Langley. [16th May, 1734—27th November, 1736.]

Admon. of the estate of Charles Conquest, doctor of medicine, of St. Paul's, Covent Garden, was, 4th October, 1693, granted to his widow Elizabeth. She survived him fifty years, and on her death is described as of the parish of St. George, Bloomsbury, admon. of her estate being granted, 10th October, 1743, to her nephew Robert Brent Lytcot.

Mary Cassey, of London, spinster, dating her will 17th March, 1725, names her cousins Anne and Mary C., Eliz. Smith, and Mary and Anthony Slauter, the residuary legatee being Eliz. Conquest. A deposition states that she "died on the Sunday previous" to 18th January, 1729—the date of probate—and had "lived for twenty years as a lodger at the house of Mr. John Sheppard, a turner, near Long Acre in Drury Lane".

Margaret Greenwood, of Brize-Norton, mentions her husband John, and her "three loving and dear children Elizabeth, Anne, and Frances Greenwood". [26th December, 1730 —31st August, 1731.]

RICHARD BLOORE, of Hatherop, names his wife Elizabeth, sister Mary Parker, niece Martha Parker, brother Hugh Frankland, uncle Thomas Brandon, Richard Brandon, son of *Richard* [*sic*, but probably an error for *Thomas*] "aforesaid" by his second wife and cousin Dorothy Grubb. [29th August, 1718—12th September, 1728.]

THOMAS EYCOTT, "late of South Cerney, co. Gloucester, bachelor". Admon. of his estate was granted, 27th June, 1740, to William Eycott, "his nephew and only next of kin". The will of John Eycott, of Cirencester, goldsmith, dated 11th May, 1737, and proved in 1751, may be that of a relative of John Eycott noticed by Cosin. He had an estate in the parish of Badginton, names his mother Mary then living, wife Elizabeth (executrix), his sons Richard, Thomas, and John Eycott, and his uncle John Shewell.

The will of Sir JOHN JERNEGAN was proved 27th June, 1737, by his widow Margaret.

TERESA, widow of Charles Trinder, of Bourton-on-the-Water, leaves to her sister Mrs. Mary Tuke a hair ring set with diamonds, Mr. Bennet Rigmaiden being her sole executor. In a deposition of two of her servants, she is described as "late of Ligny in the Duchy of Lorraine and Barr". [15th July, 1736—8th October, 1743.]

HENRY WAKEMAN, of Ashton-Underhill, co. Gloucester, gent., names his wife Frances (executrix), eldest son William, and "other children," brother Benedict, wife's father Will. Higford, and wife's brother Will. Higford. [21st February, 1723—4th August, 1731.]

JOHN PASTON, "late of Horton and now of Bath" . . . hoping, by the merits and passion of his dear Saviour Jesus Christ, and the intercession of His Blessed Mother the Virgin Mary, to be made partaker of His heavenly kingdom . . . dates his will 28th February, 1736, and desires burial at Horton near his wife Anne; names his eldest son William (who in 1726 married Mary ——), second son Clement, and third son James; da. Frances, the wife of Richard Bishop, and their children Mabel and Frances Bishop; wife Catherine, da. Mary, and grandda. Ann Paston; nephews Robert, Charles, and John Needham, of Hilston, co. Monmouth; and his brothers-in-law Henry and Richard Bostock, the latter of whom "is to have £100 for his great care of him during his illness". [Proved 10th November, 1737.]

Dame ANNE LYTCOT, of Larkstoke, in her will dated 1725, and proved in April, 1738, desires burial at St. Pancras if she die in London, names her son Rob. Brent Lytcot resid. legatee, and leaves "500 livres tournois to executors to be disposed of according to directions in a sealed packet". Admon. of the estate of Dame Anne L., "late of St. Giles-in-the-Fields, but at Paris in the kingdom of France," was granted, 11th May, 1747, to Eliz., widow of Rob. Brent Lytcot, left unadministered by him, and a further admon. was granted, 8th April, 1779, to "Fych Burgh, formerly Coppinger, Esq., one of the executors of the will of Eliz. Lytcot ".

HEREFORD.

THE PENDRELLS. Admon. of the estate of John Pendrell, late of Henfield, co. Sussex, bachelor, was granted, 18th February, 1755, to his brother Charles; and admon. of the estate of Catherine Pendrell, of Boscobel, co. Salop, spinster, was, 29th December, 1721, granted to her brother Richard P.

EDMUND ADYS, of Lyde Arundel . . . "being well . . . and fearing he may be called out of this world of a sudden," dates his will 8th October, 1724, and desires "to be buried in Pipe Churchyard near the wall," and concludes, "for fear of sudden death, I now subscribe my name ". He names his son Bernard, and da. —— Baskerville. Bequeaths "£10 a-piece to all grandchildren . . . £5 for the keeping of —— anniversary to the end of the world [sic], and 5s. each to poor Catho." [sic]: will proved 7th August, 1725.

JOHN EALES, of Droitwich, co. Worcester, yeoman, leaves to his father Thomas E., of Shobdon, co. Hereford, an annuity of £4, and names his uncle John of the same parish, and brothers Thomas (eldest) and Charles, of *Edgworth* [sic, Edgware?], co. Middx. [17th November, 1741—24th March, 1742.]

JOHN VAUGHAN, of Hunsome, directs that his body be carried by water, and interred near the grave of his late wife in Welsh-Bicknor Church: he names his mother-in-law —— Green, and brother-in-law Thomas Green; also John Cornwall, and Edith his wife, and their son Thomas Cornwall, and kinsmen Thomas, Robert, and Joseph Harper; "Mary, the wife of my nephew Joseph Griffin, of London, tobacconist"; my now wife Mary, my sister Teresa, my brother John and his wife Elizabeth, with their children John, Richard, Philip, Teresa, and Mary. He desires his executors to employ, and thus "gratify," Rob. Needham, sen., in the execution of the will. [1st September, 1716—17th June, 1721.]

THOMAS TRAUNTER, of Ross, left all his estate to Mary his wife. [10th February, 1720—16th June, 1721.]

HENRY SCUDAMORE, of Pembridge Castle, names his wife Mary (living 11th February, 1692), sons John and James Scudamore, and his grandson John Jones; da. Winifred, the wife of William Herbert (executor), and their children William and Margaret Herbert; also James, the son of his nephew George Scudamore, of Usk. [9th April, 1736; codicil, 16th February, 1737—10th May, 1737.]

ANN PYE, "of Perthieu, in p. of Rockfield," by will dated 7th July, 1720, when "somewhat infirm," and proved 24th April, 1722, left her estate to William Acton, of Wolverton, in p. of Stoughton, co. Worcester, the witnesses being Michael Lorymer and Edward and Mary Baskerville.

JOHN BERINGTON, jun., late of Winsley, now of Stafford, gent., names his wife Ann, with Charles Bodenham, Thomas Monington, Bellingham Slaughter, and Thomas Palin, guardians of his three children Andrews-John B., Eliz. B., and James B.; describes himself as "considerably indebted". [26th February, 1720—8th March, 1721.]

ELIZABETH SMALBONE, of Chipping-Lamborne, spinster, leaves 20s. to poor Catholics of p. of Llangarron, co. Hereford," and names her cousins Henry Scudamore, of Pembridge Castle, and Mary Eyston, of Hay-Hatch, "a niece of my fathers"; her grandmother Scudamore, niece Margaret Smalbone, and nephew Francis Clifton. [8th August, 1725—17th February, 1730.]

CHARLES BODENHAM, of Rotherwas, names his son Charles Stonor Bodenham, and da. Catherine, his present wife Catherine Huddleston (the settlement dating 12th February, 1731), the sister of Dame Mary, wife of Sir Francis Fortescue. Had advanced £4000 on mortgage to Edward, son of William Charleton, on the Manor of Hesleyside, co. Northumberland. His eldest son died unmarried, and his eldest da. Mary (by first wife) married John Tancred, of St. Paul's, Covent Garden, woollen draper, the settlement dating 18th August, 1760. [9th September, 1760—13th October, 1762.]

"✠ In the name of God, Amen. I, JAMES GUNTER, of Saddleboro', gent., being in perfect health . . . desire to be decently buried with little expense in the parish in which I shall dye." He left all his estate to his wife Hester, his will being attested by Catherine Prichard, Hugh Pemberton, and Charles Walker. [16th May, 1723—22nd June, 1726.]

HERTFORD.

JOHN NEWPORT, Esq., of Furneux Pelham, son of J. F. Newport, names his wife Mary and brother Thomas Heneage, and leaves £10 each to Eliz., wife of John Smith, and Mary, wife of John Barker, labourers, "das. of Eliz. Bawcock, whose death I was through great distraction and disturbance of mind . . . but without any premeditated malice most unfortunately the cause of, and of which I heartily repent". [9th October, 1737—3rd November, 1737.]

WALTER, Lord ASTON, desires burial at Standon Church, between his wife and daughter, naming his son James, da. Margaret, great-aunt Mrs. Sadleir, da.-in-law Lady Barbara Aston, and grandda. Mary Aston.

By a codicil, dated 11th August, 1747, in the form of a

letter to his son James, "he leaves £100 for prayers for his soul, viz., £50 to the two bishops in London, Mr. *White* and Mr. *Challence* [sic], to give to the most pious and wanting of their clergy to pray for me"; he adds, "You may give £10 to Mr. Wilson to pray himself, with such other good persons he thinks proper, and to distribute what he can out of it to the poor Catholics that come to the Chapel at Tixal, and £40 you may advise with Mr. Horton how to dispose of for the same purpose, and I think if the Religious Orders came in for a share, it might do very well . . . and as I believe it will not cost much, and that your sister Margaret will expect to have a service for me at her house, I would have you to pay her what is usual on that occasion, and let her know it is my desire". [4th July, 1746—15th August, 1748.]

"*White*," says the *Douay Diary*, p. 85, "was an *alias* of Bishop *Benjamin Petre*," who at the date of Lord Aston's will was Vicar-Apostolic of the London District, Bishop Challoner [*Challence*] being then also his coadjutor. Mr. Wilson was, it may be inferred, chaplain at Tixal; the *Douay Diary*, p. 87, also names one Joseph *Horton* as taking the college oath, 17th April, 1700.

HUNTINGDON.

MARGARET, widow of Ayme Gentil, of St. James', Westminster, in her will dated 3rd December, 1720, and proved 16th March, 1721, names her three grandsons mentioned in her husband's will, and her three granddas. named in that of her son John, who predeceased her; this "John Gentil, of the p. of St. Margaret's, Westminster, gent.," names his wife Catherine and his mother Margaret, desiring the Duchess of Richmond to assist the latter in her office of executrix; his three ds. were—Frances and Margaret G., and Catherine, the wife of John Cooke; to his son, "well provided for by his grandfather, he leaves his blessing and a cornelian". [30th October, 1719—6th April, 1720.]

KENT.

JAMES BLAKE, of the p. of Bromley, co. Essex, left his effects to Rob. Ashmall, Esq., of Lincoln's Inn. [4th January,

1727-8—13th January, 1727-8.] This is evidently the will of the Jesuit Father of this name, who, says Foley, *Collect. S.J.*, p. 64, was "chaplain at Mr. Mannock's, *Bromley Hall*, Colchester".

THOMAS HAWKINS.—" Nash, 2nd October, 1758. Whereas the stable and offices want new building, I therefore leave after my death all my goods and chattels to my eldest son Mr. John Hawkins, and desire that he pay . . . any such debts as may happen at my death, and as to the buildings I leave them to his discretion."

"13th September, 1763, son John Hawkins, I give you all I have except what I order you to pay by the within —— . . . to my son Hawkins Gower the first eight bags of hops"; he names also his grandson Thomas H., and adds: "—— 2s. a week to Goody Matson . . . for she had great care of me when I could not move finger nor hand . . . to my servant Samuel Woodrow, my watch, silver shoe, and knee buckles . . . and apparel . . . except swords, periwigs, and my red cloak."

"What I owe at Michaelmas."

"To Mr. Fuller £10; to the butcher £7; to Samuel [?] 19s.; hop-poles £48, £20 paid already; to you for hop-poles £25; for rent, dung, and cesses, about £35 hop-duty." No executor being named, admon. of his estate was granted, 24th July, 1766, to his son John Hawkins.

CHRISTOPHER COLLINS, of Linstead, writes: "My whole estate I leave to my daughters Anne, Lucy, and Catherine, exclusive of all my other children". His will was proved 23rd November, 1726.

GEORGE KINGSLEY, Esq., of the p. of St. James, Westminster, desires burial by his wife in the porch of that church, leaving 25s. to the clerk to see that it be done. He adds: "As my sons will none of them marry, and desiring my estate to remain in name and blood of my great grandfather William Kingsley, I bequeath my farm . . . at Ormsby, co. York, to my cousin Anthony K., druggist and citizen of London, and to his (Anthony's) sons in order of birth, Anthony, Thomas,

Pincke [?], Charles, and Thare". He names also his own sons George and Thomas (to whom, by codicil of 7th March, 1737, he left his pictures and library), and his da. Anne, the wife of George Hastings, and his youngest da. Catherine, also his wife's sister Mary Kersey. The codicil also names Thomas (son of Anthony) Kingsley as executor in the room of Sir Henry Bedingfield first named. [25th May, 1725—14th March, 1739.]

JOHN DARELL, of Calehill, desires burial in his vault at Little Chart, and names his wife Olivia, sons John, James, and Joseph, and da. Olivia. [24th May, 1739—8th September, 1740.]

RICHARD GOMELDON, of Summerfield Court. Admon. of his estate was granted, 26th July, 1719, to his sister Meliora, the wife of Thomas Stanley. His father Thomas Gomeldon, by will dated 7th July, 1702, proved 16th May, 1704, "desires to be privately buried in the night in the parish church of Selling, near his father and wife".

LANCASTER.

JOHN DARBYSHIRE, of Ashton-in-Mackerfield, yeoman, names as his executors his wife Ann and his brother James, bequeathing his estate at Pemberton to his son Henry, and at Ashton to his son John; names also his daughter Mary. [11th November, 1742—May, 1743.]

MARY CORNWALLIS, of St. Giles'-in-the-Fields, names her cousin Philadelphia Thorold, and appoints Margaret, the wife of John Yate, her executrix, though no relationship is stated. [13th February, 1727—3rd September, 1730.]

ALEXANDER STANDISH, of St. Giles'-in-the-Fields, left his house called Roundmoor, in the p. of Standish, co. Lanc., to his sister Margaret S., and names his two nephews Edward and Francis Brown (brothers), and two nieces, the widow of Laurence Brown and Mary Howard. [5th October, 1725—6th August, 1726.]

The will of WILLIAM WINSTANLEY, of St. Paul's, Covent Garden, "taylor," dated 17th September, 1733, and proved

24th January, 1735, would certainly be that of a near relative, if not the will of W. W. named by Cosin, so many Lancashire names being given : his wife Diana is executrix, and on her death testator gives "£1000 to Lady Anne Petre, the da. of the Earl of Derwentwater, who was beheaded on Tower Hill"; £10 to the Rt. Hon. Lady Winifred Nisdale, with legacies also to Rob. Scarisbrook, of Scarisbrook, Thomas Eccleston, of Eccleston, and others.

Sir WILLIAM MOLYNEUX. His first wife died in 1713, aged 58, he being 62 years of age at the time of his death in 1717. [*Lawson MS.*]

Dame CATHERINE SHERBURNE. "Memorandum that on 16th January, 1727, Dame C. S., relict of Sir Nicholas Sherburne, of Stonyhurst, being sick of her sickness whereof she died at her dwelling-house in Cork Street, in the p. of St. James, Westminster . . . having a mind to make her will nuncupative, or by word of mouth . . . Edward Strother, doctor of physic, Mr. Edmund Gage, and William Scott, being come into her chamber . . . expressed herself to them in words following . . . I give to Gilbert Talbot, of Cork Street, in the p. of St. James, my whole personal estate, and declare him my executor." Proved 11th March, 1727-8.

JOHN CULCHETH, of Gray's Inn, by will dated 20th June, 1733, and proved 7th September, 1733, left his "personal estate to his mother Mary, from whom he had received it".

ROGER CULCHETH, of "Wottenbury" (probably intended for *Wappenbury*), co. Warwick, gent., names his wife Isabel, brothers William C., George C., of London, upholsterer, and Thomas C., of Studley, co. Warwick, tanner; his two sisters —— Middlemore, of the p. of Bromsgrove, co. Worcester, and her children ; and —— Reeve, of Samborne, and her four children ; his brother Thomas being executor, and inheriting "all his estate at Wigan, co. Lanc.". [6th December, 1701—29th July, 1725.]

JOHN GRIMBALSTON, of Coughton Court, co. Warwick, in his will of 4th July, 1739, proved 16th February, 1742, " entreats his dear master, Sir Robert Throckmorton, to accept twenty guineas," and names his wife Elizabeth and da. Mary, his *brother Amor* Grimbalston, whose children were John, William, Amor, Mary, and Ann; his sisters Eleanor G. and Eliz. Briggs; sister Alice Bickliffe, whose children were John, Thomas, and Alice B.; his brother Leonard G., and nephew Leonard G.

FRANCES, the wife of Nicholas Blundell, of Little Crosby, died at Dunkirk, in Flanders, 19th August, 1763, aged 78. [*Lawson MS.*]

ROBERT TUITE, of Warrington, names his sons Robert (the eldest, to whom he left his estate at Plymouth, in the Isle of Montserrett, West Indies), Walter, and James; his das. Mary, Margaret, Anne, Elizabeth, and Eleanor; and his sister Jane, the wife of Robert Reyley, and their son Owen Reyley; Sir Joseph Tuite, bart., being named one of several executors. [13th April, 1724—19th September, 1726.]

LEICESTER.

THOMAS BLOFIELD, of Hammersmith, gent., by will, undated, and proved 2nd October, 1724, desires to be "buried by his mother and sister". Duncan Catanach, of St. Martin's-in-the-Fields, shagreen-case maker, deposes that he had known him many years: he names his cousin Mary Velson, and nephew and niece Charles and Ann Catanach; also Thomas and Charles, eldest and second sons of Charles Kinnes, of Belgrave; adding, "I give my clothes to ould Charles Kinds, all but my best suit ".

CHARLES FORTESCUE, of Husband's-Bosworth. Admon. of the estate of his widow Elizabeth F. was, 30th March, 1753, granted to Maria-Alathea-Sophia Fortescue, her da. and only child.

WILLIAM KNIGHT, of Kingerby, co. Lincoln, names his son William as sole executor of his will; the trustees, till he becomes of age, being "Robert Dolman, of York, Esq.; Edward Greathead, of Lincoln, doctor in physic; my nephew Peter Pennythorn, of Fornaby [?], and my wife Lucy K.". Others named are "my sons" Richard and Edmund, da. Lucy, my brother Alexander and his wife, my sisters —— Knight, widow; —— Pennythorn, and Anne and Margaret Knight; · brother John Knight; nieces Christian and Elizabeth, the das. of my brother Joseph Knight, deceased; uncle Mr. Edmund Stilles; my wife's mother Mrs. Lucy Jennings, and "Mr. Edmund Turner". He adds: If either "my son Edmund, or the son my wife is big of, go into Religion," his portion is to be £400 instead of £1000. [27th January, 1726; proved at Lincoln, 31st May, 1728.] The following M.I. of his sister-in-law is copied from a slab in front of the altar in Selby Abbey, Yorkshire: "Here lyeth interred the body of Mary, the wife of Joseph Langdale, gent., who died the 23rd September, 1716. *Requiescit in pace.*"

Count MIGLIORUCCI, in his will dated 18th December, 1723, and proved 23rd February, 1727, describes himself as "Peter Joseph Migliorucci, late of Florence, and now of London, merchant". His widow Lady Mary M. (*née* Nevill), by will of 6th March, 1735, proved 3rd May, 1742, left her estate to her son Cosmas-Henry-Joseph-Nevil Migliorucci.

FRANCIS RIGMAIDEN, Esq., late of Twickenham, widower. Admon. of his estate was granted, 1st October, 1747, to his da. Anne, the wife of John Crawford.

ISABELLA, widow of Francis Smith, of Queniboro', was only da. of Richard Clayton, of Keame [*sic*], co. Leicester: born in 1664, and dying 20th June, 1733, she was buried in the chancel of Ashby-Folville Church, her husband being a son of Edmund Smith. [*Lawson MS.*]

EDMUND SMITH married Amy, da. of John Sanders, of Heningsby [?], co. Warwick. [*Lawson MS.*]

FRANCIS SMITH, of Queniboro', in his (*unregistered*) will dated 10th December, 1717, and proved 15th April, 1721, names his brother Edward [?], wife Catherine, and her uncle Thomas Busby, of Ashby-Folville; apparently ob. s.p. His sister Helena (says the *Lawson MS.*) was a nun at Liege, where she died 28th October, 1722.

JOHN STEEVENS. In Saxulby Church, co. Leicester, are

the following M.I., as given by Nichols in his history of that county (iii., p. 404): "Here lieth the body of John Stevens, of Shouldby, gent., who departed this life 27th February, 1731, aged 72. . . . Also Elizabeth, wife of John Stevens, gent. . . . died 6th February, 1731, aged 85. . . . Also Winifred, wife of Morris Cam, and da. of John and Eliz. Stevens, died 13th March, 1737, in the 43rd year of her age."

John Stevens occurs in Cosin's List.

LINCOLN.

ANNE MARKHAM, of Claxby, whose will is dated 22nd April, 1727, says: . . . "I give the veil embroidered upon cambric with gold and silver, which anciently belonged to the family, and my great pair of beades, the stones spotted with gold, to my grandson Philip, eldest son of my son Thomas Markham": her son Percy is executor; she names also her grandson Thomas, second son of her son Thomas, and her das. —— Pole, and Anne and Melior Markham. [Lincoln, 10th May, 1729.]

JOHN MORLEY, of Holme, in p. of Bottesford, names his das. —— Boswell, Jane, and Anne M., and his son John; Marmaduke M. being named trustee. [13th May, 1731; proved at Lincoln, 18th May, 1731.]

MARMADUKE MORLEY, the elder, left his estate at Messingham, and his house at Twigmoor, to his son Marmaduke, and his stock-in-trade to his son and executor James; names also his son George and das. Anna Maria, Jane, and Henrietta. [29th November, 1752—Lincoln, 16th September, 1756.]

JOHN FITZWILLIAM, of Lincoln, in his will dated 4th February, 1711, and proved 1st July, 1718, names his sons Charles and William, das. Elizabeth, Anne, and Mary; his wife Anne being executrix. This Anne, his widow [12th March, 1724—Lincoln, 14th August, 1724], desires to have "six poor Catholics for her bearers to have a guinea each and 200 poor people each to have 6*d.*, each to say before taking the money, God be merciful to her soul".

Admon. of the estate of Frances Fitzwilliam, of Clixby, was

granted, 28th January, 1742, to her husband Charles, before named.

William Fitzwilliam (father of John) names his son George, cousin Percy Markham, his da. Elizabeth, wife of Thomas Ellerker, his sister Elizabeth, wife of Edward Monson, dec., and their son George M., and adds: " I give to my son John £5 to distribute for charitable uses to all such persons as do visit us, desiring *him* chiefly to be remembered as shall assist me at my death ". The witnesses to his will were Thomas Browne and John and Jane Millington. [22nd June, 1710—Lincoln, 4th April, 1717.]

Dame MARY SOUTHCOTT, of Blyborough. Admon. of her estate was granted 26th August, 1719, to her das. Catherine, wife of Francis Smith, Esq. of Aston, and Constance, wife of Thomas Fitzherbert.

MARY PORTER, of Hampton, co. Middx., says: " I desire to be buried in Kensington Church, near my son George, it not being possible for me to lye by my dear husband. . . . My daughters (Eleanor, Catherine, and Diana) may not be permitted to go to my funeral because it may injure their health." She names also her sons John, James, Aubrey, Endymion, and Richard. Her agent William Quin, of St. James', Westminster, deposed at date of probate that he had known her for fifteen years, she being lately in the p. of St. George, Hanover Square. [6th May, 1734—15th April, 1740.]

RALPH EURE, Esq. of Kensington, co. Middx., dates his will " in good health," and desires that his funeral expenses should not exceed £100. He names his son Edward, son-in-law Nicholas Stapylton, *alias* Errington, and four das. Philadelphia, Mary, Ann, and Charlotte. [1st February, 1724—25th November, 1726.]

GEORGE HENEAGE, of Hainton, names his wife Elizabeth (executrix), his sons George, Thomas, Henry, John, Robert, Windsor, and Francis, das. Elizabeth and Catherine, brother Thomas and sister Eliz. H., brother Sir George Windsor Hunloke, and grandchildren Eliz. and George, the children of his son Thomas Heneage. [4th November, 1719; codicils 26th February, 1725, and 27th December, 1731—7th June, 1732.]

THOMAS HENEAGE, of Cadeby, names his wife Winifred, and his three nephews Henry, George, and Thomas, and Catherine his niece. [31st December, 1739—15th May, 1741.]

EDMUND SOUTHCOTT, *alias* PARKER, of Blyborough. Admon. of his estate was granted, 14th November, 1725, to his widow, the Hon. Catherine S. His father's will, dated 23rd January, 1712-13, was proved in London 13th July, 1715.

JAMES HAMMERTON, of Waith, names his son James, das. Judith Buckley and Anne Calvert, and his kinsman William Loop. [25th November, 1719—Lincoln, 26th December, 1719.]

GEORGE SIMPSON bequeathed his house at Louth, "in a street or place called Fifth Shambles," to his wife. He speaks of "all his children," but names none. A witness to his will was Judith Buckley. [3rd November, 1731—Lincoln, 14th November, 1731.]

His father, "William Simpson, of Louth, taylor," and father also of William S., by will dated 2nd January, 1695, proved at Louth 12th May, 1696, left his Orby estate to his wife Elizabeth for her life, to pass at her death to his eldest son *William*. He names also his son *George*, das. Anne and Jane, youngest da. Elizabeth, the wife of Thomas Ashton, and his grandchild Mary Wilkinson, the trustees being his "loving friends" Mr. Dymoke Walpole and Mr. John Walpole, the latter and Mary Walpole witnessing his will.

THOMAS SPURR, of Louth, in will dated 4th August, 1717, and proved at Louth 14th August, 1717, by his kinsman and resid. legatee Thomas Jenkins, names his wife Bridget, sister Joyce S., and her da. Mary, kinsmen John S., and John, Richard, Henry, and Charles Jenkins, the witnesses being William and George Simpson and William Bond.

SIMON WARREN, of Dunston, farmer, names his wife Mary, his sons William, Peter, and Joseph, and da. Jane; Edward Walpole being one of three guardians of his children. [11th November, 1727—Lincoln, 8th December, 1727.]

TROTH MASTIN, of Grimolby, Grange, co. Linc., widow, by will dated 17th August, 1722, proved at Lincoln 23rd October,

1723, by her son *Samuel*, names also *his* da. Catherine, her grandda. Catherine Short, the " da. of my da. Troth," and her cousin Edward Knipe, of Grantham.

JOHN ROBINSON, of Fulbeck, names his sister Mary Coxon, nephew and niece William and Eliz. Coxon, and a nephew Benjamin Jessop, in a codicil dated 30th December, 1725. [26th April, 1722—Lincoln, 22nd March, 1726.]

WILLIAM SMITH bequeathed his Bucknall estate to his da. Mary, and his estate at Sturton-in-the-Steeple, co. Notts, to his da. Anne; names also his cousin Christopher Smith, the trustees of his daughters being his brother Samuel Mastin and Mr. Peter Medcalfe. [26th December, 1723—Lincoln, 18th June, 1728.]

WILLIAM THOROLD, of Little Ponton. On a slab in the chancel of Little Ponton Church, is the following: " D.O.M. Hic jacet corpus Gulielmi Thorold, armigeri, hujus manerii Dñi. qui pie obiit XX. die Septembris, anno Dom. MDCCXXV. R.I.P."

The following Little Ponton entries are extracted also from the Bishop's Register at Lincoln:

" William Thorold, of Little Ponton, Esq., was buried 21st September, 1725".

" Richard Thorold and Dorothy Martine were married 16th January, 1716."

" Mr. Rob. Thorold, son of Mr. William Thorold, and Mary his wife, was buried 14th February, 1686."

This last-named William T. might be the father of, or, indeed, the identical " Nonjuror " of that name, as it will be seen that his widow Dorothy, who so long survived him, might perhaps on that account have been his *second* wife. His will, being neither at Somerset House nor at Lincoln, was probably never proved. Though apparently childless, he did not however die intestate, as appears from the subjoined summary of *Close Roll*, 1 Geo. II., Part II., 15, 16. " By indenture, dated 9th February, 1726, between Dorothy Thorold, of the p. of St. Giles-in-the-Fields, co. Middx., widow and *executrix* of the last will and testament of Will. T., late of Little Ponton, co. Linc., dec., and George Thorold, Esq., *brother and heir* of the said dec.

of the one part, and William Sutton, of the p. of St. George the Martyr, co. Middx., gent., and Thomas Osborne, jun., of Gray's Inn, stationer, of the other part, the two latter became the purchasers of the Manors of Little Panton, *alias* Little Ponton and Basingham, with advowson, and Manor house of Little Ponton."

Upon the death of her husband, Dorothy appears to have resided abroad. The following summary of her will is made from the original, now among the Archives of the Dominican Priory, at Haverstock Hill:

"Dorothy *Compton*, widow of William Thorold," dating her will 11th November, 1768, from the Convent of the English Dominican Nuns at Brussels, where she died 2nd March, 1773, aged 82, names her sister Mary Arundell, "and poor relations" in England, and gave bequests to "Miss Frances Howard, of Grey-Stock," to "Sister" Mary Ann Calvert, in the Convent of the said Nuns, as also to the younger children of the late Francis Bishop, of Brailes, and George Bishop, his brother, of London.

The Rev. Raymund Palmer, O.P., also writes, that "Dorothy's *younger* sister Margaret Joseph Compton, da. of Edward Compton, of Gersby (of the family of the Earl of Northampton), by his wife Ann Merry, joined the Dominican Nuns of Brussels, was professed 1st July, 1717, æt. 22, and after being thrice prioress, died 29th July, 1768". For a further account of her, and of "Sister Mary Ann Calvert," see Dr. Oliver's *Western County Collections*, p. 155.

THOMAS SHUTTLEWORTH, of Horbling. Mr. A. Gibbons has kindly forwarded the following Shuttleworth entries from the Bishop's Register at Lincoln: "Horbling, Bap., 28th November, 1674, John, sonne of Thos. Shuttleworth, and Eliz. his wife".

"1676, July 6, Richard S., son" of the same.

"1676, July 20, Buried Richard, son of Thos. Shuttleworth."

"1679, December 10, Bapt. Edmond, son of Thomas and Eliz. S."

"1684, Buried Edmond, son of Thomas S., Esq."

One, Thomas Shuttleworth, buried at St. Pancras, dates his will 5th May, 1724, from the p. of St. George the Martyr, co. Middx. It was proved 18th May, 1724. He names his wife Mary, da. Mary, and two infant children.

. . . .

A slab in Selby Abbey Church gives the following: "Here lies interred the body of Mrs. Anne Shuttleworth, who departed this life, 19th February, 1789, aged 78 years. R.I.P."

MARY, widow of John Walpole, of Dunston, dating her will 8th January, 1744 (proved 17th September, 1746), names John, son of Stephen W., of Dunston; Mary and Ann, das. of Charles Tancred, of St. Paul's, Covent Garden, woollen draper, and her cousin Sarah Cheseldine.

The will of her da. Mary W., of Dunston, spinster, dated 15th October, 1729, was proved 12th July, 1742, when admon. of her estate was granted to John Smith, executor of the will of Edward W., dec., brother of testatrix, who survived her, but died before he administered. She desires to be buried in the Church of Slindon, names her sister Alathea, brother William, of Dunston, and her "late cousin Dymock Walpole's children, of Blankney".

WILLIAM MASTIN, of Grantham, gent., in his will dated —— July, 1734, and proved at Lincoln, 4th November, 1734, names his brother Robert M., sister Barbara Trelawney and her children, br.-in-law George Short, of Grantham, maltster, and niece Mrs. Mary Askins.

The Hon. DOROTHY THIMELBY, of St. Andrew's, Holborn, widow. Admon. of her estate was granted, 25th February, 1721, to her da. Mary Giffard, widow.

DANIEL BROWNE, of Bulby, left his Bourne estate to Peter, younger son of his nephew John Browne; his nephew Peter B., of Bulby, being executor, and his (testator's) sister Anne being residuary legatee; names also Mary Dorson, *alias* Langworth, and Elizabeth, Anne, Dorothy, and John, children of my late nephew and niece Robert and Catherine Langworth. He adds that "John, the elder son of my nephew John Browne, of Corby, co. Lincoln, is to have £10 upon the decease of my sister Anne Brown, of Bulby ". [23rd April, 1735—6th March, 1737.]

MARY CRANE, of Gedney, spinster. Her will, of which her kinsman Valentine Hilder, and Margaret Knight, of St. Martin's, in the city of Lincoln, spinster (resid. legatee), were named executors, is dated 20th February, 1730. Admon. of her estate was, however, granted, 1st June, 1743, to her niece and next-of-kin Mary, the wife of Thomas Markham, testatrix surviving both her executors.

ANTHONY VANE, of London, bequeaths "to Mr. Jerningham, goldsmith, the King of France, his picture," and names his friend Mrs. Frances Longville resid. legatee. [3rd March, 1722—26th March, 1723.]

THOMAS BOND, of Bury St. Edmunds, by will dated " 31st April" [*sic*], 1717, proved by his son Henry Jermyn Bond, 27th November, 1732, "desires, if he die in Bruges or in Flanders, burial in the Church of the Great Carmes, in the vault where Lord Dover is buried"; names his mother Dame Mary Bond, eldest da. Henrietta B. (dec.), and youngest da. Mrs. Judith B.; Sir Rob. Davers, bart., being trustee.

The will of WILLIAM MILLINGTON, of the bail of Lincoln, baker, dated 2nd February, 1759, and proved in the same year, is that, probably, of a *son* of John M. named by Cosin; he names his wife and five children—Sarah, William, Thomas, Mary, and Ann.

LONDON.

ELIZABETH PRUJEAN, of the p. of St. George the Martyr, widow. Admon. of her estate was granted, 13th June, 1746, to her son and only next-of-kin Francis. The will of this Francis Prujean, of " Sutton Gate," in the p. of Hornchurch, co. Essex, dated 5th April, 1774, was proved by his son William, 2nd August, 1780, to whom he left his estate there, and adds: " I desire burial in the vault of my ancestors at Hornchurch, near my wife, with a crucifix on y⁰ top, and a cross on my breast . . . my da. Elizabeth is to have the remainder of the term of my house in Great Ormond Street

... as also the goods in my lodging I now dwell at in Poland Street. ... A picture at 'Sutton Gate,' of the Scourging of our Saviour, I declare to be the property of the Hon. Mrs. Molyneux." He names also his son John and da. Ann, "commonly called Dame Mary Magdalen".

Evelyn, in his diary, says (9th August, 1661): "I went to that famous physitian, Sir Fr. Prujean, who showed me his laboratorie, his work-house for turning ... *also many excellent pictures*, especially the *Magdalen of Caracci*".

FRANCES FLATMAN, of St. Giles'-in-the-Fields, spinster, desires burial in that church, her will being proved in the Commissary Court of London by her servant Susan Smith. [15th May, 1734—28th January, 1736.]

Dame CLARE GULDEFORD, of ditto, leaves £20 to the poor, to be distributed by her servants Rob. Jenks and Cath. Carns, which her aunt Sarah Guldeford is to give them. [10th July, 1738—14th November, 1738.]

WILLIAM LANE, of the p. of St. Swithin, in the city of Lincoln. "I give my house, known by the name of the Three Old Tuns, in Thames Street, near Billingsgate, to my only da. Mary Lane and her heirs." He names also his two nieces Eliz. Kelly and Emerentiana Twell, the latter having two daughters Catherine and Mary. [24th February, 1728—4th February, 1730.] This, therefore, is not the Jesuit Father of that name, as suggested in *Eng. Cath. Nonj.*, p. 169.

RICHARD LEE, of Great Delce, by his wife *Margaret* had no issue, but in his will dated 25th February, 1710, with a codicil of 10th October, 1719, proved 16th April, 1725, he names his grandson Richard Lee, his sister Mary Watson, and her son William W.

Admon. of the estate of AGNES DE LA FONTAINE, of Lowick, widow (probably of John de la F.), was, 29th August, 1733, granted to her son Charles.

MIDDLESEX.

DOROTHY PANTON, of St. Martin's-in-the-Fields, desires to lie by her husband in St. Eustace's Chapel, in Westminster

Abbey, and names her son Brigadier-General Thomas Panton, her four grandsons Thomas and Henry Panton, the Hon. Henry and Hon. Thomas Arundell, and her grandda. Eliz., Countess of Castlehaven. [1st June, 1722—8th April, 1725.]

ELIZABETH RACKETT, of Hammersmith, widow, names her da.-in-law Johanna, widow of Mr. Stanislaus Bowes, late of Hammersmith, chirurgeon; also her sister Mary Hoffman, widow, the latter being with Thomas Stone, of St. Dunstan's-in-the-West, gent., executors. [20th July, 1722—24th September, 1725].

Admon. of the estate of WILLIAM PERCY was granted, 23rd November, 1721, to John Wybarne, husband of Eliz. Percy (afterwards Wybarne), and only child of W. P., late of St. Andrew's, Holborn, co. Middx., widower, she then being also dec.

MARGARET LEE, widow of Richard Lee, leaves her grandson Richard Lee her house in Gerard Street, and her niece Frances Butler her " striped crimson night gown ". She names her cousin Edward Webb, of Gray's Inn, nephews Francis and Richard Rich and William Watson, sister Mrs. Catherine Watson, niece Mrs. Mary Watson, bequeathing to her servant her " black and white striped satin night gown ". [22nd August, 1724; with codicil 12th February, 1725—12th April, 1725.]

WILLIAM WOOLFE, of St. Andrew's, Holborn, left his estate to his widow Frances. [16th January, 1737—23rd January, 1739.]

Hon. CHARLES SOMERSET, of East Street, near Red Lion Square, names his dec. wife Frances, da. of Dorothy Hanford, and cousin of Edward Hanford, of Woollashall; also his uncle Edward Hanford; leaves his boots, linen, and two best periwigs to his brother Henry Somerset. [1st December, 1720—2nd July, 1724].

MARY ROUS, of St. Martin's-in-the-Fields, widow, dates her will 27th November, 1752. One executor is Eliz. Rowbotham, to whom she leaves £5 a year from her " rents coming from Hendly House and lands in *Lancashire* and Oxford ". Her nephew, John Rowbotham, of p. of Christ Church, Surrey, brazier, deposed (18th July, 1755) that he had known her from his youth, and on the same day admon. was granted to Ann Rowbotham, widow, and sister of Mary Rouse, widow, the executors having renounced.

Sarah, the widow of John Rous, late of St. John Street, in p. of St. Sepulchre, London, distiller, names her brother-in-law John Hills, of the p. of St. Leonard, Bromley, co. Middx.; Anne, his wife; and their children John Hills, jun., and Mary-Ann Hills, her nephew and niece. [12th November, 1741—16th November, 1741.]

CHARLES BLAKE, of St. George's, Hanover Square, desires burial at the west end of the churchyard of St. Paul's, Covent Garden, "where his wives and their children lye," names his late son Charles B., son-in-law George Tilden, grandson George Tilden, and grandda. Teresa Baladine, sister of G. T., nephew Charles Blake and his wife, and niece Dorothy Blake. [7th October, 1732—1st December, 1732.] Assuming this to be the will of C. B., the "Nonjuror," he was therefore aged 95 at the time of his death.

HENRY TASBURGH, of St. Giles', names his wife Susannah, nephews Francis Tasburgh, of Bodney, and Basil Bartlett, his sister Anne Bartlett, widow, &c. His house in Devonshire Street, in the p. of St. George the Martyr, and most of his effects he leaves to his da. Mary Clare Tasburgh [27th September, 1732—10th January, 1738.], who afterwards married Sir Thomas Gerard, bart., and dying 27th October, 1768, æt. 42, was buried at St. Pancras. [Cansick's *Epitaphs of Middlesex*, p. 15.]

The will of ELIZABETH ARMSTRONG, of St. Margaret's, Westminster, widow, dated 1st May, and proved 10th May, 1742, by which she left her estate to her niece Judith, the widow of her nephew Laurence Wierex, tallow chandler, may possibly be that of E. A., the "Catholic Nonjuror".

MARGARET CALVERT, Lady BALTIMORE, names her grandda. Charlotte C., and Cecil, youngest son of Benedict C., her executrix being Mrs. Frances Errington. [15th July, 1731—21st July, 1731.]

GEORGE BROWNLOW DOUGHTY, of Beenham, co. Berks. Admon. of his estate was granted, 10th April, 1744, to his son Henry.

His widow, Frances D., of Devonshire Street, in the p. of St. George the Martyr, in her will of 31st May, 1763, names her four sons (then living) Henry, George, James, and Robert, and her three das. Frances, wife of Henry Wells; Mary, wife of Thomas Mannock; and Charlotte D., spinster; John Prujean being a witness, and John Maire, of Gray's Inn, executor of her will, proved 28th November, 1765. Further admon. was granted, 18th April, 1776, to her da. Mary Mannock.

His father, Philip Doughty, of Marford Hall, co. Lincoln (whose will of 30th March, 1710, was proved 20th May, 1710), married Elizabeth, only child and heir of William Brownlow, of Humby, co. Lincoln, a brother of Sir John Brownlow, bart.

Grace Hatcher, who by will left some estate to the Doughty family, was da. and co-heir of William Harbord, and first wife of Thomas Hatcher, Esq. of Careby, co. Lincoln, who died at Bath, 6th September, 1714. [Blore's *Hist. of Rutland*, p. 134.]

JANE FITZWILLIAM, of the p. of St. James, in the Liberty of Westminster, names her da. Jane, the wife of —— Dally, and their children Jane and Mary Dally; her two cousins Henry Cuffaud and Richard Compton, and her friends John Yate (who, with [Bishop] Benjamin Petre, witnessed her will) and Margaret Yate his wife. [2nd December, 1723—28th September, 1730.]

ELIZABETH GAZAIGNE, widow of John G., late of the p. of St. Martin-in-the-Fields, co. Middx., tailor, in her will dated 25th April, 1737, when "in pretty good health," and proved 10th February, 1743, says: ". . . I have for life the produce of 33,000 livres from the town house in Paris in the name of Eliz. Robinson, which goes at my death to my son John". She names her das. Mary Fraser and Frances Tancred, grandson Charles Tancred, and cousins Ann and Eliz. Purcell. Her husband John G. appears to have been the son of John G., of Theobald's Court, Holborn, by his wife Mary G., *alias* Adams, the will of this Mary G. being proved 6th February, 1718, O.S., by her son Anthony G.

Admon. of the estate of AURELIUS JONES, of St. Anne's, Westminster, was granted, 14th February, 1728, to his widow Mary.

Admon. of the estate of CHARLES SMALBONE, of Lamborne, co. Berks, was granted, 16th September, 1724, to his sister Margaret S., spinster.

ELIZABETH MOREN, of the p. of St. Martin-in-the-Fields, desires burial near her husband Dominic M., in the churchyard of Covent Garden, and names her sons Dominique and Charles, and her sister Mary Hinton, of Newbury, co. Berks, widow. [13th April, 1711—1st December, 1720.]

"DENNIS MOLONY, Esq., now of Gray's Inn, and late of Lincoln's Inn . . . desires burial in Sumerset House Chapel, if allowed, and if not in St. Andrew's, Holborn;" names his nephew Daniel, a nephew in Clare's regiment, and son of his sister Honora Macnamara; he gives legacies "to the late Bishop Molony's poor relations, in co. Clare . . . to Mr. Turberville, my horse, I am glad he is a good one for my friend's sake . . . £10 each to the clergy of the Portuguese, French, Spanish, and Sardinian Chapels, in London, that they may severally say and perform the service and office for the dead . . . the poor begging at the chapel door when such service is performing to have 2 guineas divided amongst them, and they to join in praying for my soul at the same time." [30th November, 1726—10th January, 1727.]

LÆTITIA LANGHORN, of St. Sepulchre's, London. Admon. of her estate was granted, 8th December, 1729, to her sister Catherine, the wife of Rob. Burton.

ANNE, Countess of SUSSEX, desires burial early in the morning, with only one coach to attend her funeral; names her grandson Thomas Barrett Leonard, da. Lady Barbara Skelton, and grandda. Anne Roper, with the other children of her da., the wife of Henry, Lord Teynham. [15th May, 1722—19th May, 1722.]

Francis Bird, of St. Giles'. Admon. of his estate was granted, 13th March, 1731, to his widow Hester, and a further admon., 5th July, 1751, to his son Edward Chapman Bird, of the estate left unadministered by the widow at that time dec.

Mary Rouge, late of the city of Paris, spinster. Admon. of her estate was granted, 17th December, 1719, to her brother John R.

Sir Henry Bond. "Translated out of French" is the will of his mother-in-law Eliz. Benoist, living 20th April, 1724, in King Street, in p. of St. James, Westminster, and "widow of the late Hon. Simon le Noir, Esq., councellor and secretary to the most Christian King": she names her grandson Sir Thomas Bond, and granddas. Eliz. and Lelia Bond. Her will was proved 1st June, 1724.

MONMOUTH.

John Jones, Esq., "late of Dingestow, now of the Dry Bridge, in the p. of Monmouth," names his wife Catherine, sons Richard (eldest) and John, and das. Teresa, Catherine, Margaret, and Cecily: one witness is Michael Lorimer. [14th January, 1725—17th May, 1726.]

Frances Watkins, now or late of Bergavenny, spinster, names her kinsman Rob. Gunter, of Bergavenny, doctor of physic, and his brother and sister John and Jane Gunter; leaves some plate to Anthony Wright, of Covent Garden, to Michael Lorimer the younger, of Perthire, and to Mary Gunter, of Bergavenny, widow. [23rd April, 1739—26th July, 1739.] The will also of Charles Watkins, of Abergavenny, son of Charles and Mary W., late of the Wayne, in p. of Tregare, dated 8th July, 1737, was proved 28th January, 1738: he left all his estate to his executor, Edward Webb, of Gray's Inn.

John Vaughan, "the elder," of Courtfield, by will of 23rd September, 1750, left his personal estate to his wife Elizabeth; a codicil of 8th April, 1754, states that "pictures, plate, and furniture are to continue as standards and heirlooms in the house". Proved 8th April, 1755.

JOHN AYLEWORTH, of Trecastle, in p. of Llangoven, names his wife Elizabeth, sister Hannah, the wife of Edward Philpot; his three nephews John Gosling, of Chepstow, cooper; Roger Cadogan, of Coytrey; and Henry Cadogan, of Kemys-Commander, co. Monmouth; with legacies to Anne, Eliz., Winifred, and Hannah, the four das. of John Prichard, of Skenfrith, by Anne his wife (testator's niece); to Winifred, wife of Mr. Herbert, and da. of Henry Scudamore, of Pembridge Castle, and to his cousin John Ayleworth, of Llandanny. [8th January, 1725—15th April, 1726.]

MATTHEW JONES, of Skenfrith, names his late parents Rice and Ann Jones, wife Alice, sons William (eldest), John, and Robert; das. Ann and Teresa, and his brother John Jones. James Powell is named as "tenant of the Wayne," the overseers of his will being his kinsman Robert Needham, jun., and his cousin Thomas Belchier. [2nd November, 1719; codicil 13th October, 1721—2nd March, 1722.]

EDWARD PROGERS was son of "William P., of Gwarindee, councillor-at-law," by Catherine, da. of Robert Berry, Esq., of Ludlow: he married Elizabeth, da. of Walter Williams, of Llanfuyst, his grandfather being Charles P., colonel of King's Guards, who married, *first*, a da. of Henry Baker, of Abergavenny, by whom he had only one da., and *secondly*, Hieronyma, da. of William Bawd, of Walgrave, co. Northampton. [Brit. Mus., *Harl. MSS.* 2291, pt. ii., f. 32.]

ROBERT NEEDHAM, jun., of St. Maughan's, died 4th April, 1720: he married, *first*, Lucy, da. of —— Scudamore, of Blackbrooke, and *secondly*, Anne, sister of Charles Pye, of the "Mynde". [*Lawson MS.*] On 4th July, 1753, admon. of the estate of Rob. Needham, late of Hilston, co. Monmouth, was granted to Robert Needham, son of dec. Ann N., widow of dec., herself dying before she had taken admon.: "the letters of admon. of said dec., granted in October, 1724, to Susanna N., widow, grandmother and guardian of the said Robert N. and of Charles N., and of John N., an infant, children of the said dec., then minors, for their use and benefit, and until they or one of them should attain twenty-one years of age, being ceased and expired by reason the said Rob. N. hath attained the age aforesaid".

Dr. Oliver, *Western County Collections*, pp. 62 and 189, writes of these "minor" Needhams, that John N. afterwards married Eliz., da. of Robert Rowe, by Prudence Chichester his wife; while of Charles, he says: " This gifted *élève* of Douay College and polished gentleman arrived at Tor Abbey, 10th December, 1745, where until the autumn of 1788, he continued his invaluable services to religion and to the [Cary] family. Retiring from the charge of the flock, he afterwards resided at the village of Tor Mohun until February, 1798, eventually dying in London, 10th September, 1802, aged 88". The *Douay Diary*, p. 63, speaks of him as *optimæ spei adolescens*, born 2nd October, 1716, and taking the College oath, 11th March, 1735.

THOMAS JONES, of Hardwick, bachelor. Admon. of his estate was granted, 8th June, 1739, to his sisters Catherine Jones and Eliz., the wife of William Taylor.

WINIFRED JONES, " widow of George Jones, of Hardwick, now in the p. of Holywell, co. Flint," by will of 8th August, 1734, proved 19th October, 1736, left her " linen and furniture in her room at Hardwick to her das. Catherine J. and Eliz., naming her brother Thomas Davies, of Trerabbott, resid. legatee".

GEORGE SCUDAMORE, of Skenfrith. The codicil to his will is dated 20th August, 1717, the will being proved 2nd March, 1723, by the two first-named of his three executors, viz., his nephew Charles Bodenham, George Morgan, of Monmouth, and his brother-in-law Robert Needham the elder.

This ROBERT NEEDHAM, by his will dated 20th February, 1720, " according to the computation of the Church of England . . . all written with his own hand . . . desires burial in a frugal and decent manner at night-time," and names his wife Susan, son Sebastian, das. Ursula, the wife of Thomas Belchier, and their da. Jane, and Susan, wife of George Pinkard, and Robert their son; his son John N. with Martha his wife, and his son-in-law John Richard Langhorn; also his grandson Robert, the son of his deceased son Robert Needham; he bequeaths his law books and MSS. of pleadings to such of the sons of his late son Robert as shall practise the law; these, his grandsons, are when "eighteen years of age to choose a profession to avoid idleness and bad company"; finally, he leaves three guineas to his niece Kimbarow Morgan, who nursed him in his illness. [Proved 25th September, 1724.]

WILLIAM PROGER, Esq. of Gwerndee, co. Monmouth, appointed his wife Catherine executrix of his will, proved 30th April, 1708, and names his "two sons," of whom Edward the eldest appears in Cosin's List, as also does his mother, who, 2nd July, 1712, married, *secondly*, William Thomas, of Brecon, a brother of Hugh Thomas, herald and antiquary. [Brit. Mus., *Harl. MSS.* 2291, and Jones' *Breconshire.*]

FRANCES PROGER, of Llantillio-Pertholey, spinster, desires burial in Bergavenny Churchyard, near her sister [Hieronyma] Mostyn, whose wedding-ring she leaves to her cousin Philippa, the wife of the Rev. Dr. Croxall; and to the wife of William Saunders, "a picture of our Blessed Lord, the Blessed Virgin, and St. Joseph". She names also her two nephews Edward and Robert Proger, and her "cousins" [*sic*] William and Elizabeth, son and da. of the said Edward Proger; cousins Catherine Jones, of Dingestow, widow, and Mary Cown, her friend Robert Cown, of Bergavenny, being executor. [26th March, 1731—17th May, 1733.]

Her sister Hieronyma married Thomas, fourth son of Sir Pyers Mostyn of Talacre, co. Flint, by Frances, his wife. H. M. was a da. of Charles Progers by his second wife Hieronyma Bawd. [*See* EDWARD PROGERS and *Harl. MSS.* 2291.]

NOTTINGHAM.

PERCY MARKHAM, of Spink-hill, names his two cousins, Cosmas Nevill, of Holt, whose son Charles was testator's godson, and William Fitzwilliam, described as "living at present with my nephew Conquest". His executors were his nephews George and Edward Markham, and there are legacies to Lady Barlow, Vincent Eyre, of Sheffield, and Vincent Eyre, of Dronfield-Woodhouse. [15th August, 1751—11th September, 1753.]

Sir GERVASE CLIFTON, of Clifton, bart., desires "to be carried to his burial by his tenantry and servants," and names his wife Anne, and sons Robert (eldest), William, Alfred, and George. [9th December, 1724—3rd April, 1731.]

EDWARD, Duke of NORFOLK, desires burial at Arundel, and names among others his brother Philip and wife Henrietta; kinsmen Charles Howard; Bernard-Edward and Henry-Thomas, the two sons of Henry Howard, of Sheffield. [21st May, 1777—9th October, 1777.]

Hon. PHILIP HOWARD, of Buckenham House, co. Norfolk, desiring to be interred in Arundel Church, Sussex, leaves his son Thomas and da. Winifred "to the care and tuition of his brother Edward, Duke of Norfolk," and his son Edward and da. Anne to the like care of his wife and executrix Henrietta. [7th June, 1745—10th February, 1750.]

NORFOLK.

Hon. HENRY HOWARD, " of St. Andrew's, Holborn, bachelor ". Admon. granted, 12th June, 1722, to his brother Philip, his mother Lady Mary H. renouncing.

ELIZABETH HEVENINGHAM, " of the p. of St. James, within the liberty of Westminster, and lately of Hatch, near Hendon, co. Wilts," spinster, names the Countess of Castlehaven, her cousin —— Weld, of Lulworth Castle, and " Mrs. Grimes ". Her executor, George, the son of Richard and Dorothy Shelton, refusing to administer to her estate, admon. was granted, 5th December, 1726, to her sister Bridgit Graby, widow, to whom also she bequeathed "the rent of her three houses in St. Martin's Lane," and whose da. Jane Graby is to receive them on her mother's death. [15th July, 1725—5th December, 1726.]

The will of Sir FRANCIS FORTESCUE, of Sawston, co. Cambridge, who also held estates at West Walton and Walsoken, co. Norfolk, dated 18th September, 1724, and of which his widow Dame Mary was named one executrix, was proved 8th January, 1730.

Dame DOROTHY YALLOP. On an altar tomb in Bowthorpe Churchyard is the following M. I. " Reliquiæ Roberti Yallop, militis, Loco, Jussu dum viveret suo, coram effoso, depositæ : obiit VII° die mensis Maii, A° Domini MDCCV., ætat 68. *Requiescat in Pace*."

And in the chancel of Bowthorpe Church : " Here lyeth the bodies of Robert, Henry, and Dorothy Yallop, children of Sir Robert and Dorothy Y., his wife, who died in infancy, 1660-1670 ".

And on another stone.

"Here lyeth the body of Dame Dorothy, the widow of Sir Rob. Yallop, of Bowthorpe, in the co. of Norfolk, Knt., to whom she bore four sons and one da. She was the eldest da. of Clement Spelman, Esq., of the co. of Middx., and one of the barons of the Exchequer: a lady no less adorned with the endowments of Nature than of Virtue ; and as the former gave her the esteem of men, so the latter qualified her for heaven, for, if the merciful shall obtain mercy, she in whom Compassion and Charity to the distressed shined so bright may justly be presumed to have met with a like return from the Father of Mercies, in hopes whereof she departed this life, the 15th day of Jan., 1719-20, and of her age 84." [Blomefield's *Norfolk*, ii. 384-5.]

Page, in his *History of Suffolk* (p. 468), says that the Bowthorpe estate was conveyed to Sir Rob. Y. for his services in the recovery of certain Yorkshire estates, the property of the Yaxleys, also a Catholic family.

Sir FRANCIS JERNEGAN names his wife Anne, sons George, John, Francis, Charles, Henry, and Edward, and das. Mary and Anne. [11th June, 1730—24th November, 1730.]

ELIZABETH HOWARD, by will dated 12th September, 1734, and proved 1st March, 1737, by her executor James Rokeby, desires burial at St. Pancras by her father " as privately and decently as 18 guineas will pay," leaves a guinea ring to the Duke of Norfolk, her uncle, and " all her effects to Elizabeth Challiner for just and good service to her parents and herself ".

JEREMY NORRIS, Esq., of the city of Norwich, in will of 30th

July, 1699, "stilo, Angliæ," proved 24th January, 1700, names his wife Teresa; former wife Anne, the da. of William Woolmer; son Jeremy, and das. Anne Reilly and Mary the wife of Thomas Seaman. He left also "£120 to poor Catholics of the city of Norwich to be put out at interest in perpetuity".

VERE HARCOURT, gent., of Little Walsingham, co. Norfolk, by his will dated 5th September, 1714, and proved 22nd March, 1717, left his estate at Clay-next-the-Sea to Lucy his wife for life, passing at her death to "such of his children and their heirs as were living at the death of the late Lady Colstone". The Rev. Vere Harcourt, rector of Plumtree, co. Notts, in his will of 30th March, 1683, proved at York, 19th July, 1683, names his eldest son Vere Harcourt (dec.), and his "*grandchild Vere*, son of his eldest son Vere and Judith his wife". This "grandson" was probably afterwards the husband of Lucy here named. Dame Anne Colstone died in 1705. The suggestion in *note* p. 177 of *Eng. Cath. Nonj.*, that Lucy was the widow of the Archdeacon of Notts, is evidently therefore incorrect.

HENRY DEVALL, of Swaffham, grocer, gives legacies to his wife Mary, to Charles Sherburne, now living with John Eyre, of Berries Hall; "to cousin Thomas Sulman, living with some ambassador in London; and to his (Sulman's) sister Mary Pell, widow, with £10 to the poorest inhabitants of Swaffham as does not take collection". [26th January, 1728—26th February, 1728.]

RICHARD BOSTOCK, of Bath, in co. Somerset, thus commences his will: "Deus propitius esto mihi peccatori: fiat voluntas tua". If dying within a day's journey of Bath, desires "to be buried between eleven and twelve at night in left-hand aisle of the Abbey Church, and that a monumental stone against the wall bear only this inscription: . . . Richardus Bostock, M.D., olim de Whixall in co. Salopiæ obiit . . . Requiescat in pace:" he names his brother Nathaniel and nephew Henry B., and three sisters Mary B., spinster, —— Thickness, and Catherine Paston, widow and executrix. [29th January, 1746—7th April, 1747.]

HELENA LAURENCE, of Castleacre, co. Norfolk, in her will of 5th October, 1741, proved 9th January, 1742, names her grandson Mat. Halcott, of Hoe, next Dereham, her son Samuel, and da. Helen, the wife of Thomas Young, of Northwold, with their son Thomas Patrick Young.

NORTHAMPTON.

DOROTHY, Lady DUNBAR, "desires to be buried about eleven or twelve of the clock in the night," and leaves to her "nephew, Cuthert Constable, the picture of Lord Dunbar and that of the Duchess of Feria, to be kept as heirlooms in his family": names her sister the Countess of Middleton, niece Lady Molyneux, and nephews John, Earl of Middleton, and his brother Charles, the Hon. James Brudenell, and his da. Caroline, Thomas, Earl of Westmoreland, and the Hon. Jane Fane. [28th December, 1734; codicils 19th August, 1738—proved 24th March, 1740.]

WILLIAM HOLMAN, of Warkworth, names his brother-in-law Henry Wells, kinswoman Eliz. Dacres, spinster; wife Mary, and nephew Rowland Eyre, with his (Eyre's) sister and brother, Catherine and Francis Eyre. [17th March, 1739—12th November, 1740.]

JULIA PULTON, of Desborough, names her father Robert Garter, sons Robert (dec.) and Ferdinand, das. Mary and Frances P., and "son-in-law Richard Wright and my da., his wife, and their three children". [20th December, 1717—21st February, 1723.]

NORTHUMBERLAND.

THOMAS DREW, of Dodington, made John Hussey, of Marnhull, executor of his will, and names his sister —— Drew, wife Frances, and *her* sister —— Gibbons: also "the son and da. of my half-sister Mary Ford. [February, 1729—1st October, 1731.] His first-named sister Frances Drew, spinster, of "Oakebole," lived at Chaddesley-Corbet: her will, dated 1st February, 1724, was proved 22nd September, 1725: Giles Hussey was her godson, and Martha, the wife of Bernard Adys, was present at her death. She also bequeathed " £40 to the Lanes of Winchester, if any of them are left; if not, to be given there to have them prayed for ".

NICHOLAS STAPLETON, of Carlton, co. York, nephew and heir of Sir Miles S., names his wife Mary, sons Nicholas, Gregory, John, and Thomas S., and his uncles George and Charles Errington, two witnesses to his will being Christopher Lodge and John Reynolds. [9th July, 1715—4th January, 1717.]

JOHN CLAVERING, of Callaly, in his will dated 25th January, 1723, witnessed by Dorothy and John Hankin and John Maire, and proved 30th July, 1751, names his late father Ralph, da. Mary, and son Ralph sole executor.

The Hon. ELIZ. WIDDRINGTON, " of St. Andrew's, Holborn, widow, desires to be buried near her da. Mary, who lies in the Church of St. Paul's, Covent Garden, and names her nieces Elizabeth, Bridget, and Ann Molyneux; " Mary, the da. of my sister Anne Widdrington, of Cheeseburn Grange "; son Edward H. Widdrington, and his da. Eliz.-Margaret, and her sister Dame Frances O'Neil. [6th June, 1730—26th January, 1731.]

"CATHERINE RADCLIFFE, formerly of Dillingston, co. Northumberland, spinster," by will dated 20th April, 1729, proved 10th July, 1744, left all her estate to Sir John Webb, of Hatherop, co. Gloucester.

GEORGE ERRINGTON, " of the p. of St. Andrew, Holborn ". Admon. of his estate was granted, 28th June, 1725, to his da. Frances E., spinster, his widow Everilde E. having first renounced : the latter, dating her will also in the same parish, 8th July, 1726 (proved 12th September, 1727), desires burial at St. Pancras by her husband and da., and speaks of her "cousins Eliz. Fenwick and Frances Errington, who now live with me ".

Their da. Frances E., of St. Andrew's, Holborn, in her will of 15th December, 1725, proved 5th April, 1726, names her cousin John, son of Gilbert E., of ——, Northumberland, and grandson of Benjamin E., late of Berwick-hill. She speaks of her "father's law books," and desires burial at St. Pancras.

OXON.

MICHAEL BLOUNT, of Maple-Durham, in his will dated 28th November, 1730, and proved 22nd April, 1740, by Michael, his son, his widow Mary renouncing execution, names his brother-in-law George-Brounlow Doughty, cousins Sir John and Matthew Swinburne, and sisters Teresa and Martha, leaving also "£300 among poor Roman Catholics"; either of his das. Mary or Frances entering Religion to have £500 in lieu of £2000 otherwise their portion, and any son "becoming a professed priest of any Religious Order" to have £500 instead of £1000.

THOMAS STONOR, of Stonor, desires burial among his ancestors at Stonor, and names his brother John Talbot Stonor, das. Winifred Howard, Anne, Elizabeth, and Penelope, and sons Thomas (eldest), Charles, John, and Christopher, " any of whom entering a Religious Order under 21 years of age to have only £500." [14th January, 1723—13th August, 1724.]

Admon. of the estate of JOHN TRINDER, of Westwell, co. Oxon, a brother of Charles T., was granted, 3rd September, 1719, to Anne, his widow.

MARY HYDE, of Stanlake, widow, names her sons Richard (eldest) and Charles, and her da. Anne, as also her nephew Francis Risdon, of the p. of St. Ann, in St. Martin's-le-Grand. Of her sons she says: " I beg of Richard for my sake to be kind to his brother Charles ". [25th March, 1732—6th July, 1733.]

ROBERT KILBY, of Souldern, names his wife Ann, nephews Gabriel and Samuel Cox, and three nieces Helena Blevin, Eliz., wife of Rev. Walter Saunders, and Alicia Cox, spinster. [30th June, 1746—25th June, 1757.]

Sir FRANCIS CURZON, of Great Milton, names his wife Winifred, brother Peter, nephew John Brinkhurst, and nieces Lady Gaydon, Catherine Brinkhurst, and Mary Barnwell. [8th August, 1749—2nd August, 1750.]

JAMES FERMOR, of Tusmore, mentions his son Henry and uncle Richard F., and leaves "£5 only to any of his five younger children who turn Religious". [25th August, 1721—19th December, 1722.]

HENRY FERMOR, of Tusmore, desires burial at Somerton, co. Oxon; names his eldest son William and brother James; "any younger child turning Religious between the ages of 21 and 30 to have only £500, but any doing so after 30 years of age to have her full share, viz., £2000". [8th March, 1743—5th March, 1747.]

CHARLES GREENWOOD, of Brize-Norton, in his will made, "In the Name of the Holy and undivided Trinity," 1st August, 1721, and proved 6th March, 1722, names his wife Ann, only da. of Francis Canning, of Foxcote (the marriage settlement bearing date 27th January, 1718); cousins Charles Bodenham, Thomas Greenwood, of Chastleton, co. Oxon, and John Dancastle, of Binfield, and appoints his father-in-law and his brother John Russell, of Little Malvern, guardians of his da. Mary G.

RADNOR.

JAMES BASKERVILLE, of Aberedow. Admon. of his estate was granted, 9th June, 1733, to his widow Mary.

SALOP.

MARY PURCELL, of London, spinster, in her will of 4th January, 1731, proved 18th January, 1739, by her sister Catherine Penson, whose husband Thomas was then dead, names her sister Winifred and nephew James, eldest son of her brother John Purcell, doctor of physic; alludes to a share of a coal mine, lately the property of her dec. brother Thomas, about which there was some dispute. The estate being left unadministered by Catherine Penson, further admon. was granted, 9th June, 1752, to Winifred Purcell.

THOMAS PENSON, of Gray's Inn, names his wife Catherine, sons John and Joseph, and da. Mary P., a further admon. being granted 1st December, 1740, to Joseph P., one of the surviving resid. legatees, Cath., the widow, then being dec. intestate. [8th June, 1736—13th July, 1737.]

FRANCIS SMITH, of Aston, in his will dated 10th April, 1700, and proved 30th April, 1701, names his wife Audrey (a da., says the *Lawson MS.*, of Robert Atwood, of Bushbury, co. Stafford), son William, and five das., Elizabeth, Juliana, Mary, Anne, and Audrey: a further admon. was granted, 19th May, 1720, to Anne his da., the widow Audrey then being dead.

The will of ELIZABETH IRELAND (widow of Thomas I.), dated " 16th September, 1718, O.S., in New North Street, near Red Lyon Square, in p. of St. Andrew, Holborn," was proved 30th December, 1718. To her son Thomas she bequeaths " all the goods she left at Abrighton, with legacies to her da. Eliz. (whose will, dated 19th November, 1717, was proved 25th November, 1730), her grandson Thomas Ireland, and her three brothers, Raphe, Edward, and Thomas Clayton.

" NATHANIEL BOSTOCK, of Whixall, in p. of Preece, co. Salop, doctor in physic," names his wife Eliz., daughters Eliz. Lowe, —— Eyre, Mary, Catherine, and Alathea, with their grandfather Stafford, and their aunt Lenoxe: his eldest son Richard (executor), and other sons, John, Henry, James, and Nathaniel B. [28th December, 1714—1st October, 1719.]

WINIFRED PURCELL, of the p. of St. George the Martyr, Queen Square, spinster, writes: " As I am a Christian I hope for salvation through the merits of my Saviour ". " To her niece Mrs. Maria Teresa Cotton she leaves her "green damasked gown and unwatered tabby"; her clothes to her brother Edward's da., of Broseley, co. Salop, naming also his two sons Edward and Thomas P., and her friend Mary, widow of the late William Lacy, and Frances Lacy their da. [21st November, 1758—21st November, 1760.]

THOMAS BERINGTON, of the p. of St. George the Martyr, Queen Square, London, in his will of 31st October, 1755, proved 29th December, 1755, names his three nephews, Dr. William B., Dr. Joseph B., and Thomas Berington, of Stock, the latter being executor; his sister —— *Clough*, four nieces, —— Berington, Frances Auben; and her two sisters, "my nieces," Eliz. and Ann Clough, adding: I leave " to my niece Philippa, now Lady Fleetwood, five guineas and my spring clock that strikes the quarters ".

THOMAS PURCELL, of the Hay, in p. of Madeley. Admon. of his estate was granted, 15th December, 1719, to his widow Catherine.

RICHARD LACON, of Linley, by will of 15th January, 1750, proved 23rd January, 1752, desires to be buried near his wife, and names his brother Rowland (executor) and the children of his two brothers-in-law, Thomas Green (dec.) and Samuel Littlehales.

The will of "ALETHEA CLIFFORD, widow, of the town of Shrewsbury," dated 9th January, 1729-30, was proved 7th May, 1737, by her grandson Richard Corbett, to whom she left all her estate.

✢

"I, WILLIAM PLOWDEN, being this 31st March, 1739, full 70 years of age and thro' God's uncommon mercy of sound judgment . . . though of fast declining health and sunk with heavy sorrows, God enable me to bear 'em Christianly ——— . . . did intend to be buried in Plowden Bow in Lidbury Church with my ancient ancestors and close to my last dear wife Mary Stonor, or in the churchyard of St. Oswald's Hospital at Worcester, but being bent upon complying with what I think will best please my present wife Mary Lyttleton, and seeing her determined to be buried by our two boys Edmund-Lyttleton P. and Charles P., I doe depart from and wave whatever moved me to the above intentions, and as a last proof that living I ever wished to please her, and dying will solely study to gain her heart. . . . I order my body to be buried in Worcester Church, near my boys . . . this to be performed in a more than commonly private manner, no pomp, no fflutter, no hearses, no coaches, no rings, no scarves, gloves, nor hat-bands, but instead thereof, 8 men to carry me to the grave and to have 5s. each, and after my corps, old Tom Blackmore—above 100—if alive, to walk mourner and to have 20s., after him 70 men of sixty, each (if so it may be) to attend unto my grave and to have 5s. each : my coffin to be of mahogany plank without covering of velvet or cloath, strong brass hasps and hinges but no pall nor escutcheons, a Brass plain crosse on the top of the coffin, under which these three letters, R.I.P., with my day of death : a large black marble to be layd over my body with 'William Plowden dyed—aged—R.I.P.'. On the church wall as near the grave as may be I will have a large white marble stone (plain mould) with a black marble cross over it, deep cut: on this white stone I will have these words, 'Here underlyes William Plowden honourably and very anciently descended, born 31st March, 1669, dyed ——': next under, I will have these words, 'Pro fide, pro rege, mala patienter sustinui, bona instanter speravi dum fui vix fui nunc sum Resurecturo, satis sed ut Bene sim pie lector precare Christum Deum quia ego credidi in ejus unam Sanctam Catholicam et Apostolicam Ecclesiam, scilicet Romanam. R.I.P.'

"All this I order if I dye at Worcester, wherever else I dye I will be buried in the parish church . . . and give £5 to the poor. . . . I give to my daughters Penelope Whitworth and Frances Slaney, to each of them the two following books, viz., *The difference between the Conversion and Reformation of England*, and that other book called *Charity and Truth*, beseeching them by the Blood of Jesus to read 'em again and again without prejudice : their dying father entreats this of them. . . . All my manors are regularly settled and will take their course, but as God has blessed me with a personal estate of some value, I dispose of it . . . with strict regard to justice and tenderness, and quite free from partiality or resentment . . . to my wife £100 . . . and whatever she calls her own (her word to be taken for it). I give her absolutely my coach or chariot, best pair of coach horses and best harness . . . as to stores, provisions, wines and all consumables she may take what she pleases for her own and her family's use. I give 20*li.* to be distributed as my executor and my eldest son know I would have it disposed of if I were under no restraint and might bequeath as fully as others may. To my eldest son I bequeath all pictures except that drawn of me in a turban, which is my wife's given her by my sister —— Goring, also all medals, coins and prints, and also half of whatever belongs to the Room where I and my family go to say our prayers . . . to my eldest son my leopard-skin saddle trimmed with gold fringe and the pistols belonging to it . . . to my faithful old servant William Thompson £20 with the horse . . . he usually rides when he travels with me . . . to Mrs. Mary Wakeman, long since married to Mr. Van Rose, a lawyer in French Flanders, £15, or to *him* if alive, if both dead look no further . . . 3 guineas to the Earl Mareschall of Scotland . . . 3 guineas to the poor of Holywell . . . 2 guineas to parson Thomas Maurice for a ring." His executor was his younger son John Trevanion Plowden, the will being proved 22nd April, 1740.

There is a tradition in the family that William Plowden's first wife, together with her newly-born infant, were poisoned by the attendant doctor; this, if a fact, together with the apparent apostasy of his daughters, and the inferences suggested by the foregoing quaint document, that the domestic reins were held pretty tightly by the fair hand of the third lady, probably contributed largely to the memory of "sorrows" when he passed his 70th birthday in settling his affairs. The books that he was so anxious for his daughters to read were Robert Manning's *England's Conversion and Reformation compared*, an 8vo volume published at Antwerp in 1725, and that of the Rev. Edward Hawarden (a missionary priest who died in London in 1735), entitled *Charity and Truth, or Catholics not uncharitable in saying that none are saved out of the Catholic Communion.*

WILLIAM HASSALL, of Berrington, in his will of 17th April, 1739, proved by his son and executor Thomas, 21st October, 1740, names his da. Anne, the wife of Arthur Lowe, and their children, William, Arthur, and Thomas Lowe, and Anne, Mary, Frances, Appollonia, Elizabeth, and Margaret Lowe; his da. Appollonia, wife of William King, and their children, William, Thomas, James, and Mary King; da. Frances, wife of Richard Johnson; grandda. Anne, the da. of Peter Hassall; da. Mary Magdalen, the wife of John Hutten, as also the children of Thomas Hassall.

CALEB HIGGINS, of Shiffnal, in his will dated 18th March, 1726, proved 29th November, 1728, names his "late wife Mary" and his da. Mary.

HENRY, Earl of STAFFORD, desires to be buried at Westminster Abbey, and mentions his brother Francis S., and sisters the Ladies Ursula, Mary, and Anastatia, with his nephew and niece William and Mary, the children of his brother John Stafford. Among the legacies are: "To my cousin the Hon. Charles Howard, of Greystoke, my carpet wrought in silk by our great-grandmother of blessed memory . . . [Anne] da. of Lord Dacre, and wife of Philip, Earl of Arundel and Surrey," and "to cousin Lady Eliz. Haccher, a hanging of green velvet wrought by the hand of Mary Queen of Scots". Of his wife he says: "I give to the worst of women, except being a wh——e, who is guilty of all ills, the da. of Mr. Grammont, a Frenchman, whom I have unfortunately married, 45 brass half-pence which will buy her a pullet to her supper, a greater sum than her father can often make, for I have known when he had neither money nor credit for such a purchase, being the worst of men, and his wife the worst of women in all debaucheries: had I known their character, I had never married their daughter, nor made myself unhappy". [2nd Feb., 1699—2nd July, 1719.]

CLAUDE-CHARLOTTE DE GRAMMONT, Lady STAFFORD, by will, "signed in London," 13th May, 1739, and proved 16th May, 1739, left all her estate to the Rt. Hon. Charles Earl of Arran.

SOMERSET.

JOHN TAUNTON, of West Lydford, names his das. Grace (then married), Mary, Anne, Jane, and Henrietta, and his sons Joseph, Thomas, and John, the last-named also having a son John. [2nd May, 1718—17th October, 1718.]

Dr. Oliver, in his *Western County Collections*, p. 69, gives the name of Thomas Taunton as his authority for the narrative of the death-bed scene of Lord Waldegrave as noticed in *Eng. Cath. Nonj.*, p. 64. Might not the words then attributed to Lord W. admit of a hopeful interpretation and be taken as a public confession of his faith, to which in his last moments he returned? "Quod si nosmetipsos dijudicaremus, non utique judicaremur." This Thomas Taunton appears to have been a nephew of Grace and Anne T., named in the will here given, and from the latter he had "received the anecdote" in question. Of them, Oliver says: "Anne T. died in 1783, aged 87, and her sister Grace, the wife of Mr. Dillon, steward to Lord Waldegrave, died in 1760, aged 82".

JOHN MOLINS, of Hull within Horsington. Admon. of his estate was granted, 9th May, 1743, to Mary, his widow.

FRANCIS CARNE, of Bath, names his wife Anne and his "unfortunate son Edward," his sister Mary Guest and her two daughters. The trustees of his estate were John Stibbs, George Stibbs, doctor of physic, both of the city of Bath, and John Hussey, of Marnhull. On 26th June, 1750, a further admon. of the estate upon the death of the widow Anne was granted to her sister Eliz. Kibbell, widow. [11th January, 1719 —31st October, 1721.]

THOMAS, Lord STOURTON, in his will dated 19th April, 1738, and proved 2nd May, 1744, names his brothers Botolph and John, nephews James and William S., and his three nieces Catherine and Eliz. S., and —— Langdale. Oliver says that he was buried at Stourton, 1st April, 1744, æt. 77, his widow, by whom he left no issue, being buried there 19th June, 1749.

"MARGARET GREEN, of Willet, in the p. of Elworthy, spinster, only child now living, and heir-at-law of John Green, late of Easton, in the p. of Bishops-Morchard, co. Devon, gent. dec., who was the eldest son and heir of Gabriel Green (the eldest), late of Bishops-Morchard, aforesaid, gent. dec., who married Dorothy Easton, of Easton, spinster, only da. and heir of John Easton, Esq," divided her estate among her servant Edward Cann, husb., her sister Anne, the wife of John Smith, of Frome, and her executor John Rowe, of Leighland, with rings to her "very much respected and worthy friends," Rob. Rowe, Prudence his wife, and their children. [11th June, 1737—13th September, 1739.] If every testator took the will of Margaret Green as a model, genealogists would certainly be saved a vast amount of trouble and research.

GABRIEL GREEN, late of Netherbury, co. Dorset. Admon. of his estate was granted, 16th October, 1718, to his widow Elizabeth.

HUMPHREY STEARE, of St. Andrew's, Holborn, gent., in will of 20th August, 1728, proved 29th July, 1729, names his wife Anne, and his "wife's da. Philippa Bourne," da. Anne, the wife of Edward Monington, and his son Robert. His widow Anne, "of the city of Bath," in her will of 16th November, 1744, proved 17th June, 1745, names also her grandda. Anne Monington, her sisters —— Baskerville and —— Gore, her niece Ann Goldney, lately married to James Wickstead, of Bath, and her husband's nephew Thomas Biggs, of Bridgwater.

JOHN COTTINGTON names his brother Francis, "mother-in-law Mrs. Catherine Cottington," his uncle Charles Fortescue, with Eliz. his wife, and their children Francis and Mary F.; cousins Charles Stourton, who had a da. Mary Langdale, and "Thomas Coleman, of London, scrivener". [16th October, 1724—3rd February, 1725.]

SAMUEL and JOHN JAMES. Dr. Oliver, in his *Collections*, p. 183, gives an interesting account of this family. He says: "Mr. William James, of East Harptree, was a wealthy grazier and possessed considerable property in the parish and at Ninton Bluett: he had hired a drover in Salisbury Market, and subsequently noticing that he did not attend the parish church, but often engaged in his devotions in the out-buildings, was led by curiosity to examine his books. Their perusal induced him to ask questions, and he became so edified with the example of his faithful Catholic servant, and so satisfied with his explanations and instructions, that he was reconciled to the Church of God." This William James appears to have died "about 1720," but in the subsequent notice of this family Samuel James is not mentioned. *John* James, a grandson of William, became a Franciscan.

ELIZABETH, wife of Samuel Rich, of Woodbridge, gives 23rd June, 1708, as the date of her marriage settlement. She left no issue, but in her will names her kinswoman Catherine Thompson. [2nd December, 1708—3rd February, 1729.]

SOUTHAMPTON.

ELIZABETH CATTAWAY, of London, spinster, names her sisters Mrs. Alice and Margaret C. She held three messuages at Stoke-Charity for the life of Frances Fox, widow. [7th May, 1727—3rd June, 1727.]

STUBBINGTON. "1749; die nono Decembris obiit Joannes Stubbington de Midhurst anno ætatis suæ 59". "1753, die vigesimo quarto Julii obiit Anna Stubbington." [*Easebourne Catholic Register.*]

AUGUSTINE FISHER, of Kilmeston, left "Holt Coppice," &c., to his wife Mary for life, passing at her death to the eldest son of his brother Charles F. [25th September, 1702—6th August, 1728.]

RICHARD CLAPCOATE, of Sopley, names his son Richard, das. Mary Allaway, Eliz. Lane, Winifred, Margaret, Dorothy C., "and other five children," with a grandda.: gives 5s. to Joseph Gildon. [3rd January, 1723—31st January, 1729.]

FRANCES, widow of Barthol. Smith, of Winchester, names her das. Eliz., Frances, Isabella, and Anastatia, the latter to have a gold cross that belonged to her (testatrix) brother James Smith, also brother William Short, aunt Margaret Short, and her godson and cousin Francis Short, of Bury St. Edmunds. [18th April, 1724—2nd October, 1729.]

JANE DESBROWE, da. of Samuel and Jane D., of the p. of St. Bartholomew, Hyde Street, Winchester, desires burial by her parents at St. James', and to be carried to the grave by six poor men who are to have 2s. 6d. each; leaves her house, &c., to Mary, da. of George and Eliz. Hine, of Kingslar [*sic*, probably Kingsclere]. [18th November, 1762—28th January, 1772.]

AMBROSE PLOWMAN, of Weeks, names his wife Elizabeth, son Ambrose P., grandson William King, and five daughters, Mary (eldest), Clare, Barbara, Anne, and Joanna. [19th February, 1724—1st April, 1728.]

GEORGE BOLNEY, leaves his "new freehold messuage at Winchester" to Elizabeth his wife, and names his brother James. [5th June, 1726—3rd June, 1736.]

JOHN WYBARNE, "senior, late of Hawkesworth, in p. of Pembury, otherwise called Peppingsbury, co. Kent". Admon. of his estate was granted, in February, 1720, to his son John (the widow Lætitia renouncing), upon whose death a further admon. was granted, 10th December, 1752, to Henry W., the second son.

Lettis Wybarne describes herself as "of the city of Norwich, widow of John W., late of Hockwell, co. Kent," her will dated 5th March, 1737, with a codicil 28th June, being proved 20th October, 1737. She speaks of her freehold manor of Flixton, co. Suffolk, and names her sons John and Henry, das. Charity and Elizabeth, and her brother George Tasburgh; and leaves "£50 to be distributed among the priests in the counties of Suffolk and Norfolk".

BARTHOLOMEW SMITH, of Winchester, allows his "mother Frances to spend £1000, any surplus of it to pass at her death to her seven youngest children"; names his brothers William, James, and Thomas, sisters Anastatia, Elizabeth, Frances, and Isabella, and his aunt Margaret Short. [8th February, 1716—24th February, 1720.]

REBECCA EDWARDS, of Longham, by will of 12th February, 1719, proved 28th February, 1722, left "the whole disposal of all her lands and goods within doors and without to her servant Mary Michel . . . no other person having the least right to anything, let her enjoy peaceably and quietly without any disturbance all my lands". One witness is John *Kippen*.

JOHN, Lord DORMER, in his will dated 4th November, 1782, when "old and infirm," and proved 10th November, 1785, names his sons Charles (eldest), James, John, and Thomas, da. Catherine, and grandson Charles.

RICHARD BRUNING, of Winchester. The will of his half-brother Charles B., of Petersfield, gent., was proved 2nd June,

1724: he names his brother George B., of Froxfield, who had a da. Eliz., his sister Anne Colstock, and niece Anne, the wife of William de la Rose.

JOHN FINCHAM, of Chalvestone, desires burial at Roxton Church, and names his wife Ann, "infant son" John, and his two sisters —— Novills and Elizabeth Fincham. [4th May, 1712—20th January, 1727.]

STAFFORD.

WILLIAM, Lord STAFFORD, in his will, proved in February, 1734, names his only son William Matthias Stafford Howard, brothers John and Paul, sisters Mrs. Mary Plowden, Xaveria, and Louisa; half-sister and brother Henrietta and Edward Stafford; nephew and niece Francis and Louisa Plowden; three das., Mary, Anastatia, and Anne; nephew George Jernegan, and his uncles Sir Edward and Thomas Southcott.

BASIL FITZHERBERT, of Gray's Inn, appoints his sister Winifred, widow of Charles Eyston, executrix of his will, dated 30th December, 1727, and proved 23rd January, 1728, and names his mother Jane and great-nephew Basil, son of his nephew Thomas Fitzherbert.

ANNE, widow of THOMAS HICKIN, of St. Andrew's, Holborn, goldsmith, names her three das.—Anne (who is in Cosin's List), Mary (dec.), the wife of Joseph Petre, and ——, wife of Major Morey. [20th March, 1725—21st January, 1727.]

ANNE PURCELL, of the p. of St. George the Martyr, spinster. Admon. of her estate was granted, 9th November, 1751, to Catherine, wife of John Byfield, niece by the sister of the deceased.

"JOHN PURCELL, of the Hay, in p. of Madeley, co. Salop, and Doctor in Physic of College of Physicians in London," in his will dated 3rd April, 1729, proved 20th November, 1732, writes: "My will and desire is that the penal statutes be never taken against my mother [Catherine], or any of my brothers and sisters except my brother-in-law Thomas Penson, to deprive them of the annuities left them by my father's will, but if they sue for more than such annuities, or for a receiver on my estates, or for any distribution of my estates, my express will is that those penal statutes be then taken against them which hinder Roman Catholics from taking interest in lands, and the rather because several of them have unfairly obstructed the probate of my brother Thomas Purcell's will . . . my will is that my brother-in-law, Thomas Penson, pay double taxes to the utmost extent for his annuities ".

From all this it may be inferred that John Purcell had renounced his religion in order to secure his estates; and it is significant, moreover, that his name does not occur among the number of the Purcell family who "registered their names and real estates".

MARMADUKE, Lord LANGDALE, names his son Hon. Marmaduke L. and da. Hon. Eliz. L., da.-in-law Hon. Constantia L., godson Marmaduke, the son of Thomas Langdale, of Holborn Bridge, and his two grandsons Thomas and Peter, sons of Sir Walter Vavasour. [8th February, 1765—11th February, 1771.]

JOHN BIDDULPH, of Biddulph, names his sons Richard (eldest) and Charles, and das. Mary (eldest), Anne, and Frances, the trustees being his brother Francis and his uncle Sir William Goring, bart. [14th April, 1720—14th July, 1720.]

FRANCIS BIDDULPH, of Gray's Inn, in his will of 14th December, 1744, proved 13th February, 1750, names his sister Lady Dormer and nephew Francis Dormer, leaving to his nephew Charles Biddulph his guns, alarum clock, silver watch, silver-hilted sword, and gold sleeve buttons, naming his nephew Ric. B. resid. legatee.

THOMAS WHITGREAVE, of Moseley, in his will dated 8th September, 1728, proved 6th February, 1729, by his eldest da. Mary-Constantia, names also his da. Mary, and his sons Charles and Francis, the witnesses to the will being John Lomax, Eliz. Merry, and Ann Moor.

HELEN GOWER, of Colmers, co. Wigorn. Admon. of her estate was granted, 12th August, 1718, to her son John, her husband William first renouncing.

Sir EDWARD SIMEON, of Britwell Priory, near Watlington, desires burial at Aston, co. Stafford, and names Edward and Thomas, elder and younger sons of his nephew Edward Weld, niece Eliz. Bridgit Weld, and the following of the Heveningham family: John H., James, son of Walter H.; Brooke H., Mrs. Mary Remington and her sister Mrs. Mary Heveningham; Christopher H., senior of Twyneforth,·co. Stafford, dead since 1736; Henry, son of Christopher H.; Edward and John, sons of the said Henry by his first wife; and James, Charles, and Thomas, sons of Henry by his second wife Mary. [15th June, 1764—28th January, 1769.]

MARY GIFFARD (widow of Thomas G.), " of Long Birch, co. Stafford," desires that "housekeeping be kept at her house at Long Birch for one whole month after her decease, to the end that her servants may have time to dispose of and provide for themselves," and names her cousins William Stourton, of Cheam, co. Surrey, and Benedict Conquest, of Irnham. [18th December, 1749—13th March, 1753.]

Admon. of the estate of WILLIAM FOWLER, late of St. Thomas', co. Stafford, widower, was granted, 1st December, 1729, to Thomas Grove, nephew by the sister of William F., for that Mary, wife of John Fowler, niece by the sister of said dec., died without fully administering. A prior admon. is dated March, 1716.

WALTER FOWLER, of St. Thomas', by will of 6th February, 1695-6, proved 28th May, 1697, left to his brother William "a gold medal of Pope Clement X. given him with his own hands," and names his sisters Gertrude F., Dorothy Grove, and her children Thomas, Gertrude, and Mary Grove; sister "Catherine F., mistress of St. Thomas, brother William's wife," his brother Thomas, "niece Casy in France," cousin Gilbert Whitehall, and kinsman Thomas Canning.

Lady MARY GERARD writes: "My body is to lye in the bed wherein I dye the space of twenty-four hours after I shall expire before it be removed, or anything taken from about it, or the pillows removed from under my head, afterwards put into a leaden coffin for eight days and kept open as long as may be without offence". Besides many of her own (the Webb) family, she names her niece Viscountess Montague; "little nephews and little nieces," the Earl of Derwentwater, Lady Ann Radcliffe, the Hon. James Philip, and Henrietta Waldegrave; cousin Charles Ireland, and "my worthy good nephew" Lord Langdale. [13th June, 1729—29th October, 1731.]

SUFFOLK.

HENRY BEDINGFIELD, of Stoke-Ash, desires to be interred in p. church of Denham, leaves his library to his three brothers-in-law Thomas, William, and John Havers; names his wife Mary and daughters, any of whom entering a Religious Order before 25 years of age is cut off from her portion. [13th August, 1730; codicil 14th August 1737—22nd February, 1739.]

Sir WILLIAM GAGE, by will dated 2nd May, 1715, and proved 23rd June, 1727, left all his estate to his wife.

THOMAS MANNOCK, of Bromley Hall, desires burial at "Stooke Church," leaves to his wife Mary for life two estates as per settlement, viz., Martell's Hall and Manor and Bromley Hall: names his nephew Peter Lynch. [1st May, 1722—21st May, 1722.]

JOHN TOURNER, of Midhurst, co. Sussex, M.D., "old and advanced in years," desires to be buried by his late wife and children at Easebourne, and names his sons William (dec.), John, and Thomas; das. Mary Bryant and Eliz. Laurance; and grandchildren Richard and Ann Heath. [13th June, 1744—14th August, 1744.]

JOHN GAGE, of Harleston, left his estate to Sir William Gage, of Hengrave, for life, to pass next to Thomas, grandson of Sir William and one of the three sons of Thomas G., of Hengrave: names John, son of Sir Will. G.; kinsmen Francis G., Edward G., of Whittlebury, co. Northton, who had a son George; also George and Henry, kinsmen and sons of the late Sir Edward G., and their three sisters Penelope Sulyard, Mrs. Mary Bond, and Mrs. Basilia Gage; Eliz., da. of Penelope Sulyard: his executrix was his kinswoman Eliz. Gage, the "da. of the late Lady Tresham". [15th June, 1718—28th March, 1723.]

DELARIVIÈRE GAGE, of Bury St. Edmunds, names her son Sir William Gage, eldest dec. son Sir Thomas; sister Mary, late wife of Francis Tasburgh; sister Henrietta, late wife of Thomas Havers, of Thelton; and nephew Richard, "now in Portugal," son of Richard Elwes by her sister Merelina. [28th March, 1744—7th November, 1746.]

HENRY JERMYN BOND, of ditto, names his wife Jane, and two sons James and Henry. [5th November, 1733—26th March, 1748.]

Sir F. MANNOCK, in his will of 17th October, 1755, names his sons William (married to Teresa Wright), Francis, Thomas, and George, and three das. Ethildred, Mary, and Ann. Admon. was granted, 1st December, 1758, to his son Sir William, his widow Frances renouncing execution. Her will, dated 13th November, 1758, was proved 30th May, 1761, all her estate going to her son Francis Mannock.

JOHN TASBURGH, of Flixton. His will, dated 1st November, 1698, was proved by his widow Frances, 19th September, 1719. In her will of 27th June, 1724, proved the following 20th July, she says: "I desire burial at Holt about midnight, my heart to be sent over to Bordeaux in France, and deposited in the same chapel there where my son John lies interred (over whose body is a white marble stone), and a black marble stone set up over it. She names her aunt Mrs. Catherine Matthews; sisters Dame Margaret Conyers and Mary Migliorucci: her friend Frances, the wife of William Woolfe, of p. of St. Geo. the Martyr, co. Middx., is to educate and be guardian to "Margaret Frances, da. of my da. Margaret Tasburgh, dec. Others named are her father Henry and uncle Thomas Nevill, aunt Dame Frances Wintour, niece Harriet Conyers, cousin Percy Markham, and kinswoman —— Napier. Her daughter Margaret Tasburgh describes herself in her will of 26th November, 1720 (proved 12th July, 1721), as "now residing in Dublin and only surviving da. of John T., of Flixton".

EDWARD SULYARD, of Haughley Park, desiring burial at Wetherden, names his wife Eliz., sister Eliz. Dunne, brothers Ralph, Philip, and William, and his two nephews, the sons of last-named, Edward and Francis S. [2nd August, 1733—22nd January, 1745.]

CATHERINE MARTIN, of Melford, by will of 16th February, 1724, with codicil of 13th March, 1727, proved 15th December, 1727, left her estate to her brother John Martin and to George Yate, who, with his da. Lady Mannock, of Giffords Hall, were joint executors.

JOHN TYLDESLEY, now of Bury St. Edmunds, co. Suffolk, gent., names his wife Jane, two das. Frances T. and Bridget Hanne, and grandda. Bridget Hanne. [8th February, 1734—1st April, 1735.]

JOHN STAFFORD, of Bury, names his da. Anne, wife of Dr. Nathaniel Bostock, and their da. Anne, wife of Vincent Eyre; da. Tyldesley, and grandson John Bostock. [9th April, 1712—3rd May, 1717.]

SUSSEX.

HONORA BROWNE, of Easebourne, widow of Stanislaus B., left £5 to each of her four das. that should be living at her death, and names her sons Francis and Mark, the latter to have her property in Spain, he being also resid. legatee and executor. [19th September, 1721—30th December, 1724.]

THOMAS STUBBINGTON. "1755, Die decimo Decembris obiit Elizabetha Stubbington anno ætatis suæ 64." [*Easebourne and Cowdray Catholic Register.*]

EDMUND LEWKENOR, of Easebourne, by will of 1st November, 1730, proved 27th September, 1731, left his estate to his brother Anthony, and a guinea to Ann Fitzhenry, da. of his sister —— Roberts.

JOHN HEATH. "Die tertio Novembris, 1749, obiit Anna Heath anno ætatis suæ 61."

"Die decimo nono 1756 [*sic*] obiit Johannes Heath anno ætatis suæ 61." [*Easebourne Catholic Register.*]

FRANCIS CROUCHER. "1745, Die 24th Julii obiit Franciscus Croucher, de oppido Midhurst postquam in infirmitate confessus, sanctissimo viatico refectus, et sacri olei unctione roboratus esset."

Also in the same year is the following entry: "Franciscus Croucher obiit die decimo Decembris anno ætatis suæ 83". [*Easebourne Catholic Register.*]

RALPH CROUCHER. "Die nono Julii, 1747, obiit Rudolphus Croucher, de Midhurst, anno ætatis suæ 59".

"Die quinto Decembris, 1749, obiit Rudolphus Croucher, de Midhurst, anno ætatis suæ 77." [*Easebourne Cath. Reg.*]

Sir WILLIAM GAGE, of West Firle. His will, dated 13th July, 1737, with codicil of 20th January, 1739, was proved 10th May, 1744.

JOHN TOURNER. The *Easebourne Cath. Reg.* has "vigesimo septimo Februarii, 1752, obiit Joannes Tourner, de Easebourne, anno ætatis suæ 81". Admon. of the estate of John Tourner of Easebourne, widower, was granted, 14th March, 1752, to his son John T.

ANTHONY LEWKENOR, of Wotton, by will of 18th December, 1734, proved 23rd May, 1737, left his estate to Anne Lloyd and her heirs, and names his brother Robert Malbon, dec., and cousin Richard Goble. This Robert Malbon, of Easebourne, by will of 21st August, 1733, proved 19th January, 1734, left his estate to his br.-in-law Ant. Lewkenor.

NICHOLAS TOURNER, sen., of Midhurst, names his wife Anne, son John, and da. Martha Taylor. [4th June, 1722; with codicil 3rd June, 1725—5th March, 1729.]

ANTHONY KEMP, of Slindon. Admon. of his estate was granted, 30th July, 1753, to his da. the Hon. Barbara Radcliffe, wife of the Hon. James Bartholomew Radcliffe, commonly called Lord Kinnaird, his widow the Hon. Jane Kemp renouncing.

FRANCIS ROBOTHAM, of the p. of St. Andrew, Holborn, gent., names his wife Sarah and da. Sarah, the wife of John

Leeremans, with their son James L. [30th July, 1737—12th December, 1737.]

JAMES AVELIN, of Storrington, names his wife Anne, da. Elizabeth, the wife of John Ellis, with their sons John and Thomas Ellis; also his grandda. Eliz. Smith. [11th January, 1721—14th June, 1726.]

Sir WILLIAM GORING, of Burton, desires burial at Burton, and names, besides his wife, Richard and Charles, eldest and second sons of his nephew John Biddulph; Francis, the brother of his nephew John Biddulph; and his "little niece Mary, eldest da. of the said John B. and Mary B. his wife"; also a cousin Cotton Plowden. [22nd January; codicil 22nd February, 1723; proved 17th March, 1724.] His widow, Dame Dorothy Goring, by will dated 2nd July, 1729, and proved 8th June, 1737, desires "to be buried in the church of the English Sepulchrines at Liége, all her English servants to have their charges borne to London". She names her brother William Plowden, nephew John Trevanion Plowden, nieces Mary and Anne Plowden, and her "little niece Mary Biddulph," her nephew Francis Biddulph being executor.

Sir GEORGE MAXWELL, of Cowdray, left the residue of his estate to his executor Mungo, eldest son of Robert Maxwell, of Gelston, in the Stuartine of Kirkcudbright, by —— Lindsey, his second wife. [20th July, 1715—14th June, 1720.]

PHILIP CARYL, of North, "being aged" at date of his will, 21st April, 1733, proved 17th February, 1735-6, names his son Philip, gives £100 to Lady Lucy Herbert at Bruges, and £60 to Lady Bagnal at Gravelines, the resid. legatee being Mr. Matt. Farine, a tobacco merchant at Dunkirk.

RICHARD ROWT. On a sheet of paper that has found its way to a curious collection of loose MSS., which, together with a folio volume, make up the *Cowdray, Easebourne, and Midhurst Catholic Register*, are the following Memoranda in the handwriting of Mary Rowt:

"These are my family that is dead" [*signed*], "Mary Rowt".

"Martha Taylor dyed 22nd July, 1726."

"My great-grandfather, Nicholas Tourner, 8th May, 1731

[? 1736]. Ann Heath, 7th October, 1727. Francis Tourner, 13th January, 1734. My grandmother, Margaret Harris, 20th February, 1736. Ann Croucher, sister, 30th June, 1744. Aunt Elizabeth Harris, 4th June, 1747. Mary Luttrell, 13th December. My father, *Richard Rowt*, 8th February, 1748, anno ætatis suæ 73: my mother, Anne Rowt, 14th April, 1760: my brother, Richard Rowt, 6th February, 1738: my brother, Peter Rowt, 29th August, 1763 [? 1769]: my aunt, Martha Harris, 18th January, 1773."

In the same handwriting also are the following: "Mr. Tourner of Easeborne's family: Eliz. Tourner, 17th December, 1726; Mary Tourner, 16th October, 1741; Catherine T., 6th June; Elizabeth T., the mother, 11th August, 1746; Nicholas T., William, and John, I don't know the date, and the father, John T.; Thomas Tourner, the last that died, 23rd May, 1774; Mary Browne, Mr. Mark Browne's first wife, 7th January, 1741; Mr. Mark Browne dyed in February, I don't know the day, 1755". But the register has in another part:

"Die Septimo Februarii, 1755, obiit Marcus Browne".

SURREY.

JOHN WESTON, of Sutton Place, by will of 22nd November, 1724, unsigned—but William Woolfe, of the p. of St. George the Martyr, deposes to his handwriting—desires burial in the chapel of the family at Guildford, and adds: "Whereas the miserable condition and sufferings of the poor Catholics of England is very deplorable, in consideration thereof I bequeath to the poorest and most needy of them £250, to be divided amongst 500 poor, which is 10s. a-piece". He names his sister and brother Woolfe, nephew John Woolfe, aunt Mary Weston, sister Anne Weston, his da. Melior-Mary Weston being sole heir and executrix. The will was proved 17th March, 1730-1.

WARWICK.

CATHERINE WILLOUGHBY, widow, who held an estate at Kingsbury, was a da. of Thomas Cholmley of Bransby: she died in 1733. [*Lawson MS.*]

JOSEPH GRIFFIN, living at date of his will (1st July, 1728, proved 12 days later) in New North Street, in the p. of St. George the Martyr, co. Middx., leaves to his wife Mary his furniture there, with coach and chariot: he names his sisters Winifred and Teresa Griffin, mother-in-law Mrs. Flora Levery, uncle John Vaughan's four younger children, and the following *cousins:* "Cousin James Baskerville, son of Thomas Baskerville, dec., who was son and heir of my aunt Baskerville, dec.; cousins Nicholas, James, and John, brothers of the said Thomas Baskerville; cousins Mary Whitaker, Anne Hinderson, Thomas Cornwall, George Cornwall, James Cornwall, of Watling Street; John Cornwall, of the Castle Tavern, Drury Lane; and the son and da. of the said John Cornwall by the first wife; cousins John-Vaughan Sadler and Nathaniel Pigott: there are legacies also to Francis Prujean, of Ormond Street, and Anne P., his wife, and to ——, wife of Postern Stary, and to Robert Freeman of Henley-in-Arden.

HUMPHREY SPARRY, of Edgbaston, desires to be buried at Edgbaston, near Anne, his wife, and names his three sisters Magdalen Atmore, Eliz. Lea, and a sister married to William Spurrier, who had a son Thomas; nieces Jane Ellis and Mary Thompson; cousins Mary and John Sands, and Humphrey, son of another cousin James Sands. [5th January, 1725—17th March, 1725-6.]

LAURENCE PETRE, of Spernall, widower. Admon. of his estate was granted, 18th April, 1752, to his son George.

TERESA KNOTTISFORD, of p. of St. Giles-in-the-Fields, co. Middx., desires burial at Studley, near her husband, and names her son Charles, three das. Catherine, Teresa, and Bridget, wife of Laurence Petre; sister Philadelphia Woolmer, three grandsons Charles and John Knottisford and George Petre, and nephew John Fortescue. [4th June, 1720—22nd September, 1726.]

JOHN REEVE, of Birmingham, gent., names his wife Anne, son Thomas, and da. Anne. [7th November, 1727—12th December, 1727.]

Dame ANNE THROCKMORTON desires burial at Coughton, "near her dear mother": leaves £35 to "Mr. Bonaventura Giffard," and 5gs. to "Mr. Benjamin Petre": names her cousins John, Francis, Mary, and Catherine Hyde, of Hyde End, they being brothers and sisters: also Sir Thomas Manby and his two sons, Edward and Robert Manby: four grandchildren: Sir Robert Throckmorton, who is to have a fine wrought book and gold enamelled cross: Anne Petre, Anne Widdrington, and William Wollascott, who is "to have one large silver candlestick that was generally used to light me up and down": great-grandda. Mary Petre: three other grandsons Thomas and Martin Wollascott and —— Widdrington: a "beloved friend Charles Coffin," and servant William Hockley, and a diamond cross, watch, chain, and £200 to her grandda. Frances Wollascott, afterwards revoked by codicil, she "having since entered into Religion and become a professed nun". [14th June, 1724; first cod. 15th February, 1725; second cod. 24th September, 1727; proved 9th August, 1728.]

FRANCIS CANNING, of Foxcote, in his will of 10th July, 1732, with codicil 26th January, 1733, proved 12th March, 1733, names his father Richard, eldest son Francis, and youngest son Richard Canning, "da. Ann Greenwood, widow," and her infant children Charles and Mary Greenwood; brother Richard C., sister Eliz. C., his "brother and sister —— Elliot," and their nine children, his nephews and nieces, viz., Humphrey, Nathaniel, Edward, Richard, Anne, Winifrid, Apollonia, Margaret, and Frances Elliot; his nephew and niece —— Betham, and their son (his godson) Richard Betham; aunt Mrs. Mary Audeley; kinswoman Eliz. Conquest, cousins Mary, Charles, Constantia, and Hannah Busby, and John, the son of Hannah Busby; cousins Richard Lacon, Nathaniel Pigott, and Rebecca Pigott, his wife, and grandda. Apollonia Canning: notices his "law-books," divides his library between his sons, and asks all legatees to be in harmony with each other.

EDWARD FERRERS, of Baddesley Clinton, was married in 1712, his wife Teresa dying in 1734. [*Lawson MS.*]

ELIZ. BALDWIN, of Brailes, widow, in her will dated 24th August, 1723, and proved 5th September, 1728, names her brother John Baughan, and her two das. Mary Baldwin and Eliz. the wife of Thomas Travor. Possibly she was the wife of Edward B.

FRANCIS CARINGTON, Esq., of Wootton, co. Warwick, in his will of 31st January, 1748, codicil 19th May, 1749, proved 1st June, 1749, names his wife Mary, uncles Charles and William Smith, sister —— Wright, da. Mary-Teresa, four sisters-in-law Teresa, Martha, Eliz., and Ann Englefield; two brothers-in-law Sir Henry and Charles Englefield, and his father-in-law Edward Webb, of Gray's Inn, and adds: I give "to Mrs. Bridget Pain £5 5s. to pray for me . . . to the monks at Douay £300 to say as many masses for me at our Lady's altar as their duty will allow of, and a high mass every year . . . £20 a year for the maintenance of a priest at Wootton, and for the poor".

WESTMORELAND.

Dame WINIFRED STRICKLAND desires "to be buried by her husband at St. John's Chapel"; names her son Thomas, grandsons Thomas and Gerard, brother Trentham, brother King and his wife, sisters —— Aston and —— Blood, and cousin —— Griffith; also "Sister Bonaventura of the Third Order". She adds: "My book-case and arrears of pension are to go to Mother Abbess, two parts for masses for my soul, the other part to obtain the prayers of the holy community". From this it would seem that upon her husband's death she entered a religious house. [28th February, 1725—30th March, 1726.]

WILTS.

The Hon. HENRY ARUNDELL, the elder, now (19th May, 1720) residing at Wardour, left by will of that date, proved 21st August, 1721, "to Mr. James Morgan, of Southampton Street, in London, £100".

FRANCIS COTTINGTON, of Fonthill-Giffard. Admon. of his estate was granted, 19th December, 1728, to Dame Winifred Golding, widow and guardian of Francis Cottington, son of F. C., of West Wickham, co. Bucks, widower, until he attain the age of 21 years.

His stepmother, "Catherine Cottington, of the city of New Sarum, widow," appoints Mrs. Catherine Fielding "universal legatee," her will, proved 7th January, 1740, being witnessed by Ursula and Sarah Fielding and Eliz. Stoddart.

GAYNOR CRUSE, of Wootton-Bassett, widow, by will dated 14th January, 1717, from "the p. of St. Nicholas, in the city of Worcester," and proved 5th December, 1718, bequeathed her house property, in the p. of All-hallows, in city of Hereford, to her nephew John Kelly, *alias* Lloyd.

CHARLES WOOLMER, of Fonthill-Giffard, names his wife Mary (executrix), brother Francis W., and sister Mary Berkeley. [30th May, 1716—23rd April, 1719.]

THOMAS KNIPE, of Semley, in will of 24th August, 1719, proved 19th December, 1720, names his nephews George, Thomas, William, John, and Edward K., and nieces Eleanor, Mary, Catherine, and Anne.

HENRY, Lord ARUNDELL, widower. Admon. of his estate was granted, 23rd June, 1726, to his son Henry Lord Arundell.

GEORGE KNIPE, of Semley, names his brothers John and Edward, four sisters Mary, Catherine (both in Paris), Eleanor, and Bridget, wife of John Mandeville, and godson George Mandeville. [6th September, 1734—17th February, 1735.]

THOMAS CHAMPION, of Sutton-Mandeville. Admon. of his estate was granted in November, 1726, to his da. Anne, the wife of William Lewes. The will of his mother, Joan Champion, of Odstock, widow, dated 30th March, 1719, was proved 24th October, 1726. She names her son Thomas and his present wife Anne; her second son William C., who had two sons William and Thomas; her two grandsons Anthony, the son of her third son Anthony, dec., and Henry, son of her da. Mary, the wife of Henry Carew, of Muckleshall, in p.

of Holdenhurst; and her grandda. Anne, "the wife of William Lewes, of Common Garden, in Russel Street, London, bookseller".

WORCESTER.

THOMAS GROVE, Esq., of the city of Worcester, "desires to be buried near the place where his wife designs to be buried"; names his two nieces (sisters) Mary Ann and Rachel Micham, and his da. Rebecca, wife of Richard Fitzgerald, and alludes to "his study of law-books". There are also the following bequests: "£5 to the gentleman that assists me at the time of my death . . . £5 to my friend the Rev. Dr. Edward Combe . . . and £50 to my friends at Mr. Worthington's house, called the English House at Bornheim". [24th June, 1730—14th November, 1730.]

BRIDGET HORNYOLD, of Blackmore Park, widow, names her sons John and Anthony H., das. Frances, wife of Edward Hanford, and their son Robert Hanford, and Bridget, wife of Christopher Atwood; also sister Ursula Hornyold, and brothers Ralph H. and William Windsor. [27th March, 1721—13th March, 1722.]

WILLIAM ATWOOD, "late of the city of Worcester". Admon. of his estate was granted, 2nd May, 1732, to his three principal creditors, his widow Sarah and da. Sarah having first renounced.

Another William Atwood, of Powick, in co. Worcester, in his will dated 1st May, 1740, and proved 17th June, 1740, names his das. Ursula and Mary, and his brother Thomas Atwood, "doctor of physic".

WILLIAM ACTON, of Little Wolverton. His will was proved 26th May, 1727: he names his sons William (eldest), Vincent, Perkins-Richard, and das. Barbara and Ann.

ANTHONY HORNYOLD, of Hanley Castle, names his wife Mary Magdalen, brother John, son Anthony, and father-in-law (executor) William Berington. [4th June, 1739—17th April, 1740.]

WILLIAM GOWER, son of W. G., of Colmers, in his will of 10th August, 1721, proved 16th March, 1726, names his mother Helen and cousin John Coyney.

JAMES GRIFFITH, of Longford, by will left "everything to the poor except £5 to his sister Anne," and adds: "No poor body to go away from my funeral without a penny loaf and drink". [16th January, 1734—7th June, 1737.]

ANNE, widow of Rowland Bartlett, of Hillend, in her will of 12th December, 1734, proved 13th February, 1742, describes herself as "of the city of Worcester," and besides those named in her husband's will, names her son Basil, da.-in-law Bridget, and godda. Anne Cassey.

JUDITH BERKELEY (widow of John B.), of the p. of St. George, Bloomsbury, by will of 3rd December, 1746, proved 1st January, 1752, left her estate chiefly to her servant and executrix Eliz. Pye, with "£5 to Mr. John Smith (lodging with Mr. Harles, coachmaker in Holborn) . . . or to the person who shall succeed to serve me in the capacity he doth, if he die in my life-time". [This was probably the Jesuit Father of that name who died in London, 4th August, 1754, aged 85. Foley, *Collect.*, 718.] She gave a legacy also to "Ann Howell, living near Spetchley". John Maire and Will. Hodgson attested her will.

FRANCIS WOOLMER, "of the city of Worcester, gent., aged and infirm," at the date of his will, 16th November, 1722, proved 19th June, 1723, names his da. Brace, the wife of Edward Hunt, and sister Mary Berkeley, of Spetchley, widow.

EDWARD SHELDON, of Beoley, names his wife Elizabeth, eldest son William, and nine younger children—"Edward, Ralph, Harry, Mary, Frances, Catherine, Anne, Barbara, and Elizabeth," any da. entering Religion to have only an annuity of £10 : also his brothers Ralph, William, and Henry, kinsman Thomas Overbury, and two goddas., viz., Catherine, da. of his cousin William Sheldon, of Winchester, and Frances, da. of Richard Bishop, of Brailes. [2nd May, 1736—23rd July, 1736.]

WILLIAM MINSHULL, by will dated from Aylesbury, 30th January, 1741-2, and proved 8th March, 1742-3, his wife Mary being executrix, and one trustee also being Frances, wife of John Temple Howse, of Bierton, left to his only son William all his books and medals, &c., with legacies "to the widow of Mr. Charles Howse, now of Buckingham, and to her das. Frances and Sarah H., as also to Francis Howse, of Aylesbury, surgeon, and to Ann Howse, of Bierton, spinster".

He was son of Richard Minshull, by Anne, da. of Francis Finch, of Rushock, co. Worcester, his wife Mary being a da. of Philip Box, of Caversfield, co. Bucks [Lipscomb, *Hist. of Bucks*, ii. 590]; his sister-in-law Catherine, the widow of Richard Minshull, and da. of George Blount, by her will proved 20th March, 1740, desires "burial at St. Martin's-in-the-Fields, near Mr. Minshull and da.," and adds: "I give to the poor at each door of the chapel in Golden Square, one shilling, and 10s. to the poor of my own door in Marlboro' Street".

SOPHIA AUBREY, widow of Thomas A., by will dated 22nd March, 1714, from St. Giles'-in-the-Fields, and proved 19th December, 1718, left her interest in the Shipston estate to her two nieces Mrs. Mary Galloway and Mrs. Eliz. Galloway, with £50 to her sister Mrs. Susannah Reynoldson.

WORCESTER CITY.

RICHARD KETTLE. His name occurs in the years 1727 and 1730, in the *Worcester Catholic Register*, privately printed in 1887.

JOSEPH HARPER, of p. of St. Nicholas. Several of this name also appear in the *Worcester Catholic Register*, one, Joseph H., being entered as "reconciled to the Church, 22nd December, 1724".

CITY OF YORK.

DOROTHY BEDINGFIELD, of York, succeeded her aunt Frances B. as Superioress of St. Mary's Convent, Micklegate Bar, the "leasehold house" evidently referred to in *English Catholic Nonjurors*. Dr. Hutch, in his *Biography of Mrs. Ball*, the foundress of the *Institute of B.V.M.* in Ireland and the Colonies, writes, p. 40: "This lady (Dorothy) . . . was so revered by all classes for her many virtues, that several of the nobility attended her obsequies on 20th October, 1734".

The will of WILLIAM HUNGATE (undescribed) dated 19th August, 1706, and proved 6th February, 1720, is worth recording here for the following connections that he gives: " My three nieces, —— Smalley, and Lucy and Mary Hungate; my brother —— Hammond, and his son Gervase Hammond; my cousins Eliz., sister of Robert Dalton, of Thurnham, lately dead; Eliz. Butler, and Helena and Mary Middleton". His executors were his nephews Dr. Hungate and William H. (brothers).

Admon. of CHARLES, Lord FAIRFAX, bachelor, was granted, 29th November, 1715, to his mother, Lady Mary Hungate.

EAST RIDING OF YORK.

Admon. of the estate of JORDAN METHAM, late of the p. of St. Andrew, Holborn, was, 9th February, 1725, granted to his widow Catherine.

HANNAH ELLERKER, of Doncaster, spinster, in her will of 6th July, 1716, proved 2nd August, 1717, names her four sisters Jane and Anne E., Sarah Short (who had a son Thomas S.), and Eliz. Wright; her two nephews William and John E., nieces Eliz. Furnace and Hannah Bingley, and cousins Catherine and *Thomas* E.

Hon. ELIZ. CRAYTHORNE, by will dated 28th February, 1727, and proved 29th November, 1739, left all her estate to her sister the Hon. Mary Cockayne.

HENRY CUTLER, of Hayton, by will dated 19th November, 1715, left his household goods, &c., to his widow Elizabeth, to whom admon. was granted 8th April, 1730, his executors dying in his lifetime. He names the eldest son of Egerton

Cutler, clerk, his nephews Cutler Wainwright and Francis Willy, and sisters Magdalen Rutherford and Grace Smith. To his niece Jane Wainwright he leaves "£250, provided she marry a man worth £500 in debtless goods". Further on he adds: ". . . if any of my sisters come to want I give them £20 per annum . . ." or ". . . if they shall want a physician or other necessary in sickness, they shall be provided for out of my estate at Dodworth . . . and if any of my heirs or their successors shall by good fortune raise their estate . . . to be worth £800 per annum, then all my tythes I give to an orthodox minister in the Protestant religion, according to the establishment of the Church in King Charles the Second's time, to the chapel of Barnsley; if not orthodox according to this intent, then to the minister of Silkstone if such; if not, to the poor of Silkstone". Hunter, in his *Deanery of Doncaster* (ii. 266), gives an elaborate account of the Cutler family, and names Henry C. as second son of Sir Gervase C., and one of seventeen children, of whom fourteen were girls. Egerton C. named in the will was a son of Sir Thomas C., an uncle of testator. Sir Thomas "served under the Duke of York at sea, and was afterwards four years and a half in the French service".

Sir MARMADUKE CONSTABLE left his estate in trust to his own right heirs, a codicil of 16th April, 1746, naming his nephew Sir Carnaby Haggerston. [August, 1745—16th February, 1747.]

WEST RIDING OF YORK.

Admon. of the estate of "Sir CHARLES INGLEBY, servientis ad legem in hospitio servientium ad legem Chancery Lane," was granted 9th February, 1720, to his son Thomas.

Hon. BERNARD HOWARD, of the p. of St. George the Martyr, co. Middx., in his will dated 21st May, proved the following June, 1745, names his four brothers Hon. Charles, Thomas, Henry, and Philip, giving to the first-named his book and furniture.

CHARLES TANCRED, of St. Paul's, Covent Garden, in his will of 10th May, 1725, proved 28th November, 1733, names his son Thomas, then married, and his two das. Mary and Ann. The will of Frances Tancred, of St. Paul's, Covent Garden, widow of Thomas T. aforesaid, dated 26th March, 1748, was proved 20th March, 1753. She names her sister Mary, wife of Thomas Fraser, apothecary, and Ann F., their daughter; her three das. Eliz. Tancred of Liege; Ann, wife of Thomas Webb; and Henrietta, wife of Robert Kirby; leaving her "business of a woollen draper" to her sons-in-law, "both of St. Paul's, Covent Garden, Esquires," in trust for her eldest son John, second son Walter, and da. Barbara T.

DOROTHY HASTINGS, "one of the das. of Ferdinando H., late of the p. of St. Giles-in-the-Fields," dates her will 31st January, 1721, proved 6th July, 1725, the chief legatee being her servant Ann, wife of John Barker.

MARY HORNCASTLE, of Balne, in p. of Snaith, co. York, single woman, in her will dated 22nd August, 1754, proved 17th December, 1754, names her brothers Joseph and John H., "also Mary, William, Eliz., John, and Joseph, all sons and das. of Joseph H., of Balne". Perhaps a relative of Will. H. [See *Eng. Cath. Nonj.*, p. 311.]

Dame MAGDALEN GASCOIGNE, "late of the p. of St. Ann, Westminster, widow". Admon. of her estate was granted, 22nd February, 1722, to Mary Foster, spinster, and attorney for Henry Curwen, of Workington, co. Cumberland, brother of said dec.

NICHOLAS STAPLETON, of Carleton, by will of 29th June, 1742, of which he named his brother John S. and Sir Edward Gascoigne executors, mentions his das. by Charlotte Eure, his first wife, and appoints his present wife Winifrid guardian of his children Thomas, Miles, Nicholas, John, Charles, Gregory, Eliz., Winifrid, and Monica, any da. entering Religion to have only £500. His executors dying in his lifetime, admon. of his estate was granted, 2nd August, 1750, to his widow Winifrid, he then also being described as "late of Carlton, but at Hammersmith, co. Middx.". A further admon. was granted,

3rd March, 1769, to his son Miles S., the eldest son Thomas renouncing.

MARY STAPLETON, "late of the city of York, but at Bath, co. Somerset, widow, and executrix of Nic. S., *formerly* Errington," desires burial at Carlton by her husband if dying in England, or if beyond sea, her heart to be brought over and buried by her husband. She names the following: My sons John (oldest) and Thomas S., uncle Sir Myles S., "son-in-law" Nicholas S., of Carleton, with his children Philadelphia, Mary, Charlotte, Fanny, and "Master Stapleton"; also Eliz., sister of said Nicholas S. "My da. Mary, wife of Ralph Clavering, and their children Mary, Ralph, Nicholas, Nancy, Franky, Winifred, and Catherine Clavering; da. Catherine - Hester Stapleton; "relations" Sir Basil and Lady Dixwell; cousins Eliz. Plumton, who had three sisters, Mary, Catherine, and Nelly Gascoigne; cousins Eliz. Mompesson and Mary Christmas; "my brother Joseph Sandys and his wife; grandmother Lady Peyton and Aunt Lady Swan". To her son and executor she adds: "I am sure, my dear Jacky, you'll never forget to pray for my poor soul. . . . Give £10 to the Benedictines at Brussels, and what you think proper to the good nuns at Antwerp, Louvain, Cambray, and Gravellines." [11th May, 1734—20th June, 1735.]

NORTH RIDING OF YORK.

JOSEPH PATTISON, of Six-Hills, co. Lincoln, held an estate at Leake, in the North Riding. "1692. Anne Paddison was buried February y⁰ 10th." "1703. George, y⁰ son of Joseph Pattinson and Margaret, his wife, was born 14th December." [*Bishop's Reg.* at Lincoln.]

THOMAS, Lord FAUCONBERG and Viscount HENCHKNOWLE, desires burial at Coxwold, and names his sons Thomas and Rowland Bellasis, das. Mary, Ann, and Penelope, brothers John and Rowland B., the executors of his will being his wife Bridget and Sir John Webb. [6th March, 1714—7th May, 1719.]

JANE TOOTELL, late of the p. of St. Andrew, Holborn. Admon. of her estate was granted, 16th July, 1718, to Henry Trapps, guardian of her infant children Eliz. and John Tootell.

ZACHARY S. MORE, of North Loftus, whose marriage settlement with Anne, da. of Richard Harnage, Esq., is dated 16th August, 1706, "desires burial at Loftus near Mr. Danby's grave," and names his eldest son Zachary Harnage More, *second* son Thomas, and da. Anne M., all minors; brother Thomas More and sister Bridget Hoskins, giving to his sister "Barbara More, now at Lisbon, in Portugal, £10 per annum," with a like sum to Mr. Tobias Battersby, brother John Collingwood and goddas. Eliz. Hoskins and Ann Collingwood, naming also in a codicil his nephew John Collingwood. [23rd January, 1728—20th June, 1732.]

CUTHBERT CONSTABLE, of Constable-Burton, co. York, names his wife Elizabeth, eldest son William (to whom he left his library), and Marmaduke Tunstall, of Wycliffe, executors of his will; also son Marmaduke and das. Cecily and Winifred. [14th March, 1746—27th May, 1747.]

WILLIAM SALVIN, of Easingwold. Born in 1662, he married, in 1702, Anne, niece and heiress of Thomas Reynes, of Easingwold: dying in 1726, he was buried at St. Olave's, Marygate, York. [*Lawson MS.*]

GERARD SALTMARSH, "of the county of York, gent.," in his will of 28th December, 1732, proved 5th February, 1733, by his executor "Mr. Ralph Clayton," names his brother Edward S., and his three nephews Philip S. and his son, and Mr. Peter Vavasor, of Willitoft.

PHILADELPHIA THOROLD, of Southampton Street, Bloomsbury, spinster, left by will dated 29th May, and proved 11th December, 1735, "£5 to Mr. *Benjamin Petre*, who lives with Mr. George Jernegan, and to Mr. *Challoner*, who lives with Mrs. Brent".

The collection known as the "Forfeited Estates Papers" at the Public Record Office, from which many extracts were given in *Eng. Cath. Nonj. of 1715*, is again the source of the following pages. This further and still larger selection will be found of great interest, throwing, as it does, so much light upon the sufferings and adventures of English Catholics of that period.

[*Forfeited Estates MS.*, A. 23.] " Dame MARGARET ANDERTON, sworn this 15° Maii, 1718, upon her oath, saith that Sir Laurence Anderton, her son, was, whilst he was under her care, educated in the Romish Religion, and she doth believe that he doth still profess the same; that before he was one-and-twenty years of age he was sent or did go over to the College at St. Omers to study and for his education, and is now (as this deponent verily believes) in parts beyond the seas."

[*Id.*] FRANCIS ANDERTON, Esq., sworne this 30th May, 1718, saith that he was married about 10 or 11 years since to the sister of Sir Henry Bedingfield, with whom he had £5000 portion, and that before that marriage part of the estate . . . some £500 per annum, was settled as jointure . . . and that Mr. Eyre, of Gray's Inn, drew the said settlement, and that Mr. Edward Bedingfield, dec., was one of the trustees, and that he, this deponent, was in possession for about two years before the said marriage, and during the life of his elder brother James, who was then beyond seas, and is since dead, who conveyed the same to this deponent . . . that he hath constantly paid about £50 or £60 per annum to his elder brother Sir Laurence Anderton, who is now about the age of seven or eight and thirty years, and was educated in and doth still profess the Romish Religion, and that when he was about the age of 15 or 16 he, the said Sir Laurence, was sent over to the seminary at St. Omers to study and be instructed in his religion and for his education, and that he remained in the same college for the purposes aforesaid for the space of seven years or thereabouts; and further, this deponent saith that he hath heard the said Sir Laurence Anderton own that he was a monk. FRANCIS ANDERTON.

[A. 24.] RICHARD COTTON, gent., Quartermaster in the regiment of dragoons commanded by the Hon. Brigadier-General Honywood, saith that after the rebellion was suppressed at Preston he, with some dragoons belonging to the said regiment, was ordered to reside at the house of Francis Anderton, Esq., commonly called Sir Francis Anderton, at Lostock, to take care of the goods . . . among which were . . . a large clock like a church clock in the gate house or porter's lodge . . . that several of the goods were very good, and particularly a scriptore, as rich and as fine as ever this informant ever saw, and must have been very valuable. [15th December, 1716.] RIC. COTTON.

[A. 55.] Dame MARGARET ANDERTON in her will dated 17th August, 1720, of which John Gillibrand, of Chorley, was executor and resid. legatee, names her da. Mary Blundell, grandsons Robert and Henry Blundell, and her granddas. Bridget, Margaret, Mary, Anne, Frances, and Elizabeth Blundell.

MS. 29 A. gives in detail the case of Sir LAURENCE ANDERTON v. FRANCIS ANDERTON.

[B. 62.] " CHRISTOPHER CLARKSON, of Preston, co. Lanc., said that Edward Kitchen is uncle to his wife and is a Popish priest; that the said Kitchen goes by the assumed name of Smith, and hath for several years last past received the rents of certain lands in Higher Walton, in the p. of Walton-le-Dale, . . . known by the name of Shutlingfields; that the usual residence of this said Kitchen, *alias* Smith, was at Bank Hall, in p. of Broughton, where he officiated as a priest of the Church of Rome, but sometimes came over from thence to Walton to receive the rents of the tenants of his said estate of Shutlingfields, which rents are applied by him to the support of himself and other popish priests." [19th November, 1716.]

[*Id.*] " WILLIAM GREGSON, of Barton, in p. of Preston, saith that Mr. Edward Kitchen, *alias* Smith . . . officiated as priest at Bank Hall, and he hath seen Papists *in great numbers* go to and return thence upon holy days; and the said Smith hath shewn him the said house, and in particular, a Room above stairs, which had forms and conveniencys in it, which induces this informant to believe that it was the said Smith's chapel." [12th December, 1716.]

To the above "information" the following memorandum is added: "Examine one, Moore, who promised to attend at the office . . . the man is a Protestant, but his wife is a Papist, who probably prevented his coming; this man or his wife can prove Kitchen a Popish priest ".

[*Id.*, p. 20.] JOHN HARRISON, of Bodarstone, in p. of Blackburn, linen-weaver, saith that Henry Wilcox, of Houghton, box-maker, was actually in the town of Preston. at the time of the late rebellion there, viz., upon Thursday, 10th November, 1715, and that this informant did then see Henry Wilcox walking in the streets of Preston, in company with several persons that have been since condemned and executed on account of the rebellion, and that he, the said Henry Wilcox, had then a cockade in his hat which was a mark to distinguish the friends of the Pretender by. In witness whereof, &c. [21st November, 1716.] The mark of
JOHN + HARRISON.

[B. 62, p. 100.] WILLIAM MOORE, Esq., "Master of the References," and acting for the Forfeited Estates Commissioners, writes to them from Preston: . . . "I have found Mr. Chaddock, the present [1716] Mayor of Preston, on all occasions a very hearty and zealous man for the Government, nor can I in this place having named the Mayor omit taking notice of the town of Preston, which, though by reason of its healthful situation, was usually made the winter residence of a great many Roman Catholic gentlemen in the neighbourhood, and was taken possession of by the rebels in the late rebellion, and thereby unfortunately became the scene of an action wherein so many gallant men of His Majesty's troops lost their lives. Yet I should do it injustice if I did not say that there is not any town in Great Britain, in proportion to the number of its inhabitants, that can truly boast of more hearty friends to His Majesty, King George, than are to be found in Preston! and during the late mobs, those preludes to the late rebellion, it was not in the power of the enemies of the Government to raise any tumult there, which must in a good measure be attributed to the Rev. Mr. Peploe, the parson of the town, who, during the late reign, though placed as it were in the midst of a college of Popish priests,—there being no less than six Popish chapels in his parish,—had the honesty and fortitude to declare on all proper occasions, as well from the pulpit as in his conversation, that nothing humanly speaking could secure our Religion and our laws but the succession of the crown as settled in the most illustrious House of Hanover, and who, since His Majesty's accession to the throne, has shown as eminent a zeal for his royal person and Government; for, on the approach of the rebels to Preston, he, with the best of the townsmen, retired to His Majesty's troops, and returned again with General Wills to the attack of the town, for which the rebels burned his barn and plundered his house, to his damage at least £200—a very considerable loss to a clergyman of his small preferment and numerous family; and I must take the freedom to say that as this worthy divine's having yet met with no public favour for his services and sufferings (though as well qualified for preferment in the Church as most of his order) must be a matter of great pleasure to the Papists and Jacobites, so it must be no less cause of discouragement to the friends of the Government! I have presumed to be the freer on this subject from the directions I received at Preston from some of the Hon. Commissioners to lay a memorial before the Board relating to this gentleman, and I flatter myself I shall soon have an occasion to congratulate him on his having been recommended with success by the Hon. Commissioners to the royal favour. . . .

"The Lord Molyneux has a deposition made against him by his gardener that shows his lordship to have been as directly concerned in the late rebellion as any man that was executed for it. There are also other depositions relating to his lordship, which, tho' they do not so fully come up to the point, yet it was the opinion of several persons well affected to His Majesty's Government with whom I discoursed that it had been no difficulty to have fixed another direct evidence upon his lordship. . . .

"There are several depositions of which I have also taken copies relating to Sir Nicholas Sherburne, a Roman Catholic of a very great estate, and I was informed that there was also a letter of his found upon the late Lord Derwentwater, or some other person taken at Preston by the King's troops, in which he wishes good success to their undertaking, or words to that effect, and I was further informed by a gentleman in his neighbourhood, who came to me at the office in Preston, that he was very well assured, had proper methods been taken and encouragement given, it had been no difficult matter to have fixed sufficient evidence upon him. . . .

"The family of Thomas Clifton, of Lytham, Esq., a Roman Catholic of a very considerable estate, seems to have been very deeply engaged in the late rebellion. George Clifton, his brother, is actually outlawed on account of that rebellion, and I have the copies of several depositions taken against the eldest son of the said Thomas Clifton, and one Mr. Mayfield, his steward, relating to their being concerned in the rebellion, that are very plain and direct! This Mayfield was taken in Preston by the King's troops on the surrender of that town, and at the earnest solicitation of Mr. Shawe—as I was informed—was admitted to bail; but the man was so conscious of his guilt that he left his bail in the lurch, and is said to be fled to France, and yet the recognizance is not estreated! And the eldest son of the said Thomas Clifton has absconded ever since the action at Preston, and is said also to be fled to France, and yet there have been no proceedings by way of outlawry against either of them. There are also some depositions against the said Thomas Clifton himself, and I have been assured by a clergyman of the Church of England in his neighbourhood, a very zealous man for the Government, that . . . was there but proper encouragement given there might be a cloud of witnesses produced that would fix the matter plainly upon him. And I must say that I found it the general opinion of the friends of the Government in and about Preston that the family of Clifton had been unaccountably screened from prosecution! And they did not stick to name the person, which I shall avoid doing here, because in some other matters he seems to have acted heartily for the Government. If Mr. Townley and Mr. Tildesley were acquitted by their jury for want of evidence (as I have often heard suggested) I am sure it was not because evidence sufficient could not be had, for there are a great many depositions against them so direct and plain as had those persons been produced as witnesses it must have made a jury, even of Jacobites, ashamed to have acquitted them.

"I have also taken copies of the depositions against the Cottons, and was there an inclination to trace that affair to the bottom, I have been assured the matter would not be very difficult.

"I also took copies of some depositions taken formerly by Sir Henry Hoghton and Thomas Molyneux, Esq., against one Thomas Whitehead, relating to his having been engaged in the late rebellion. This I did at the request of Mr. Greenhalgh, a Justice of the Peace for the county, who, but a few days before I left Preston, had committed the said Whitehead for high treason to Lancaster gaol on other depositions lately taken by himself, that, if there should be occasion on his prosecution to produce other witnesses besides those who had sworn against the said Whitehead before him, he might also make use of those who had sworn against him before Sir Henry Hoghton and Mr. Molyneux. This commitment of Whitehead, which was a little before Christmas, gave a sensible concern to the party who seemed to have gained new courage from the Lord Townshend's dismission from being Secretary of State, insomuch that several of the persons outlawed for high treason on account of the late rebellion began to appear publicly in the country! And I was informed that the Popish priests were everywhere spiriting up their people by assuring them that they would see an unexpected turn in their affairs! which probably proceeded either from what was then publicly discoursed that there would be an universal change in the ministry or from their having some private intelligence of the intended invasion from Sweden."

WILLIAM MOORE.

[B. 62, p. 22.] THOMAS BROWNE, of Dalton-in-Furness, co. Lanc., yeoman, saith that about two years ago he took of one, Mrs. Mary Richardson, 26 acres of land in Dalton, for 3 years, at £3 per annum, clear rent and also paying all taxes and charges whatsoever, and particularly a rent of four nobles per annum, to Her Grace the Duchess Dowager, of Mountague; that the said Mary Richardson is housekeeper to one —— Taylor, a Popish priest, and though this informant has paid his rent to the said Mary Richardson, yet the said —— Taylor is looked upon to have the profits of the said premises, and that Mary Richardson only acts under him, and this informant further saith that he has always heard and believes that the said premisses are settled to Popish and superstitious uses. [21st November, 1716.] THOS. BROWNE.

[*Id.*, p. 30.] JOHN SALLOM, of Clayton, in p. of Garstang, deposes, 27th November, 1716, that Mr. Richard Shuttleworth, of Turnover Hall, in the p. of St. Michael, near Garstang . . . was engaged at Preston in the late rebellion, and in attempting to make his escape from Preston was killed by the King's troops.

[*Id.*, p. 35.] 27th November, 1716. THOMAS FORD, jun., of Liverpool, co. Lanc., gent., saith that James Almond, the elder, of Speke, near Liverpool (who is proved to be a Popish priest by the information of Richard Hitchmough, of Garston) is possessed of a house in Union Street, Liverpool, now in the possession of one —— Hawett, widow of Richard Hawett, of Liverpool, merchant, for which house she pays £6 6s. per annum.

[*Id.*, p. 37.] The same THOMAS FORD also deposes, 28th November, 1716, that the township or village of Ulveswalton, with the land thereunto belonging (lying within Leyland and adjoining to Extonburgh, *alias* Euxton, about six miles from Preston . . . and now the reputed inheritance of William, Lord Molyneux, of Croxteth), belongs to some Popish priests or Jesuits, and that Lord M. is only a nominal trustee for some Popish priests or Jesuits, or for some other superstitious use for the township of Ulveswalton.

[*Id.*, p. 72.] Also that the Hon. HENRY HOWARD, brother to the Duke of Norfolk, is a Popish priest, and has a pension of £200 per annum paid him out of the Duke's estate. [14th December, 1716.]

[*Id.*, p. 73.] Also that Lowick Hall, the reputed inheritance of THOMAS CLIFTON, Esq., of Lytham, about four miles from Preston, belongs to some Popish priests, or is appropriated to some other superstitious use. [14th December, 1716.]

[*Id.*, p. 87.] Also that an estate called Brin Hall, lying near Ashton, co. Lanc., and now the reputed residence of Sir

WILLIAM GERARD, of Garswood, belongs to the body of English Jesuits or to some other superstitious use: also that out of an estate called the Hall Wood, lying in or near Melling, within six miles from Liverpool, and now the reputed residence of Robert Molyneux, of Mosborrow, is an annual pension of about £20 paid to some Popish priests for saying Mass at the said Hall on several particular days in the year. [22nd December, 1716.]

[*Id.*, p. 17.] WILLIAM SHEPHERD, a servant of Lord Molyneux, sending a report to William Moore of his "discovery of an estate granted to superstitious uses," also adds: ". . . I have sent you a small present of brandy: I should be glad to know it proved acceptable: I should be glad you would please to drink my health in one bottle with your landlord William Harrison: the rest are entirely at your service. I heartily hope it may prove good: Sir, I hope as I have been truly free and plain in the matter without equivocation, so I hope that falling into so good hands as yours in whose power it lyes both to be favourable and do justice to all, so *I doubt not only of a third part as you proposed at first*" [Mr. Moore writes in the margin: "This was a mistake, for I told him a *trustee* of a superstitious estate, dicovering it before 24th November, 1716, was entitled only to a *fourth* part"], "but of all the reasonable kind usage that in an honest fair way can be hoped for, for I do assure you I have had an endless hurry about that business, and I do not know that I have had so much of it as I have spent on that account, so I rely wholly upon your kindness, which will ever be acknowledged to his power by your humble and obedient servant, whilst William Shepherd." Mr. Moore adds in margin: "The above letter was directed, for Mr. Moore, at Mr. William Harrison's, saddler, in the Fryar Gate at Preston, and was dated 25th November, 1716. At the same time the said Mr. William Harrison, at whose house I lodged, received a letter from the said Mr. Shepherd, dated also 25th November, 1716, of which what follows is a copy."

"Honest William; I have left a lease and assignment in Liverpool to come by Gornal this week which I desire you'll show Mr. Moore, and afterwards keep them till I see you, or send them to my mother's . . . pray give him my humble service, and with the lease come 4 bottles of brandy, which I beg you'll also give him, one of which I could wish if he please you and he would together drink my health . . . I have not tasted the brandy, but a friend of mine promised to get right good, and I pay for such, and should be ashamed if it should prove otherwise. I had designed to have made a further addition of a dozen lemons, but could meet with none. The things come directed for *you*. I forgot to desire my friend to pay the carriage, but if he hath not, pray pay it, and I'll return it with thanks for all troubles. I doubt not but in a fair way he'll be so kind as to show me all the favour he can, and as he proposed at first *allow me a third part. I paid not for the postage of his letter, because I supposed him free,* which, with many thanks for all troubles, is from your friend and servant whilst

" WILLIAM SHEPHERD."

But Mr. Shepherd's obsequious and diplomatic despatch to the government official, and the more confidential letter to his friend the saddler, seem alike to have met with a cold reception, as appears from the subjoined memoranda of Mr. Moore, who writes: " I did not think it proper for me to return an answer, but got Mr. Harrison to do it, the copy of whose letter to the said William Shepherd here follows :

" Preston, 13th December, 1716.

" Sir, — I received the lease and assignment . . . Mr. Moore thanks you for your intended present to him of four bottles of brandy, which I could not get him to accept nor taste a drop of it, but bid me tell you it was not out of any disrespect, but because he was under an obligation to take nothing; so there the brandy will remain at my house till I receive further orders from you.

" I am, Sir,
" Your most humble servant,
" WILLIAM HARRISON."

Mr. Moore appears to have remained at Preston until almost the end of December, 1716, leaving " the keys of the office with Mary Harrison, the saddler's sister," and writing with great particularity to one of the Commissioners on 22nd

December [C. 93]: ". . . You will find in the closet of the Commissioners' Room a few penns, some ink, both black and redd, three rheams of writing paper, some very large imperial paper, and some other things which I thought proper to leave for yours and the Surveyor's use ".

Five days later he writes (apparently from Chester) [B. 62, p. 106], 27th December, 1716: ". . . I think it my duty to acquaint the Hon. Board that I have been very well informed that Lord Molyneux has summoned in all his tenants to fill up their leases, which are generally for three lives, and that the Papists in general are either doing the same throughout the county, or else making conveyance of their estates to Protestant trustees, to evade the late Act for seizing two-thirds of the estates of Popish recusants for the benefit of the public; and I cannot without some indignation say that I apprehend some persons who would be thought friends to the Government are busily concerned in these transactions. And I am humbly of opinion that, without some proper clause of retrospection in an act of Parliament to be passed the next sessions, the two-thirds of the estates of Popish recusants will be of little benefit to the public."

[C. 85.] Letter from CHAMBERS SLAUGHTER, Esq., to George Treby, Esq., one of the Commissioners:

" Preston, 5th February, 1716-17.

". . . 'Tis to be wished that strict orders might be given to the Justices, but particularly to those of this country, that ye oaths should be again tendered to all persons without distinction, as well Protestants as Papists, being assured that several of the former have been neglected, though equally obnoxious as the latter. . . . If anything drops from me unbecoming to suggest, please to impute it to zeal and not conceit, being very desirous of approving myself,
" Sir,
" Your most obed. servant,
"CHAMBERS SLAUGHTER."

[C. 91.] Sir HENRY HOGHTON, M.P. for Preston, also writes to the "Commissioners of Enquiry" at Preston from Penrith, 3rd September, 1716:

"Sir,—I am sorry I had not the opportunity of waiting on you and the other Commissioners before I left the country. I hope you had a good journey to Preston. . . . This evening, Mr. Thomas Fletcher, of Hutton Hall, a good gentleman of a good estate in this country, tells me an acquaintance of his, one Mr. John Tiffin, can make several discoveries of real and personal estates belonging to the rebels, as also of some estates given to superstitious uses. *Mr. Fletcher, who was formerly a Papist, but now a Protestant,* and zealous in the interest of ye Government, I presume also knows of some estates given to superstitious uses. . . . If you think proper to offer the oaths to any about Preston, I could mention some who call themselves Protestants, and yet I believe won't take the oaths if tendered. . . .

"Your sincere friend and humble servant,

"H. HOGHTON."

[*Id.*] "Warton, 3rd October, 1716.

"To the Commissioners of Enquiry at Preston. Gentlemen, —I received your obliging letter, and take it as an uncommon favour that you are pleased not to lay any positive injunctions on me to make my personal appearance before your Honours, as I am very sensible you might justly have done. The journey would have been entirely fruitless; for I do hereby most sincerely profess, declare, and protest, upon the word of a Christian, gentleman, and *priest*, that I do not know of any estate . . . whatsoever, in this or in any other part of Great Britain, or any other His Majesty's dominions . . . applied to superstitious uses or appertaining to any college, seminary, monastery, convent, nunnery, church, chapel, &c., of the Romish Religion. I have often heard in general that the English Jesuits have considerable estates and possessions in this kingdom under borrowed names, as also large sums in the public stocks, but as to any particular whatsoever I can give no account in the world, as I am ready to declare upon oath in the most solemn form and manner, if at any time required. I hope, honoured Sirs, that I need not use any further argument to engage your belief in this matter. I think I have given more than ordinary proofs of my sincere zeal for the Protestant Religion and hearty affection to the present establishment and His Majesty's Government by an uniform series of loyal words and actions, and the whole tenor of my conversation. I am, with all respect and submission, Honoured Gentlemen, &c., W. AYLMER."

William Aylmer was instituted to the vicarage of Warton, in Lancashire, on 7th May, 1714, which he appears to have held till his death in 1734. In a volume of sermons in the British Museum is "A Recantation Sermon against the errors of Popery, particularly Transubstantiation, preached at St. Martin's, Oxford, 20th September, 1713, before . . . the Bishop of Oxford . . . the Mayor, Aldermen, &c., and Bailiffs of that city by *William Aylmer, lately Professor of Divinity in the Roman Church*. Published at the desire of his lordship. Oxford, 1713." No wonder that the Commissioners sought out this terrible apostate!

[C. 92.] JONATHAN MAUGHAN, to the Commissioners, dated from Wolsingham, 17th November, 1721 : "Captain Lancelot Ord was taken prisoner in the late rebellion at Preston, made his escape from prison, fled beyond the seas, and there continues. The tithes of Ancroft and Tweedmouth belonged to his three younger brethren—viz., John Ord, who was executed in the rebellion; Mungo Ord, who died in the same rebellion; and Francis Ord, who was kept in prison until set free by the Act of Indemnity, these tithes being held by lease under the Dean and Chapter of Durham at a very small rent. Mrs. Eliz. Ord, sister to the above-said rebels, renewed the lease three years since."

[*Id.*] Letter to a Commissioner:

"Sir,—Being very uneasie at my being kept out of the money due to me out of Shuttleworth estate for so many years, and having more pressing occasion for money at this time, I beg of you and the rest of ye gentlemen that I may be p^d as soon as possible, which will greatly oblige your most obed. servant, THOMAS CLARKE.

"18th November, 1721."

[B. 62, p. 89.] 22nd December, 1716. WILLIAM WALL, of Preston, desires that, if possible, his name might not be made use of in his information (furnished through William Moore) to the Commissioners, he being *the only attorney in Preston* that has made any information for the benefit of the public. William Moore writes himself to the Commissioners to hope they will indulge him in this.

[*Id.*, p. 93.] 27th December, 1716. ". . . WILLIAM MASSEY, Esq., of Puddington, co. Chester, died about a year ago, and by his will left £500 to his sister, who is a professed nun at Douay, and £5 to Thos. Brockholes, of Standish, co. Lanc., who is a Popish priest, and who also has an estate in Standish Wood . . . which he holds as a priest of the Church of Rome, and is to go always to Popish priests. The mother of Sir Nicholas Sherburne, of Stonyhurst, gave an estate near Chipping, of £60 per aunum, to Charles Panket, a Popish priest, to go at his death in a succession for ever to Popish priests for their maintenance and support, the said Charles Panket, now living in the house called Chipping Lane, to which the estate so given him as aforesaid belongs."

[C. 98.] A letter endorsed "To the Hon. the Commissioners for Forfeitures, these":

"April 3, 1717.

"May it please your Honours: Upon search of Mr. Nevill and Mr. Timbrell, &c., in relation to our affair in Oxfordshire, I have happily succeeded, and have found where he lives, but my friend tells me he cares not to medle, and is somewhat shye till I can present him with some small sums of money, and likewise divers other priests, &c., who has already discovered about £1400 or £1500 per annum—near £700 in Essex, £400 or £500 per annum in Lincolnshire, £400 per annum in Kent; and engages to discover more in Oxfordshire and most counteys in England; £3500 made over to Doway by a former Member of Parliament, but in his travells turned abott of ye said place, and his brother will be the chiefe witness in this affair.

"I am, your honours most obed^t most humble serv^t,

"THOMAS CARR."

[This somewhat obscure letter would almost seem to refer to Hitchmough, who was turned out of Douay.]

[T. 2. *Miscell. Papers relating to George Talbot.*]

Maryland, 12th October, 1717.

In a series of "Interrogatories proposed and offered by his excellency JOHN HART, Esq., governor of Maryland . . . unto Charles Carroll, Esq., of the city of Anapolis," one is as follows: "Do you know of any lands or sums of money that are applied to superstitious uses in the Province [Maryland] for the maintenance of any Popish Bishops, Priests, Jesuits, or any other Regular order of the Romish Church, or of any Seminaries that are for the education of youth in the Romish Persuasion?"

"Answereth that he doth not know of any lands . . . that are applied to superstitious uses in this Province, but believes that some priests in this Province are possessed of some tracts or Parcels of land taken up by themselves in their natural capacities under the common conditions of Plantations and pursuant thereto, or by those under whom, for valuable considerations, they derive, and verily believes that the yearly value of them is so inconsiderable as hardly to afford a bare subsistence for those who are possessed of them, much less to make any fund for education of youth in any Popish seminaries."

"Do you know of any persons concerned in the late rebellion who were possessed of any estate at that time in this Province, or at any time since 24th June, 1715?"

"Answereth that he doth not know of any such person . . . save what he said before of James Talbot" [son of Colonel George Talbot, which James T. was in Newgate as prisoner, "taken for the late rebellion"].

[C. 100.] JAMES BLACOE, of Barton, co. Lanc., taylor, upon oath, 7th January, 1715, saith: "That on Tuesday morning, ye 8th of November last, Mr Thomas Whitehead, sonn of Mr. Richard Whitehead, of Matside-in-Claughton, Thomas Green, of Myerscough, who carried a gunn with five or six more in company, came to this informant's house to search for militia arms, and some of the company knowing this informant's brother to be a militia souldier, demanded to have what arms they had for the service of the Northern Rebels then coming towards Preston, but the rest of the company this Informant knows not".

[T. 33.] 10th December, 1715. WILLIAM BAINES, of Preston, husb., "saith he was in Preston when the Rebels entered the town on Wednesday, 9th November last, and continued there until the town was surrendered to the King's troops, during which time this Informant remembers John Leyburn, of Nateby, Esq., came to the Mitre Inn . . . on Thursday, 10th November, armed with a case of pistols and a sword by his side; and the said John L. had two servants, both of them well armed with pistols and guns, and that they mounted their horses when the King's troops came before ye town with all their arms and accoutrements, in order to go and oppose the said troops . . . that Albert Hodgson, of Leyton, Esq., came to lye with Mr. Leyburn at the Mitre on Thursday night, bringing his sword and pistols along with him to the Mitre, and he saw the said Mr. Leyburn and Mr. Hodgson with cockades in their hats . . . very active and busy among the said rebels . . . that he saw John Brockholes, of Claughton, jun., arrive . . . and above 9 men with him, armed in the like manner, and come to the Mitre to ask for quarters for himself and those men, his soldiers as he called them . . . and that on Saturday, when the King's troops came to towne, one of those men bid this Informant farewell, for he was going either to kill or be killed . . . that he also saw John Dalton, of Thurnham, Esq., come into the town well armed, with a drawn sword in his hand, waving it about at the head of his company . . . of over 20 men, all on horseback, and well armed, with each man a sword, musket, and case of pistols . . . and that on Friday, 11th November, he saw Edward Tildesley, of the Lodge, Esq., come into town at the head of his company . . . of near 100 men . . . that Captain Francis Leigh, brother to Peter Leigh, of Lyme, Esq., came on Thursday, 10th November, to the Mitre, with sword and pistols in his holsters and pistols in his breast, and 6 or 7 men with him . . . and Richard Townley, of Townley, Esq., with a cockade in his hat . . . with 12 or 14 men with him, all with cockades, swords, pistols, and guns on Sunday morning, marching amongst the said rebels to oppose the King's Forces . . . and that on Sunday morning, whilst the action was . . . he saw Sir Francis Anderton and John Trafford, of Croston, gent., mount their horses . . . and ride to join the rebels in opposition to the King's Forces ... and that on Thursday morning Edward Boswicke, of Manchester, came to the Mitre Inn aforesaid, with the said Captain Francis Leigh, and had a cockade in his hat, a sword by his side, and a case of pistols in his breast, and when he, the said Mr. Boswicke, lighted and came into the backside, he said: 'Now for King James' ... and this Informant further saith that Mr. James Singleton came on ye Saturday at night to enquire for General Foster, and said he must send some assistance to my Lord Derwentwater."

[C. 101.] CHAMBERS SLAUGHTER writes to the Commissioners from Preston, 23rd April, 1717.

" ... I would be glad of your opinion in relation to rewards for ... small discoveries *which several poor Fellows come to ask after*, and I am not able to give an answer to, and *to refuse them any will be a great discouragement to services of that kind.* There is much discourse in the country about the explanation and prolongation of ye Registering Act and gives the enemies of the public a great handle in infusing into the minds of the meaner sort a design of ye Parliament to repeal that Act, and other suggestions upon the late change that the Commission will be dissolved, which makes me the more desirous of a little light, being wholly in the dark myself and not knowing what to say in opposition."

[C. 102.] Contains—*inter alia*—"An Account of ye Names of Severall Persons in Preston who are Harty and Zealous in His Majesty's interest, Recommended to ye Hon. Commission for Inquiry into ye Rebels' forfeited estates, to make use of them as they shall have occation." A list of names of trades, &c., is given under each of the following headings: " viz.—

"Gentlemen bred up to ye Law, quallifyd for clarks and able to assist in severall kinds.

. . . .

"Persons quallifyd for surveying land . . . and appraising goods &c.

. . . .

"Persons proper to attend ye office, to run upon messages & arrants about ye town.

. . . .

"Persons that are good Footmen, proper to be sent upon Messages about ye Country if 50, 60, or 100 miles.

. . . .

"Persons proper to be sent to seize or apprehend persons on any account.

. . . .

"Names of such persons at whose houses the officers, clarks, and servants may be entertained and lodged at.

. . . .

"Persons using professions & trades recommended to ye Hon. Commissioners to make use of y^m. as they have occation." The first named on this list is Dr Thomas Whaley, physition . . . who "lives out of town but is often in it".

[*Id.*] "THOMAS PARRY, of the Cross Keys at Holywell, co. Flint, innholder, sworn and examined this 10th July, 1718, saith that about sixteen years ago he did treat with Cap. Peter Pennant, of Bighton, one of the Justices of the Peace for co. Flint . . . (and landlord of the Inn at Holywell wherein this deponent doth now inhabit) in order to take the Inn and did agree to take it at a rental of £11 13s. . . . Deponent never paid any rent to Mr. Winne, a Romish priest who lived in this deponent's house. . . . That Sir Peirce Mostyn and Mr. Roberts, of Herques, had a lease of the Inn . . . that 2 years since, Mr. Wilmott came to Deponent's house and hath ever since boarded there for £6 per annum . . . that he did always apprehend Mr. Wilmott to be a very poor man, and hath heard Mr. W. say that at the time of his being taken up in the chapel in this deponent's house, he (Wilmott) had but 15s. in the whole world . . . and deponent further saith *that he is very certain that there never was any gold lace for the use of the altar there or for any other use in the said chapel save only such as was stitched round a red vestment* [the words in italics are erased], and that at the time when the furniture of the chapel was seized by virtue of a warrant of this Hon. Board there was nothing taken away from Deponent's house save only a pair of sheets which was immediately returned to this Deponent's servant, and that he hath not heard that anything was taken away from the Starr, save only the furniture of the chapel there, nor hath Deponent heard of any complaint of any Loss of goods in the said town or of any misbehaviour of any of the officers that seized the same or of the soldiers that came with them, and that the civil and quiet deportment of the officers and soldiers during their stay at Holywell is the frequent discourse of the inhabitants there.

"The mark of
✠
"THOMAS PARRY.
"Robert Floyd at Starr."

[*Id.*] PETER PENNANT, of Bighton, Esq., saith that about the year 1704 he let the house known by the name or sign of the Cross Keys at Holywell to Sir P. Mostyn and Mr. Roberts for a fine of £50, under the yearly value of £5 5s. for lives of deponent and his mother, who is now living . . . Roberts being dead.

18th July, 1718.

[C. 44.] Depositions of PETER CHARNLEY, of Lytham, yeoman, dated 27th December, 1715, and of Andrew Dobson, of Bryning-cum-Kellamore, co. Lanc., husb., 28th December, 1715, relative to the part taken by the Cliftons in the rebellion.

Several of the servants of Thos. Clifton and others are mentioned, some of whose names also occur among those who "registered their names and real estates"—*e.g.*, William Walmesley, groom to Mr. Clifton; James Sanderson, of Little Plumpton, yeoman; William Bennett, of Westby; and "Nicholas Sanderson, young Master Clifton's man".

Andrew Dobson deposes that on Thursday, 10th November, he went to Lytham Hall, where he found twelve or more persons who were all to go with the young Mr. Clifton, and after dinner that day and drinking a glass of ale in the cellar it was agreed that all the company should make themselves ready and come to Lytham Hall at seven o'clock the next morning, Mr. Mayfield desiring all the company to get their horses shod that night.

[C. 43.] A letter from W. FETHERSTONHAUGH to the Hon. the Commissioners of Enquiry, dated October 2, 1716, saying he was told by the wife of John Sanderson that the rent of the house she inhabits, being the property of George Clifton, was settled to "pious uses".

[C. 116.] WILLIAM SEDGWICK, of London, merchant, maketh oath that he never heard of any ship laden with salt or coals that was to be consigned to him by his brother-in-law, *Chambers Slaughter*, and he doth not believe that the said Chambers S. has at any time since his first being chosen an officer under the Hon. Com. for Enquiry either near Blyth or any other place load any ship to this deponent.

[C. 57.] CATHERINE COLLINGWOOD, widow, sworn and examined this the 22nd Octber, 1718, saith that she knows John Collingwood of Eslington, in Northumberland, and that he is a reputed Roman Catholic, and that she has seen him at Mass.

[C. 64.] The petition of CATHERINE COLLINGWOOD, one of the das. of the late Henry Lord Viscount Montague, and relict of George Collingwood, dec., sheweth—

That by reason of the attainder of her said late husband, and a defect in her marriage settlement occasioned by ye ignorance or negligence of ye lawyer concerned in drawing it, your petitioner is deprived of her small jointure, and her three daughters of ye moderate portion settled upon them by the said marriage settlement ; that by reason that she and her daughters (without any injustice in the Court) thus deprived of the slender provision which was intended for them . . . they are reduced to extreme necessity. That . . . your Petitioner hath applied to His Majesty, who hath had the Royall compassion to refer her petition to the Attorney-General, who hath ordered the allegations of the said petition to be made good before him tomorrow, in the evening ; that her councel advises her to produce the settlement of William Collingwood, father of the said George Collingwood, to enable the Attorney-General to judge of the defect in your petitioner's settlement . . . and further prays that her councel may have a sight of the said settlement.

[*Id.*] 5th November, 1718. ROBERT COLLINGWOOD, upon his oath, says that there was due to him $3\frac{1}{2}$ years' arrears of his annuity at Pentecost last. Charles Collingwood makes a similar deposition. *Both* of them say that their annuities were always paid them tax-free, and that there will be due to them each 4 years' arrears at St. Martin the Bishop in winter, which is the 11th day of this Instant November.

Christopher Metcalf, of the p. of St. Giles, co. Middx., gent., saith that he and his brother, Thomas Metcalf, have for several years paid the said Robert and Charles Collingwood their annuities by order of George Collingwood, their nephew, but have paid none to them since Lady Day, 1715.

The Commissioners, however, were probably unaware that these two claimants of unpaid annuities were Jesuit Fathers.

[D. 49. *Miscell. Papers concerning the Derwentwater Family.*]

"The late Col. RADCLIFFE devised his estate by will to ye Lady Mary Radcliffe, but by private instructions part of it to be in trust for the late Earl of Derwentwater or his heirs, and other part for superstitious uses, y^e maintenance of priests, Popish seminaries, or monasteries. The Lady Mary R. is a great bigot, and therefore was thought a fitt person to be intrusted with y^e disposal of Legacies left by nuncupative wills for superstitious uses. Examine s$^d.$ Lady Mary and Mr. Jenison, her priest, allso Mr. Jackson, late of Durham."

[D. 50. *A Case for the Commissioners*, &c. This is a paper endorsed " Mr Pengelly's opinion ".]

THOMAS RADCLIFFE, Esq., being seized in fee of divers manors, lands, &c., by his will, dated 30th June, 1705, gave all his manors, real estate, &c., to his sister, the Lady Mary R., for her life, and from and after her death . . . to James, then Earl of Derwentwater, his heirs and assigns for ever. The said Thomas R. soon after died s.p., to whom the said James, Earl of D., was nephew and heir-at-law. Lady Mary was at the time of the devise a Roman Catholic within the statute 11 and 12 King William, by which she is rendered incapable of taking by the will, so that the premises vested in the said Earl of D. and his heirs, and by his being attainted of High Treason became forfeited, and are now vested in the commissioners and trustees. The Lady Mary R., under pretence of the said will, has been in possession of the premises ever since the death of the devisor, Thomas R., the Commissioners having but very lately had the discovery made to them of this matter.

Query : " Whether Lady Mary, being a Roman Catholic, can take by this devise for her life ?"

Reply : " I conceive that she, being a Roman Catholic, is disabled, and incapable to take such estate for life by force of this devise ".

Query : " If she cannot take, what will be the proper method for the Commissioners to get into the possession of the premises —whether by taking possession by their officers or by bringing ejectments ?"

Reply : " This estate, having continued in the possession of Lady Mary, and Lord Derwentwater not having the profits thereof, I think it is most advisable to bring an ejectment, wherein the point of law arising upon the statute 11 and 12 W. III. will be determined properly before the Commissioners to change the possession." [27th November, 1721.]

THOMAS PENGELLY.

[*Id. Petition to the Commissioners of Ladies Catherine and Eliz. Radcliffe.*]

... " Sheweth that your Petitioners having £100 a year a piece secured to them for their lives by their late father Francis, Earl of Derwentwater, dec., issuing out of lands . . . allowed to John Radcliffe as first son of James, late Earl of D., and therefore so long as the said John R. lives the said annuities are secure, but inasmuch as the next person in remainder after the death of the said John without issue male is a forfeited person, your petitioners may not be secure, and for that it is all their subsistence and that they are in years and very infirme, your Petitioners pray your Honours to appoint a day for hearing their claims that it may be secured to them in case of the death of the said John Radcliffe."

[*Id. To the same: Ralph Gowland on behalf of the Hon. Lady Mary Radcliffe of Durham.*]

". . . prays that they will dispense with her personal appearance, being in a very weak condition and unable to take so great a journey without the utmost danger and hazard of her life, having been a long time confined to her chamber and frequently to her bed by an ill state of health."

"*Memorandum*: if she deliver a full and just [acct. ?] by 14th February, granted."

[*Id.* To the same: ANNA MARIA RADCLIFFE, widow of James, Earl of Derwentwater, on behalf of her eldest son, John R.]

". . . Sheweth that your Petitioner did some time since put in two claims on the estate of her dec. husband, he being but tenant for life with remainder to his 1*st*, 2*nd*, and 3*rd* sons: that the s^d. John was eldest son of the said late Earl (an infant under age), who by reason of the attainder for high treason of the said late Earl his father hath been kept out of all the profits of the estate to his very great loss and detriment. . . . Petitioner prays Com^rs. to appoint a day for hearing her claim."

[*Id.*] "The same to the same on behalf of her da. Anna Maria Radcliffe . . . who apart from the portion granted by her father hath nothing else for her necessary support and maintenance."

This and the foreg. petition were "dismissed".

[*Id.*] Petition of JAMES ROOKE, Esq., and MARY, Countess of DERWENTWATER, his wife.

". . . Sheweth that your Petitioners have long since entered their claims for a rent charge of £1000 out of estate of the late Earl of Derwentwater: that there are now several years in arrear due to your Petitioners, who have nothing else to support themselves and family withal, and as their title is independent and paramount the late Earl or his sons, your Petitioners pray the Comm^rs. to appoint a day for the hearing of their claim, without which they are not able to subsist any longer."

A note adds, "as soon as possible". This last petition would seem to have been granted, 19th June, 1719. [*MS.* 47. D.]

[D. 59.] Decision of Commissioners in Essex House, London, to dismiss the claim of [*Bishop*] "Benjamin Petre of the p. of St. Giles-in-the-Fields, gent.," to £100 annual payment out of the Manor of Whenby, &c., the estate of Lord

Derwentwater, Tuesday, 1st December, 1719, *he not appearing to support his claim.*

[C. 104.) *Inter alia*, a paper endorsed *Holywell*, and evidently an inventory of some of the spoil from the "Starr" or the "Cross Keys".

	oz.
"Remonstrance,	7
Plate, about,	96
	103

Books about 150, vestment suites 12, albs 8, amices 10, cushions 3, antependiums 7, sideboard cloaths 6, Pictures 6, curtains 2, Altar-hangings."

[C. 105]. An amusing sheet from the Commissioners' accounts is the following:—

"Laid out by Eliz. Evans for necessarys used in the Town's hall for the Hon. His Majesty's Com^{rs.}

"For flowers for the flower pots, 6 times, 3*d*. a time,	01. 6
For cleaning the Hall and Council House 7 weeks, shee referrs and leaves to their hon^{rs.} pleasures,	10. 6
Paid for the flower Potts,	00. 6
	12s. 6"

[C. 116.] "William Brining of Woodplumpton, co. Lanc., yeoman, saith that Edmund Fishwick, late of Newsham, co. Lanc., was seized of an estate in Newson called Crowboe, consisting of two messuages and 30 or 40 acres of land, held in part of Sir Nicholas Sherburne of Stonyhurst and in part of John Warren of Plumpton, and ... that Edmund F. had told him in his last sickness that he had given the said estate to William Sheppard (now servant to Mr. Blundell of Ince) ... and another person to maintain a Popish Priest, and that he (deponent) then desiring E. Fishwick to do something for his poor relations, he said they could not do him so great kindness as the Priests, and thereupon said, all that ever I have shall go for Pious uses ... that E. F. died about 10 years since and ...

that William Sheppard who is a Papist let the estate and receives the rents.

"The mark of
+
"WILLIAM BRINING.
"Preston, September 13, 1716."

[*Id.*] A document endorsed "Paper of Mr. Brooke delivered by Sir Richard Steele".

"To the Hon. Commissioners, &c., appointed to enquire of estates of certain traitors, &c.

"With most humble submission to your Honours:

"Those clauses which relate to estates given to superstitious uses, I . . . pray leave to lay before your Honours such methods as may probably answer the intention of the Act of Parliament."

After giving a summary of the Act granting a fourth part of a "superstitious estate" to any trustee "discovering" it between 24th August, 1716, and 24th November, 1716, the paper continues: "Your Honours are the most knowing how few trustees have made discoveries pursuant to the directions of the s$^{d.}$ Act; wherefore I beg leave to assure you that trusts of that nature are so very secretly managed that, for the most part . . . none are privy to them but the . . . persons principally concerned, who [not] being fearful of others, will always keep them concealed, unless some expedient be found to oblige or force them to discover and give account of all such secret transactions, the penalty of not appearing or not discovering the trust in them reposed being only £40, and imprisonment till paid. Which s^d fine of £40 it may be believed they will sooner pay than discover and loose the Fortunes they are entrusted with, and also bring themselves under the penalty for being accountable for mean profits, &c. As to the continuing the clause of paying the mean profits or repealing that respective clause, I most humbly submit, may it please your Honours: When Roman Catholics are summoned to take the oaths to the Government for preventing the two-thirds of their estates being applied to the use of the public, as per Act of Parliament, if they were to take the oath following:

"I, A. B., do solemnly . . . swear . . . that I am not now, or ever was, entrusted with or concerned in any estate, real or personal, demised, bequeathed, or given by any person to the use of . . . the Church of Rome, or any funds or allowance for educating, feeding . . . youth in any seminary, school, or Religious House, &c. (by the Papists often called Pious Uses) in any part of Europe . . . and that I do not know of any such trust, &c., reposed in any other person . . . nor of any estate belonging to the clergy or Religious Orders of the Church of Rome . . . all which I declare to be true . . . and I have not, never had, or do believe, or in anywise expect any forgiveness, pardon, remission, releasement, absolution, or any other manner or way of *Indulgence* from the *Sea* of Rome, meaning by or from the Pope, or any Prelate, or Ecclesiastic of the Romish Church . . . in case I do now here in the presence of God and of this hon. assembly equivocate, &c. . . . So help me God!

"It may reasonably be thought that if they will not save their own estates by swearing against their consciences, they will not take a false oath to preserve the revenues of their Church.

"And in case any person refuse to take this oath and be interrogated, then the Com$^{m.}$ be empowered to sequester estates and imprison such person refusing, wheresoever the estate can be discovered, and the same disposed of for the use of the public.

"May it please your Honours:

"The countenance I have received from some persons of distinction hath obliged me to present to your Honours the before mentioned method to deal with those the said Act aims at, whose economy or Church government of the Popish clergy in England I shall present unto you in the best manner I can. The great body of Ecclesiastics are divided into several branches. . . .

"The seculars or clergy are entirely governed by their Bishops in spiritual affairs and temporal interest (viz.), the Prelates receive all moneys and the revenues of estates left to superstitious (by them called pious) uses, and have the immediate government and direction of colledges, monasterys, &c. Their numbers were commonly four, but at present I can only be certain of three: these are Giffard (Metropolitan) and Witham residing here; the third is Ellis at Rome.

"The other Orders are called Religious, and are nominatively Monks, Fryers, Jesuits, Anchorites, and Carmelites: these Religious are subject to the Bishops in spiritual but are governed by their superiors in temporal interests, and they have the care of all abbeys, priories, monasteries, &c., and receive such sums of money yearly as are left to their use for their support.

"The nature of Trusts given to the aforesaid uses is such that the very members of the Body are unknowing from whence their vast revenues do arise. The superiors themselves do many times receive large yearly sums appointed for their uses, and know not who is the Donor, so jealous and fearful they are of being discovered, or any light given of their secrets.

"For proof of what I shall humbly offer to your Honours, if you shall please to summons Sir Charles Ingleby, Knt., and councel for the Jesuits; Mr. Piggott, of the Temple, London; Mr. Aire; Mr. Beddingfield; Mr. Fitzherbert, of Gray's Inn, councel for the others, to answer interrogatorys, 'tis highly probable many estates given or assigned to the aforesaid uses for thirty years past may be by them discovered. I pray that a particular regard may be to examine Mr. Aire touching Sir Henry Fletcher's estate, who is become a Fryar.

"*Monks.* The monks, a very opulent order of Religious in temporal interest, are governed by a Superior or Lord Abbott, and he has the care of all their Abbeys, Priories, &c., to whom all revenues and interest are paid, and the whole Order are accountable to him. His office is for life.

"*Fryars.* The community of fryers consist of several distinct Orders, as Franciscans, Augustines, Mendicants, &c., having one Superior only, to whom all revenues are paid, and to whom all monastic jurisdiction doth belong: his office is elective and continues by one year.

"*Carmelites.* This Order is governed by a Superior, and nothing differs from the former in Dignity and Power: his office is likewise elective annually.

"*Jesuits.* The Jesuits are the most political and most opulent of all the Orders. Amongst these Religious is a Provincial who governs them, whose dignity and power is the same with the last, only in some cases he is subject to the

General of that Order, whose station they look upon to be greater than that of a Bishop: his office is also elective and triennial.

" 'Tis evident that the whole interest of the English clergy and Religious of the Church of Rome centres in the chiefs before mentioned, which must consequently consist of vast treasure to support so many and so great seminarys in Forreign parts, which is obvious are founded and maintained by the English donations. But such is the conduct of these great Rulers that the inferior clergy do not know the circumstances of the Body nor from whence their revenues do arise. By which it may be conjectured that the secret is locked up in those who have been the chosen governors and their councel, who are only such as have been Principles themselves. Therefore, with all humble submission, I think no expedient can be proposed to discover the treasure which rests in their hands but by apprehending those Principles and strictly interrogating them as your Honours shall think fit. I'm sure I may venture to say they have vast sums in the Public Funds and Stocks uncomatable any other way, for no other persons are concerned for them; sometimes the chiefs themselves receive great yearly sums which they are directed to dispose of for certain purposes without knowing from whence they come, or what the settlement was; which was evidently manifest to me when I had made all submissive addresses to the trustees, and used my endeavours to oblige them to grant me the right due to me: I was not only slighted with much railing language, but absolutely denied the sight of the deeds relating to my wife's interest; then I found myself obliged to prefer a bill against the trustees of Mrs. Catherine Winford for the money due in right of my wife. They pretended it was a secret trust, and that gave them discretionary power to pay or not to pay that legacy. *At that time, being of that religion,* I was so cautious of injuring the Church that I went to the Bishops and all the Superiors of the Religious Orders to know if they were concerned in the trust, and to give them notice that if I could not find justice among them, I would proceed in Chancery: they all professed ignorance and were free that I might sue the executors, viz., Atwood and Purcell, which I did with success, by which I had a perusal of the deed (*whereof I have made a discovery to your*

Honours) which appoints a certain sum of money as a Perpetual Fund for educating youth at St. Omer's. At that time the Provincial of the Jesuits, since dead, was a near relation to my wife, and very helpful in recovering our right. He was surprised when I told him the tenour of the said deed that such a thing could be and he not know of it.

"I beg pardon for this digression, but . . . before the aforesaid methods are put in practice . . . it is worthy of consideration whether the Commisioners have power by this Act to detain or punish them any further than by a fine of £40: if not, they will unquestionably pay the said fine and evade the interrogatorys. On ye contrary, if the power is sufficient, I'm apt to believe that a right method being taken in the interrogations will prevent equivocation and be an expedient way to come at the clergy's effects which is resting in their own hands, and will discover the methods they take in managing their treasure.

"It may be necessary that the Penalty on Trustees being accountable for mesne profits should be repealed, upon condition any discovery be made upon their own oaths, but in case a discovery be made by the testimony of any other person, then to be continued; for the consequence of so great a Penalty upon the trustee may induce him to forswear himself to preserve him and his posterity from utter ruin."

CATHERINE WINFORD, "of the p. of St. Giles Holborn, co. Middx., spinster," in her will dated 8th December, 1698, which was proved the 11th of January following in the Prerogative Court of Canterbury, offers her house and land at Bayton called the Summer Pole, in the co. of Worcester, for the sum of £150, to her cousin Thomas Winford prothonotary of Astley, in that county, eldest son of Henry W., dec., directing her executors (George Atwood and his son William, with Richard Purcell, of Clement's Inn) to pay a number of small legacies with the proceeds, while if her cousin refused the Bayton property it was to be sold for its full value. The following are among the legatees named: John and Henry, 2*nd* and youngest sons of aforesaid Henry Winford, with their 3 sisters Eliz. W.,——Geeres and Wilmote: *cousins* William Winford and his brother Dr.

Edward W., Dorothy Digby and her sister——Howes, John Digby, Anthony Hamerton, Henry Yaxley, Winifrid Atwood, of Beverie, Anne Petre, who has a little enamelled cross set with green stones: four uncles Richard St. George, Knevett Hastings, Charles Hastings, and Ferdinando H., Dorothy, Eliz., and Ferdinando Hastings, children of the latter: Theophilus and Charles, sons of my cousin Walter Hastings. Besides her godda. Katherine Hammerton, who has £20, others of that family named are Mr. Hammerton, of Dunsby, and his sons and das. John, William, Elizabeth, and Olivia Hammerton. Two of the witnesses to the will are Dorothy Hanford and Richard Canning. The will concludes thus: " to the intent they shall see my will executed . . . according to my intentions I leave to my executors the residue of my estate ".

But Catherine Winford, on the day that she made her will, secretly executed a lengthy and important Codicil, which from its very nature she evidently neither expected nor intended her executors to "prove" with the will. Indeed so many plain-spoken Catholic bequests would have rendered publicity impossible in those times. Her executors were therefore carrying out her wishes *to the letter* in regarding this codicil as "a secret trust" and nothing more. Unhappily, however, as we have seen, litigation ensued in consequence, and Chancery proceedings resulted in the final deposition of the original codicil among the "Forfeited Estate Papers" in the Public Record Office, of which the following is a summary:

[*Forfeited Estates.* W. 43. *Will of Catherine Winford.*]
" Whereas in my last will *bearing date with these presents* I . . . left the . . . residue of my estate to my executors, I now further declare that as I have given in the said will several legacies, particularly one to my godda. Mrs. Catherine Hammerton to whom I design a larger guift than in my will expressed or *what I am willing should be known to any but my executors, upon whose secrecy and fidelity I confidently depend* . . . in case my godda. Catherine Hammerton become a Religious woman, that is to say, a nun, my executors when she is professed shall give the portion which the house she fixeth in shall require provided it do not exceed £300 . . . or if she marry

with the consent of trustees she is to have £200 . . . provided
the money come not into the hands of her father John Hammerton." Other bequests are: ". . . £400 to raise £20 a-year
to maintain a student at St. Omers or at some colledge of
y*e* [*blank*. MS. *cut*] to be educated there in order to become a
Religious man of whatsoever God shall give him a vocation to.
And my will is that my relations of the Hastings or Winfords,
if any of them will accept it have the first offer to be preferred
to this place, and next to them one of my cousin Hammerton's
sons . . . and next . . . the son of Mr. John Fraser, of Worcester, Thomas Fraser . . . provided that his parents have not
wherewith to pay for his being so educated, for that this is
intended for such as are poor . . . but if there shall be none
such found to put into the place there . . . then the son of any
that is a gentleman and so poor that his parents cannot pay for
him . . . is to be presented." There are legacies of £10
downwards "to those of the Society of Jesus of the English
Province, to Mr. Thomas Roper, George Loup, Henry Humberston, John Mannock, Leo Randle, Martin and Thomas
Russell, John Stanford, Thomas Gavan, Edward Levison, Mr.
Berriman the younger, Charles Wharton, Francis Gibson, Dr.
Kemble, James Griffith, Thomas Busby, Messrs. Floyd, Sutton,
Piercy, Brett, Fleetwood, and little Mr. Baskaville . . .
to the poorest Priests that are about London £15: to poor lay
Catholics about Worcester £10 . . . all these charities being
given for the benefit of the souls of my father, mother [sisters],
and my own. To the English Discalced Carmelites £20
towards a foundation of a house or convent for them, also to
the Catholic boarding school at Hammersmith £10 . . . £5
each to the 2 children of Mr. Henry Yaxley, to be given to his
cousin Mr. Howes to apprentice them. Next, I give to my
Lord Bishop Giffard my great silver crucifix, humbly begging
his remembrance of my father and my mother. My large
picture of our Saviour upon the Cross I give to the District of
the Society of Jesus of Worcestershire, and my best suit of
Church stuff, with the chalice of sylver and all things belonging
to it, I give to that Catholic church or chappell that shall be
first set up in Worcestershire, with the obligation of praying for
the soul of my father, mother, and myself. For the rest of my

ERRATA IN

"ENGLISH CATHOLIC NONJURORS OF 1715."

Page 18, line 2, *for* "James" *read* "Jones".
,, 30, line 20, *for* "Jessica" *read* "Teresa".
,, 40, line 6, *for* "Lewis Dyre" *read* "Sir Lewis Dyves".
,, 73, line 38, *for* "mutatu" *read* "mutatus".
,, 80, line 38, *for* "Charles" *read* "Chambers".
,, 163, line 25, *for* "Martin" *read* "Mastin".
,, 164, line 21, *for* "1723" *read* "30th March, 1726".
,, 170, line 15, *for* "Delee" *read* "Delce".
,, 343, line 8, *for* "216" *read* "116".

church stuff my will is that my executors give it to some priest that wants some for the help of the Poor. I give to Mrs. Appolonia Yates a pair of white cornelian beads of five tenns with a Reliquary set in gold the shape of a heart. I give to the Monastery of Poor Clares in Dunkerk my biggest gold ring which was my mother's wedding ring and £10, and of my 5 mourning rings, I will that one be put to a coral pair of beads and given to my cousin Dorothy, da. of my uncle Ferdinando Hastings . . . another with coral beads to cousin Dorothy Digby, and the three others with beads to the three das. of my cousin——Conquest. . . . To my godda. Catherine Hammerton, gold ear-rings, hair gold ring, a sylver cup with 2 ears, another sylver cupp with a cover to it and a little box for counters . . . to the wife of William Gibson, Esq., a gold ring that I commonly wore upon my thumb in which is a silver ring of St. Xavier's . . . I give £10 to my cousin Christiana Hastings, who is gone into Germany . . . £10 to the English Carthusians at Newport where Mr. Hall is now Prior, and my residuary estate is to be employed in binding poor Catholic children apprentices." 8th December, 1698, in presence of C. Lamport, Margaret Boucher, and Catherine Knowles.

This codicil, of course, does not appear at Somerset House. It is endorsed thus: "This writing was delivered by Mr. Richard Purcell, of Clement's Inn, ye 1st of Feb., 1716, and he then swore he *concielled* it by order of Geo. Atwood, Esq."

MS. S. 94A describes this *Francis Brooke* as "of the parish of St. Bride's, co. Middx., gent," the date of the "information" he gave relative to the will of Catherine Winford being 30th January, 1716. Probably he married Catherine Hammerton.

[C. 116.] Letter to the Commissioners.

" Pleas your Honours.

" Presuming that y^r· Honours will shortly proceed towards Northumberland, where I know y^r· Hon^{rs}· will find much difficulty in discovering the Rebels' Estates, I thought it my duty as being a true well-wisher to my country to acquaint you that there is a gentleman in Hexham, his name Warburton, who for four years past hath been employed in making a survey of that county, in order to compiling a Book of the History and

Antiquities thereof, and hath lately published a large Map of that county which shewes the owners of every individual estate, as advertised in the *Evening Post*, on Saturday, 25th August, 1716. He is singularly well effected to the Government, as my Lord Townsend can inform you, and hath been very serviceable thereunto during the whole course of the late Rebellion, and I doubt not but will at your Honours' request (notwithstanding his many solicitations to the contrary) frankly discover the estates which the rebels enjoyed. He lately shewed me 6 large volumes in folio MS. of his own collecting, in which there is a particular account of every acre of land and the tenure by which they are held, so I think it may be absolutely necessary for your Honours to write to the said Mr. Warburton, to be assisting to your Honours in that affair, and am,

"Your Hon^r unknown friend
"and humble servant,
"T. R.

"Newcastle,
"8th October, 1716."

This was evidently John Warburton the herald and antiquary.

[*Id.*] Memorial of WILLIAM GIBSON [*Steward* to Lord Derwentwater] to the Commissioners, reminding them that in November, 1717, he gave information to them relative to the marriage settlement of the Earl of D. with a da. of Sir John Webb; he concludes: "Your memorialist humbly prays that y^{r.} Honours will be pleased to reserve for his use such a share as he humbly apprehends himself intituled unto by the Act of Parl^{t.,} having been greatly oppressed by the enemies of the present happy Constitution on account of the said information..."

From a memorandum attached to the "memorial," it may be inferred that this miserable informer probably gained his end.

"*Will further consider*: 12th March, 1719."

[*Id.*] *Northumbria*. A paper endorsed "Matthew Robson's certificate for £7".

"Whereas Matthew Robson, of Bellingham, in ye said county, hath come before me this present day and taken his corporall oath, that on Friday, the 14th October last, he was coming from Alnwick Sessions, where he had been about his lawful occassions, and coming to Rothbury in his way home he was intended to refresh himself, and before he lighted off his horse, one Robert Talbot, one of the Rebels, came to this deponent and told him that he must go and speak to the gentlemen at the market place, where a great number of the Rebels was assembled in Rothbury aforesaid; upon which he went with the said Talbot to the gentlemen in the market place, where among others, Mr. William Charlton, late of Readsmouth, in the s$^{d.}$ county; one of the rebels came to this deponent in a great passion biding God d——n this deponent, and told him he wisht to have his masters there—meaning the Justices of the Peace—whom if he had there, he knew how to take care of them; telling this deponent he was one of them that was for breaking their caball, shaking his whip at this deponent, telling him he would let him know y$^{t.}$ it was not brook yet, and thereupon ordered some to take his horse from him; upon which one William Dod, one of y^e said rebels, took the horse from this deponent, saddled and bridled, and this deponent's sword and buff belt, puting him under a guard during the space of three howers, threatening to slay or shoot, and so releast him, but kept his said horse and all the things above mentioned, which this deponent saith was realy and *bone fide* worth, the time when taken from him, the sume of £7 British money. All which he hath averd upon oath before me, the 1st September, 1716.

". . . coram me.
  "WILLIAM LORAINE."

[W. 32. *Widdrington Papers. Letter to the Commissioners.*]
  "BLANKNEY, LINCOLNSHIRE,
    "2nd October, 1718.

"Sir,
"This is to certifie the Board y^t y^e Honourable Coronell Ralph Widdrington died y$_e$ 22nd of June last, according to y^e Inscription upon his coffin, and was layd in y^e vault lately belonging to y^e Family, June 28th.
  "Yours in all observance,
    "JOHN CONEY, Curate.
"I had not y^e honour to receive y^r letter till y^e 29th of September last, otherwise you should have been informed before."

[*Id.*] April 7th, 1718.

FRANCIS FOOTE saith that on Saturday, 5th April, he made enquiry at the house of the late Lord Widdrington, for the place of abode of Eliz. Widdrington, his sister, and of Helena Fairfax, of London, spinster, and could not receive any satisfactory answer. That same afternoon the said Lord Widdrington sent him word that he knew not the place of their abode, but would send me the Person who entered their claims to inform me, which as yet he hath not done, nor given any further intimation thereof; only an unknown person came this morning as from Lord Widdrington to him and said, Helen Fairfax might be now at Wakefield, in Yorkshire, or thereabouts, but he could not be certain, nor did he pretend to know anything touching the place of abode of ye above-mentioned Eliz. Widdrington.

[W. 29.] *Widdrington Papers.* " Observations on the claims of RICHARD TOWNELEY and his wife MARY" (whom he married 15th April, 1713), "one of the das. of William, late Lord Widdrington".

"The will of his lordship bears date 26th March, 1694; he dyed 10th February, 1694-5."

Extracts from the will are as follows:

"To my da. Apollonia W. £2000, and my das. Eliz. and Mary £1500" for a marriage portion, and £100 yearly portion till marriage . . . provided they live in England. . . . Such of my sons or das. as shall depart out of this realm of England and settle to remain beyond the seas . . . to have nothing of his or her portion . . . and any so doing before the age of 21, that portion to be divided among the rest.

"Apollonia, under the age 21, went beyond sea and became a nun professed in or about August, 1701."

[W. 31.] *Widdrington Papers.*

One of these gives an "Inventory of the Goods in Widdrington Castle . . . apraised 14th December, 1716". An item is: "In the chappell, a pulpit, 9 forms, 5 small pictures, and 26 prints".

"In the chappell" also at Stella were "a large grate, an old table, 12 old stooles, a forme, and a parcell of old books".

"Peter Potts, Esq., of Newcastle, deposes, 21st November, 1716, that he has in his possession 5 cases of drawers or cabinetts that were the goods of Lord Widdrington . . . and were delivered to deponent's servant about January last by Mr. Lambert, his lordship's steward . . . deponent valuing them at £25 or £30."

"William Ogle, Esq. of Cawsey Park, co. Northumberland, deposes, 23rd November, 1716, that about 13th December, 1715, lord Widdrington's steward, Mr. Lambert, came to him and desired to lodge 2 boxes of goods which deponent believes did belong to yᵉ said lord in his house: that accordinly yᵉ boxes were left in a closet in this deponent's house, where they still are [and that Mr. Lambert has the key of the same]."

Lord Widdrington's steward contrasts favourably with the steward of Lord Derwentwater: he is probably identical with Cuthbert Lambert, named in *Eng. Cath. Nonj.*, p. 204.

Another paper among this collection says: "Widdrington Castle, the estate of lord Widdrington, was, on 30th March, 1720, sold for £57,100 to Christian Cole, Esq., for and on the behalf of the Government and Company of undertakers for raising the Thames water in York Buildings"!

The sheriff of Lincoln also, in a letter to the Commissioners dated "Lincoln, 6th October, 1716," writes:

"May it please your Honours,
         "In obedience to your Honour's precept . . . I have made enquiry after all such persons in this county as have been concerned in the late unnatural rebellion, but don't find any save the family of the Widdringtons, and pursuant to your honours' commands have been at Blankney House to secure the goods there belonging to that family, but was informed they were all sold except these few mentioned in the enclosed. . . . .
                    "THOMAS BECKE."

This "enclosed" list purports to be "a perfect Inventory of the goods and chattells of the late lord Widdrington or Mr. Peregrine W., his brother, taken and siezed in Blankney House, co. Lincoln, 3rd October, 1716". The only item of any interest is, "in the hall, a large long table, supposed to be an heirloom".

While, however, nothing seems to have escaped the greed of the Commissioners, the following draft, evidently designed for the royal signature, affords an interesting evidence of the noble determination of the unhappy Widdrington family to allow no worldly consideration to rob them of apparently the only "heirloom" that remained—viz., the Ancient Faith:

[W. 31.] "Whereas in and by an Act of Parliament made in the 4th year of our reigne, entitled an Act for vesting the Forfeited Estates in Great Britain and Ireland in trustees, &c. . . . the estate of William, late lord Widdrington, a papist, attainted for the late unnatural rebellion, was vested in trustees . . . and whereas by the said Act a power is reserved to us to make such grants as we shall think fit for the support and maintenance of the children of the said lord Widdrington during his life out of the lands, &c. . . . which were the inheritance of his late wife Jane, lady Widdrington, *dec.*, and mother of the said children, not exceeding £700 *per annum.* But by the same Act it is declared that where we shall make any such grant, disposition, or provision for the use or benefit of any child or children of any such forfeiting person, *every such child shall be educated in the Protestant Religion*, and not be of force any longer time or term than such child shall continue to be of the Protestant Religion and shall publicly profess and practice the same, and in every such grant an express condition to be inserted to that purpose, and whereas since the making of the said Act we have not made any . . . provision for any of the said children of the said William, late Lord Widdrington, *who have not given any satisfaction of their being educated in the Protestant Religion, but have by one of our principal secretaries of State signified to the Commissioners that they might proceed to sell the said estate.* . . . And whereas the Commissioners have since June last contracted with Joseph Banks, of Revesby Abbey, co. Lincoln, Esq., for the sale of the said estate, and sold it to him . . . without any . . . regard in respect of our power aforesaid. . . . Now know yee that at the humble request of the purchaser, and to extinguish our power of making such grants, and for the better enabling the Commissioners to complete the sale, wee of our especial grace . . . have released and discharged . . . all the estate of the late Lady Jane

Widdrington, dec., of the said power for charging the same for the support and maintenance of the children of lord Widdrington . . . to the intent that the said Joseph Banks may quietly enjoy the said lands. . . . Given under Our Privy Seale at our Palace at Westminster, the —— day of ——, 1719, and in the sixth year of Our reign."

[*Id.*] " I, whose name is hereunto subscribed, residing at Pontoise, Physician in ordinary to the King, doe hereby certify that I have for these several years attended Mrs. Elizabeth Widdrington in divers distempers, and particularly for two months the distempers which she has been subject to at several times are (amongst others) violent fitts of the apoplexy, of the cholick, of vomitting, the feaver; all which accidents do render the said gentlewoman so feeble, that she is not in a condition to undertake the least journey without the hazard of her life, and consequently it's deemed that a journey to England is not practicable in the present state of her health, which I certify to serve the said gentlewoman as far as it's reasonable. [Dated at Pontoise this 8th day of May, 1719.]"
"GAUBRIN."

[D. 82.] *Dicconson Papers. Petition of Hugh Dicconson, gent., to Commissioners.*

" . . . Sheweth that your Petitioner hath entered his claime for a remote remainder expectant on the failure of issue male of William and Roger Dicconson, his brothers, which Roger hath issue a son Edward, now living; that upon notice that your Honours had appointed a time for the hearing of his claim he did resolve to be present. But being at Douay, in Flanders, was there taken so ill that he cannot undergo a journey to London without endangering his life . . . and he prays to be excused personal appearance."

. . . .

" Edward Dicconson, gent., maketh oath that he . . . being in Flanders with his brother Hugh on 13th November last . . . did set out for London about 14th November, at which time deponent left his brother Hugh dangerously sick in Flanders, and wholly unable to travel by reason of his languishing condition, the Phisitian saying . . . it would endanger his life to travel." [12th December, 1718.]

[*Id.*] "Thomas Carter, of St. Margaret's, Westminster, deposes . . . that William Dicconson, late of Wrightington, co. Lanc., Esq., was concerned in the Lancashire Plot in 1694, but then acquitted. In 1695, or at the time of the assatination plot, the said William was convicted of Recusancy. Two years afterwards, in 1697, he made the deed of settlement on Mr. Roger of all his estate in Lincolnshire.

"*Query*: 'Whether that settlement is good, had William a tytle to grant, or Roger to take, both being Papists?'

. . . .

"Edward Dicconson, the fourth son of Hugh D. (dec.), claims . . . a large sume of money of Roger's Lincolnshire estate. . . . Edward D. was indicted upon the statutes for taking orders in the Church of Roome, and coming and staying in England contrary to the said statute, and outlawed for the same in the years 1700 or 1701."

[G. 10.] *Gibson Papers.*
Memorandum dated 5th April, 1716, from the Fleet Prison, signed by George Gibson, late of Stonecroft, co. Northumberland, and now of London, gent., relative to a farm let on his estate; witnessed by Edward Swinburne.

[G. 9.] *The same.*
"John Armstrong, of Corbridge, co. Northumberland, aged 46, maketh oath that he has been parish clerke of Corbridge upwards of 20 years, and for all that time and long before knew Thomas Gibson, late of Stagshaw-Close House, and some time of Stonecroft . . . father of George G., who was concerned in the late rebellion (which said George . . . this deponent believes dyed a prisoner in Newgate, att London), and saith that Thomas G. departed this life about the beginning of August last . . . and deponent was present and see him buryed in Corbridge Parish Church, in the same burying place where one of the wives of the said T. G. was formerly buryed.

"Jur. apud Hexham . . . 1st November, 1720."

[L. 16.] Dorothy Langdale, wife of Jordan Langdale, Esq. (son and heir apparent of Philip L., of Southcliffe, co. York, Esq.), and widow of William Walmesley, late of Lower Hall, co. Lanc., Esq., by her will dated 11th January, 1715, and proved 21st May, 1718, gave legacies to her brother John Dandy and his da. Ellen and to her sisters Jane, the wife of James Marsden, and Margaret, wife of Dr. Hesketh.

[S. 94A.] JOHN TAAFTE, of Chester, gent., maketh oath, 25th July, 1717, that Catherine Massey, sister to the late William Massey, of Puddington, co. Chester . . . hath been a nun for many years in the Convent of the Poor Clares at Bruges . . . that he saw her about 30 years ago in her habit "shut up within ye grates," and that she hath a legacy of £500 under Mr. Massey's will . . . and further . . . that Thomas Brockholes, a legatee in this will is a Popish Priest, and he has often seen him in the reign of the late King James officiate as such in the chapel at Whitehall, and was Mr. Massey's confessor at the time of his death.

[*Id.*] EDWARD POOLE, of Newhall, co. Chester, gent., maketh oath that Joseph Gerrard, of Killough, co. Monmouth, Esq., under his will of 9th April, 1705, devised property to such pious uses as John Berington, of Winsley (a professed Papist), and Charles Watkins, of the Wayne, co. Monmouth, should think fit, and that Charles W. was a priest and often officiated at Killough. [22nd October, 1717.]

[*Id.*] JOHN WALMISLEY, jun., of Wigan, says that the rent of some land at Hardshaw, co. Lanc., settled to superstitious uses, is paid to Humphrey Orrell, of Parr, tanner, who is a Papist, and only a trustee for that estate; and further that when the rebels surrendered at Preston, he (deponent) and Captain Gregg, who lives near Manchester, did pursue and take Robert Kellett, servant to Sir Francis Anderton, as he was endeavouring to make his escape. [3rd November, 1716.]

[*Id.*] RICHARD HITCHMOUGH deposes, 7th October, 1716, that he knew Mr. Lawrence Breers, and hath frequently seen him officiate as a priest . . . also that his sister, Catherine Breers, is a nun in the English Monastery at Gravelines: that Mr. Breers has an annuity of £20 out of an estate called Walton Hall, near Liverpool, Catherine B. also having a rent charge of £12 from some estate which passes at her death to the same monastery for ever.

He also deposes that Mr. Richard Hulme, who now lives with the Hon. Richard Molyneux at Much Woolton, is a Benedictine Monk, whom he has often seen officiate. [7th October, 1716.]

[*Id.*] RIC. HITCHMOUGH adds further, 1st October, 1716, that Thomas Young of Blackread, near Wigan, is a secular priest, where also he has an estate, on which he built a large house and chapel, where he usually had a numerous congregation of Papists ... and that the said Thomas Young having thereby run himself into debt, at a general meeting of the secular clergy at Park Hall in 1708 ... desired the assembly to assist him with £100 out of their common fund. The assembly—at which Hitchmough himself was present—voted him the money on condition of his depositing some deeds with Mr. Barlow, vicar-general and president of the assembly.

[B. 58.] *Correspondence relative to Hitchmough.*
Letter of a Commissioner to Rev. Mr. Hitchmough.

"Sir,—In answer to yours of the 14th, I am ordered to acquaint you that you may depend upon the favour as well as justice of the Commissioners when the proper time shall come to consider of your Reward for the Discoverys which you have made, which by the Direction of the Act will be when the estates are recovered, until which time they have no power to grant such a certificate as you mention." [21st May, 1716.]

. . . .

The Commissrs. to the Rt. Hon. the Lord Chancellor.
"Essex Street, 6th February, 1716-17.

"My Lord,—We think ourselves in duty to the public obliged to recommend to your notice the Rev. Mr. Hitchmough, of Liverpoole, in the county of Lancaster, as a proper person to be preferred ... to some benefice in your Lordship's gift. He formerly was a priest of the Church of Rome, but has left the Communion of that Church about five or six years, during which time he has lived in extreme poverty and very much persecuted by the Papists, upon some occasions even to the hazard of his life. He is *a man of a good character*, and has been hearty and zealous in his service to the Public by giving us information in relation to estates settled to Popish and superstitious uses. . . ."

This letter failing to awaken the Lord Chancellor to a sense of his duty, it was followed by another to the same effect, three years later:

"16th March, 1719-20.

"My Lord,—We hope your Lordship will give us leave to lay before you the case of Mr. Hitchmough of Preston, formerly a Priest . . . but now in the Church of England: he is zealously affected to the present government: . . . *he has a wife and several young children* and is extremely poor and is still rendred more unfortunate by the continual vexation of *the adverse party too powerfull in those parts:* We therefore recommend him to your Lordship's favour. . . ."

This letter, as we know, resulted in the presentation of Hitchmough to the living of Whenby, in Yorkshire, in November, 1720 (see *Eng. Cath. Nonj.*, p. 343). The Registers of that parish, which appear to be in a tattered and imperfect condition, throw no light upon his after career.

[B. 58.] *The Commissioners to Hugh Dreisdale, Esq., Major of Regt. of Dragoons, commanded by Sir Charles Hotham.*

". . . Information having been laid before us that there are two Popish Chappels at Holywell, in the co. of Flint, in which are a great quantity of plate and other valuables given to superstitious uses, we have directed our Precepts to . . . Richard Hitchmough, clerk, and . . . [others] to seize and secure the same; and we, adjudging it to be for the service of the Publick that our officers should be supported in the execution of the said precepts . . . desire you would detach such a number of the soldiers under your command for the purpose . . . as you shall think proper . . . and for so doing, this shall be your justification.

"Town Hall, Preston, 27th June, 1718."

[B. 62, p. 44.] RICHARD HITCHMOUGH, of Garston, co. Lanc, clerk, saith that Mrs. Mary Egerton, late of Hardshaw Hall, near St. Helens, in the township of Windle and p. of Prescott, by her will, devised to one Mrs. Mary Cottam the estate of Hardshaw Hall, subject to a rent-charge of £20 per annum, to be paid to Mr. John Ince, of Ince Hall, Wigan, in trust for the Popish secular clergy, for ever: Deponent hath also been informed by Mr. Thomas Golden, now proprietor of the said estate, that Humphrey Orrell, living near Parr, co. Lanc., usually received the rent-charge, and paid the same to Mr. Ince for the aforesaid use. [3rd December, 1716.]

[C. 91.] Letter from Ric. Hitchmough to Francis Foote, Esq., one of the Commissioners:
"Preston, 13th October, 1717.
"Honoured Sir,—. . . You may perhaps remember when I was at London, I told you I should be very glad you would solicit my affair as to what belonged to the Commission, and I repeat the same now, in case you think and find that the Commission goes forward, which I am much afraid of: for we have a parcel of people in these parts who make it their business since the Act of Grace to persuade the world to the contrary, and, indeed, I must needs own they vent their assertions with such assurance, as though they were absolutely certain it would be as they wish. I doubt not but by this time you are able to judge how matters will be carryed, and if you would please to favour me so far as to impart your thoughts to me upon the receiving of this you would much oblige, honoured Sir,
"Your most humble and obed. Servant,
"RICHARD HITCHMOUGH.
"Turn over. William Sidall, the tenant of Phiswick Hall, who, I believe, holds the greater part of that estate, was with me the other day, and tells me there is a very honest Protestant who would gladly be his partner for the whole, if the Popish tenant may be turned off, and in case he is not, himself must be forced to leave the farm, for he is grown so impudent of late, and so much encouraged by Dick Jackson, that there is no living with him: he begged of me to represent it to you, and begs the favour of your answer."

[C. 93.] Letter from Henry Wiswall to Rev. Ric. Hitchmough, at Preston, dated from Ormskirk, 28th June, 1718.
"Sir,—I spent the greatest part of yesterday to find out the person I spoke of who married old Mr. S——le's maid, and was tenant at Hall B—w— afterwards, whilst the old gentleman lived: After I had found him I took him to an alehouse—

under pretence of renewing our old acquaintance—and there asked my questions as near as I durst for being suspected. I will only tell you that he's but a lukewarm Papist, may be easily brought to our own shape, and will absolutely answer what will be wanted from him. . . . The will which Mr. H——ys must produce is of a priestcraft contrivance. . . .

[After expressing a hope to have the Hon. Commissioners' approval of his proceedings, he adds]: ". . . I expect . . . an account this evening of some seculars, regulars, &c., but, I doubt, rather *irregulars*, of whom at our next meeting we shall talk, and till then you may depend upon my silence and watchfulness. I write this doubly for fear of a mistake.

"Your most humble Servant,
"HENRY WISWALL."

[C. 92.] Richard Hitchmough to the Commissioners.

"Honoured Sirs,—I cannot avoid troubling your Honours with a fatall accident which happened this morning about 11 a'clock. A violent fire brok out, first in the Barn of one of my parishoners at Pool Rice, which immediately set fire to his dwelling house; the man's name is Thomas Dresser, who by the judgment of all his neighbour has lost near £200; he was at church himself when the accident happened, and when he came to his ruined habitation found that he had not a penniworth of goods saved besides his cattle. All his implements of husbandry, corn, brass, pewters, and all his wearing apparel, in a word, all he stood possessed of, were all consumed in the violent conflagration in the space of one hour. The design of this letter is humbly to supplicate your honours to lay this poor sufferer's condition before our next new Lord if he may have commiseration on him. The man has been all his life a very industrious person and a very good liver, so humbly begging your honours' pardon for the trouble of this, I am, Honoured Sirs, your honours' most dutiful, most humble and most obed*t*. Servant. RIC. HITCHMOUGH."

RICHARD HITCHMOUGH did not long enjoy the living of Whenby, the "Bishop's Certificates" for the Arch-diocese of York giving 20th April, 1724, as the date of the next presentation to the vicarage, then vacant "per mortem naturalem

Richardi Hitchmough ". This appears to be the only record of his death, nor is any trace of him to be found in the probate registry either of York or of London.

The following summary of further depositions by RIC. HITCHMOUGH is also taken from *MS. S.* 94A.

R. H. "very well knows Brinhall, near Wigan, now in the possession of one Richard Holne, son of John Holne, *dec.*, who formerly rented Brinhall, and that monthly the Jesuits of this county met at Brinhall to settle their accounts . . . and that Mr. Thomas Gerard, a Popish priest, told this deponent that the Brinhall estate, worth about £150 a-year was given to the . . . English Jesuits by Sir William Gerard, of Garswood, bart., to receive the profits of it until the Roman Catholic Religion should be re-established in England . . . and deponent hath been further informed that an inquisition was taken at Warrington concerning divers lands given to superstitious uses . . . among which was Brinhall . . . the Record of such inquisition now being either in H.M. Court of Exchequer at Westminster, or in the Petty Bag Office in the Court of Chancery." [31st October, 1716.]

. . . .

That Mrs. Jane Johnson, of Crosby, by will, devised £300 towards the maintenance and schooling of two youths, viz., Edward, son of Edward Molyneux, of Altkar, and Richard Smith, son of Mrs. Margaret Smith, who is now the wife of Thomas Widdowson, of Bootle . . . the money being paid to some Popish College beyond seas to make the said youths priests. [1st November, 1716.]

. . . .

That an estate at Wolston, in p. of Warrington, worth £70 per annum, and another at Farnsworth, in p. of Prescot, worth £18 per annum belongs to the Benedictines, while one called Croftsworth, in p. of Winwick, of £30, belongs to the Jesuits.

. . . .

That Mr. Wolfall, of Ormskirk, holds £200 for the secular clergy.

. . . .

That Sir William Gerard, of Garswood, settled £50 per annum on the English nuns at Gravelines, besides . . . £30 annually to his brother Thomas, a Jesuit . . . residing at Garswood.

. . . .

That Lord Molyneux, of Croxteth, settled £60 on his son William and the English Jesuits, as may appear by the marriage settlement of the said lord's eldest son with Mrs. Brudenall, which deponent remembers to have seen while chaplain to Lord Molyneux.

. . . .

That Robert Molyneux, of Mossborough, gave £10 per annum to superstitious uses.

. . . .

That John Savage, now Earl Rivers, is a Popish secular Priest, and receives £500 per annum from James, Earl of Barrimore.

. . . .

That Fitchborough Farm, an estate of £50 per annum, in Bunbury, co. Chester, belongs to the secular clergy.

. . . .

That £200 per annum out of Painsley, 10 miles from Stafford, the estate formerly of Philip Draycot, and a farm called Rishton Grange, 2 miles from Newcastle, co. Stafford, worth £80 per annum, is settled to the Popish secular clergy at Douay.

. . . .

That Mr. Whitgreave, of Moseley, besides maintaining a priest in his house, gives £30 per annum to like uses.

. . . .

That there belongs to the Popish chapel at Wolverhampton £100 per annum; Mr. *Higgins* [Hickin] being temporal trustee.

. . . .

That a rent charge of £100 a-year is settled and paid to a Popish Bishop named Witham.

. . . .

That a rent charge of £200 out of Medesley Manor, 10 miles from Drayton, co. Salop, late the estate of . . . Brooks, Esq., dec., goes to the Jesuits at St. Omers.

. . . .

Finally, that £100 a-year from the estate of Lord Fauconberg, at Sutton, in Cheshire, goes to the College at Douay. [19th June, 1717.]

[*Id.*] "THOMAS FLETCHER, Esq. of Hutton in the forest, co. Cumberland, deposes, 12th September, 1716, that he knows Thomas Roydon, a priest who inhabits a tenement called Lewhouse, in p. of Wetherall, co. Cumberland, at a £25 rental, held under the Duke of Portland, and that about four years agoe, being in company with the said Roydon, he told this deponent that the tenement was his upon trust for the support and maintenance of two priests officiating in the northern parts, viz., himself and one Lodge, *alias* Bates.

"Deponent, who is lord of the manor of Twisleton, in the West Riding of York, saith further that about five years ago one Columbus Ingleby, Esq., a customary tenant of that manor, told deponent that he wished to alienate a customary messuage, for that it was not his own, but a trust given to superstitious uses. . . . This messuage was conveyed by deed to Sir William Gerard, bart. . . . the affair being chiefly transacted by one Gilpin, a priest.

"Further, that Sir Henry Fletcher, bart., after having settled his real estates *upon deponent, being his nearest relation in name and blood*, did go beyond the sea to Douay, in Flanders, and some time before he went did show to this deponent what he called his church plate, being both gold and silver, there being an altar and candlesticks, all of solid silver, and pixes, chalices, Beads, crosses, and crucifixes, all of solid gold: the covers of mass and other Bookes in gold, and a large circle of gold set with large diamonds, in which the consecrated Host was to be exposed on solemn days. The said Sir Henry Fletcher likewise showed to this deponent several other valuable pieces of plate, all which he told deponent were for the use of a chapple he had built at Douay . . . and to the best of deponent's knowledge, all the aforesaid pieces of plate might be worth £1000 or upwards, over and above the said circle of gold set with diamonds, which this deponent (being not skilled in Jewells) can't set any true value upon. . . . Sir Henry F. left all the plate at the house of one Mr. Thomas Hickin, goldsmith in Holborn, London, where . . . it remained some time after Sir Henry went to Douay, and actually was there at the death of the late Queen Anne. Sir Henry Fletcher dyed at Douay in May, 1712 . . . making Henry Eyre, of Gray's Inn, and

Percival Hornsby, of Middlescough, Cumberland, gent., his executors . . . the said Eyre and Hickens were entrusted with the plate and can give an account of it. . . . That Sir Henry dyed very rich and left several small sums of money to the use of the said chapel at Douay."

[B. 58.] *Letter to Sir John Eyles, bart., signed by five of the Comm^{rs.} of Enquiry, and dated "Office at Preston, 14th September, 1716".*

"Sir,—You have enclosed a copy of part of an information laid before us relative to a great quantity of plate, &c., given to superstitious uses. . . . You have likewise a warrant to the Sheriffs of London and Middlesex to seize the same, which we pray your particular care of, and recommend to you to see it obeyed in the best manner that may be; and being apprehensive that Higgins may be unwilling to obey our warrant and to prevent the discovery as much as he can of the said plate, &c., we have also sent you enclosed a summons for him to attend us at Preston to be examined in relation to the same, but we would not have this summons served without you see an absolute necessity for it, occasioned by his stubborness...."

The Commissioners certainly lost no time, only five days elapsing between the "information" of Thomas Fletcher, given at Preston relative to the plate, and its seizure at the bankers' in Holborn, as recorded in *Eng. Cath. Nonj.*, p. 343.

[F. 16.] *Sir John Eyles to the Commissioners.*

"London, 18th September, 1716.

"Gentlemen,—I *instantly* upon receipt of your letter yesterday went to Sir John Fryer, one of the sheriffs, and served him with your precept, and without loss of a moment's time we went, together with the under-sheriff, a city officer, and a constable, to Mr. Higgins, and with as much civility as the nature of our errand could admit, acquainted him with our business: at which he first seemed surprised and denyed the having such things, at last owned he had had them, but that he had formerly sent them away to Flanders, or delivered them to Sir Harry's order. This not satisfying us, and threatening to search his house (where, by the way, I believe, had your warrant been more general, we should have found other things secreted), the wife, after her husband, being under apprehension of some ill consequence to himself, had slipt out of the house, produced three boxes which she said belonged to Sir Henry Fletcher's executors, and contained all that Mr. Higgins had of ye things mentioned in the warrant. . . . Particulars are given in enclosed memorandum. After this was done, I told her I expected her husband to give me yet further satisfaction as to other things that were wanting, or else . . . I must serve him with a summons to appear at Preston: accordingly he came to-day to the Guildhall and told the sheriff and me he had . . . nothing more except a tabernacle of silver belonging to ye Altar, which he brought with him . . . but the sheriffs thinking themselves not authorised to take possession of it . . . he took it back again . . . promising to deliver it to your order. . . . Thus stands the case as to this seizure, which amounts to 212l. 00z. 12dwt."

MSS. F. 6, 9, and 15 complete the story of Sir HENRY FLETCHER, as the following summary will serve to show. An elaborate septempartite Indenture, dated 31st October, 1710, sets out the settlement of his real estate, which Sir Henry Fletcher, of Hutton in the Forest, co. Cumberland, made upon his kinsman, Thomas Fletcher of Moresby, Esq., previous to his setting out for Douay, one party to the indenture being Catherine, a sister of Sir Henry, and the wife of Lionel Vane, of Long Newton, co. Durham.

[F. 15.] Sir Henry, by will dated 10th May, 1712, left several small legacies to his nephews and nieces, George, Henry, Walter, Lionel, Elizabeth, Alice, Catherine, and Mary Vane, and to Margaret, Alice, Mary, and Lucy Bowes: to his cousins, Thomas Fletcher, of Hutton, and Harry, son of John Fletcher, as also to Marcus Fletcher, Mrs. Dorothy Herron, Charles Grimstone, his servant; Mr. Massey, of Puddington, and to Thomas Hickins, the "goldsmith in Gray's Inn," his executors and residuary legatees being his "trusty servant," Percival Hornsby and Henry Eyre, of Gray's Inn.

But on the same day he also executed a secret codicil, just as Catherine Winford did, and of which the following is a summary :—

" To the English Rector at Douay, with the obligation of
saying 800 masses for my soul, ... £100

To the same, for beautifying the church,	£100
To the English Colledge near St. James' Church in Douay, with the same obligation for 400 masses,	50
To the English Benedictine Monks at Douay, for 400 masses,	50
To the Scotch Jesuits at Douay, with the same obligation for 400 masses,	50
To the English Poor Clares in Ayre,	100
To the Bishop of Arras, to be disposed of to the poor of his diocese,	400

"I leave to the Church of the English Recollets in Douay all my church plate, both of gold and of silver, and what are sett with diamonds, to be putt up att our Blessed Lady's Altar: to them alsoe I leave my church vestments: I give to the aforesaid Rector my two large silver payles I used to sett my bottles in, and which are in one of the boxes att Mr. Hickins', goldsmith, wherein is my table plate, to make, with my other church plate, two Holy Water Potts for their church in Douay . . . also my two ffyne pictures with silver frames, one whereof is of our Blessed Saviour, to be putt up in their church . . . I give unto the Bishop of Arras my gold watch and chaine for himself . . . *and I ordain this present writing . . . to stand in as full force and power as if it had been inserted in the body of my will.*" [10th May, 1712.]

Previously to this, however, Sir Henry F. wrote to his solicitor, Henry Eyre, of Gray's Inn, under date 23rd August, 1711: ". . . I also desire that my Little Red Box that has in it my prayer book with the gold cover, my gold Beads, a gold medal, 2 gold crosses, one having a diamond crown and the other a gold crown, gold Holy Water bottle, silver relick case, silver repeating watch, p^r· of Beads of Blood Stones, with a silver cross with silver medals: a silver cross with a silver crown: [my gold cross with a diamond crown has a gold chain to it], all which are in the custody of Mr. Hickins, the goldsmith, and that I desire may be sent to the English Recollets at Douay, in Flanders, that am,

"Sir,
"Your obliged & humble Servant,
"HENRY FLETCHER."

On the other side of foregoing MS. is " Mr. Grimstone's receipt ": " . . . Received of Thomas Hickins one gold basin & cruetts : one gold spoone : one gold chalice and Patin, and one Black Vestment of Velvet " [together with the plate named in the letter] : Exam. *Thomas Penson*. [See *Eng. Cath. Nonj*., p. 219, as also his will.]

. . . .

Another paper, enumerates among the "plate seized a little box for frankinsence, a large silver lamp, thurible, and bread box, all which things are delivered as belonging to the Altar." [17th September, 1716.]

After this a couple of Jews "valued the plate" at £831 15s. 9d., the silver tabernacle weighing upwards of thirty pounds, the silver being estimated at 5s. per oz., with the exeeption of the "Glory silver gilt with diamonds," the silver of which, weighing 31oz. 17*dwt*., at 4s. 6d. per oz., was valued at £49, or the whole at £56.

. . . .

Percival Hornsby also deposes, 17th April —— " . . . that the original directions of Sir Henry F. to his executors are in the hands of Mr. Bruno Cantril, a Romish priest now at Douay . . . that none of the legacies were paid except the watch and chain to the Bishop of Arras . . . that there were 2 notes due from Mr Hickin, the goldsmith . . . to Sir Henry F. in the hands of Mr. Nicholas Fortescue, a Romish priest who lately lodged next door to Mr Hickin. . . . Deponent can't take upon him to say that Nicholas Fortescue is an Agent of the College of Douay, but confesses that he has seen him there."

Thomas Fletcher also further deposes, at Preston, 11th October, 1716, "that he knows George Carter, of Castlesteeds, Thomas Wytham, of Workington, and Thomas Warwick, of Warwick . . . all to be Popish Priests of the Benedictine Order, and believes those priests know of lands settled to superstitious uses, particularly an annuity settled by the Lady Mary Ratcliffe, at Whenby, in Yorkshire, and several other lands to the same use . . . and that there now lives at Corby, in Cumberland, one Sherburn, a reputed priest, whom deponent has heard hath some great office or dignity in the Church of

Rome, and that he is concerned in the Revenues of Benedictine Colleges at Douay and Paris."

Three years later, *i.e.*, on 19th January, 1719, Thomas Fletcher, in ironical gratitude to the memory of his cousin Sir Henry, to whose munificence he was indebted for every inch of the estate he then held, presented "a Memorial to the Commissioners," reminding them of his "depositions . . . that the Plate had been seized and sold, and *your Memorialist has received his share, for which he returns humble and hearty thanks, and hopes he is also entitled to his share of the money bequeathed by Sir Henry Fletcher's codicil*"!

The next design, however, of the Commissioners, was to rob the poor of the money bequeathed them under Sir Henry's will but before doing so they thought it best to take counsel's opinion, and therefore submitted the following case to Sir Edward Northey, on 11th April, 1720. With what result will presently appear.

"Sir Henry Fletcher being possessed of considerable personal estate in England and Flanders, and residing at Douay, makes his will, and after several legacies devises his residuary estate to his executors . . . but *by a codicil*, among other legacies, devises £400 to the poor in the diocese of the Bishop of Arras. Sir Henry dyed at Douay, in 1712.

"*Qy.:* Whether the said £400 . . . is to be construed superstitious within the statute against superstitious uses?

"*Reply:* I am of opinion the devise to the Bishop of Arras of £400 to the poor . . . is a good, Christian, charitable, and not a superstitious use, for although the Bishop be a Papist, he is only a trustee, and it will be the same as if the trustee were a Protestant; and although Arras be in a Popish country, yet it was never thought that giving to the poor in such country was superstition, for the poor of all persuasions are objects of Christian charity, and even in the Stat. 1 E. 6, cap. 14, which gave to the king all chantreys and destroyed all superstitious uses being at that time, takes notice in the preamble, that what was so given might have been given to godly uses, among which one is for maintenance of the poor, and this charity is encouraged by the Stat. 43 Eliz., cap. 4, and it's plain this is neither a Popish nor a superstitious use."

. . . .

As to the costly Altar plate, the last scene of this somewhat eventful drama is laid in an auction room, as appears by a paper endorsed "Sale of the Altar Plate—12th March, 1716-17," and of which the following is an exact copy.

"Genteilemen,—You have here exposed to sale by the Hon. the Commissioners of Inquiry . . . an altar of Massey Silver: 6 large candlesticks: a mass book with silver cover: a silver Tabernacle: a silver book cover: a silver crucifix and . . . church plate of 231*l.* 4*oz.* 15*dwt.*, together with a gold chalice weighing 1*lb.* 8*oz.* 13*dwt.*, and a silver *glory* gilt and set with large diamonds.

"Genteilemen,—The method of this sale is by auction to the highest bidder, and the goods are put up altogether at £800 only: no less than 20*s.* to be advanced on each bidding: the money to be paid into the exchequer within 7 days after sale, and upon certificate for the same the goods to be delivered to the buyer."

The auction must have been a "Dutch" one, for in another handwriting is added the following: "Mr. John Bland, of Lombard Street, bought the same at one hundred and three pounds biding.

"Vouched: JNO. MANSERGH."

Or more probably the purchaser gave £103 *in excess* of the original £800.

Thus ends this melancholy story. It does not appear that Sir Henry Fletcher entered Religion. No doubt, however, had his life been spared, the priesthood was his intention. Dodd merely says of him (iii. 452), that "he was educated a member of the Church of England, and lived many years in that profession. At last he became a Catholic, and, leaving England, retired to Douay, where he fitted himself up a small apartment joining to the Convent of the English Franciscans, and died there, May 19, 1712, in the 54th year of his age, having before built a noble church for the use of those religious men."

Burke, in his *Extinct Baronetcies*, says that "Sir Henry lies buried at Douay, in a magnificent Chapel which he built for the Community at his own expense, and that with him the Baronetcy expired. At his demise, his sisters, as heirs-at-law, prosecuted their title to the whole estate, but after much litigation it was agreed that *Thomas Fletcher, of Moresby*, should enjoy the . . . Hutton estate for his life, and if he died without issue, then Henry Fletcher Vane, Esq., should inherit the whole property. Mr. Fletcher, of Moresby, *did die s. p.*, and the estates passed to the Vane family."

[*Id.*] *A letter signed by all the Commissioners and addressed to the Lords of the Treasury.*
"Speaker's Chambers,
"21st August, 1716.

"My Lords, We are obliged again to trouble you with a complaint against the Fees demanded at the Exchequer, and to beg your Lordships' immediate interposition. We lately ordered one Salter to pay into the Exchequer £2 12s. 6d., which money he had in his hands belonging to Ralph Standish, Esq., who stands attainted of High Treason. He informs us that the fees demanded for his paying this money amounts to 12s. 6d. If a stop be not put to such demands, the Public will be in a great measure deprived of the Benefit intended."

. . . .

[*Id.*] *The same to the same.*
"Essex Street, 31st January, 1716-17.

"My Lords, Your letter directed to us at Preston came not to our hands till our coming to town. In obedience to your Lordships' commands, we have considered the Paper intituled Proposals humbly offered in behalf of the poor Prisoners and others now under an attainder of High Treason, and are of opinion therein proposed can't possibly raise so much money for the benefit of the Publick as will be by sale of the estates, when the Parliament shall think fit to expose them : *and we likewise are of opinion that this proposal sets the Roman Catholic Interest very near in as good a condition as before the Rebellion : whereas if they are divested of their estates, and Protestants succeed, the Roman Catholic Interest in those Northern Counties must be intirely ruined : this project seems so intirely impeachable and unreasonable that we are of opinion it deserves no further consideration.*"

[B. 99.] *Papers concerning the Breers family.*

ROBERT BREERS, of Wigan, gent., in his will dated 22nd April, 1708, names as joint executors "Elizabeth, my now wife," Thomas Hesketh and Christopher Gradwell, and, referring to an indenture dated 13th May, 1707, mentions "Roger, my son and heir, with Bridget, his wife": there are legacies also to his son Thomas and his cousin Perpetua Wilkinson. Attached to the will is a paper giving the following note: "A true account of your children's age, as follows:

"Thomas Breers was born 16th September, 1692.
"Bridget   ,,   ,,   15th February, 1693.
"Mary   ,,   ,,   1st February, 1696.
"Margery   ,,   ,,   25th December, 1698.
"This is all with our humble service to yourself and family:
    "I rest,
      "Yours to command,
        "JOHN SHEPHERD."

[B. 143.] *Miscell. Papers relating to the Butler family. Henry Butler to the Commissioners of, &c.*

"19th July, 1717.
"May it please your Honours:
    "That I, Henry Butler, Esq., late of Rawcliffe, co. Lanc., but now of Castletowne, in the Isle of Man, about 8 years since being very much indebted and desirous to discharge the same as far as I could and to make provision for my younger children, did convey all my estate to Richard Butler, my son, who, being an inconsiderate, rash young man, did engage himselfe in the late horrid rebellion, for which he was tryed and executed.

"Reserving only £60 a-year for maintenance of my wife and self . . . and my son having forfeited the estate, which is now in the hands of ye Government, the tenants and receivor of Forfeited estates refuse to pay me my Annuity for want of an order from your Honours . . . which I humbly beg your Honours will please to grant to the said receivor to prevent mine and my wife's being starved for want of food and raiment. We having no other dependance or livelihood in the world besides the said annuity, and we being both well-stricken in years, are altogether incapable of any means to assist ourselves, and must inevitably perish if not relieved by your Honours. In which deplorable condition I humbly beseech your Honours' early order for payment of my said annuity to prevent our destruction, and Mr. Elstob being now gone into Yorkshire, I intreat your Honours will signify your pleasure to Mr. Whalley, of Preston."

. . . .

[*Id.*] "The widow of Mr. Ric. Butler, uncle and heir-male to deceased Ric. Butler, of Rawcliffe, convict for late rebellion, humbly proposes to become farmer of his estate in behalf of her two infant sonns, *who she offers to be educated Protestants*, by Mr. Cawthorn, of Wyersdale, and that he for their use may be the farmer: he is well affected to his Majestie, and is very solvent and responsable. 21st June, 1717."

. . . .

[*Id.*] *Thomas Fletcher's information and observations on claims on the estates of Richard Butler.*

"12th July, 1718."

He examines the grounds and pretexts upon which various parties have laid claim to the estates, among whom are "Henry Curwen, Esq., whose claim," he says, "is void, he being a Popish Recusant Convict".

"Mary Butler"—another claimant—"then was and now is a Papist. . . ." He continues as follows:

"In the reign of King James II., the ancestor to the late Earl of Derwentwater gave a rent-charge of £20 per annum upon the lands of Castlerigg and Derwentwater for ye maintenance of a Popish priest to reside there, but after some time, the Papists being quite extinct in those places, the fund was removed and paid to a priest of the Benedictine order residing at Whenby, in Yorkshire. The priest who last resided at Whenby was one John Potts, a Benedictine Monk.

"About the year 1709, Thomas Salkeld, of Whitehall, Thomas Howard, of Corby, John Warwick, of Warwick, *and Thomas Fletcher, then of Moresby, co. Cumberland*, Esqs., petitioned the late Lord Derwentwater to have the sum of £20 per annum restored to a priest residing in Cumberland, which was granted, but the petitioners not agreeing among themselves, and some disputes hapning between the secular and regular clergy, the

Cumberland project failed, and the £20 was paid to the monk att Whenby."

[From this it is evident that Thomas Fletcher, the donee of the estate of Sir Henry Fletcher, was an apostate, and that Sir Henry Hoghton was correct in describing him as "formerly a Papist".]

. . . .

[*Id.*] *Thomas Fletcher to the Commissioners of Enquiry at Preston.*

"19th September, 1716.

". . . If your honours will favour me so far as to send me some assistance, I'll be master of what's in these two countys in a fortnight's time, for the tennants will do everything as I direct them. . . . Mr. Slaughter, or whoever is sent to me, must take his road by Kendal, from thence to Keswick, where my Lord Derwentwater's estates lye, and come to the Royal Oak Inn, where he will either find me or hear of me. . . . If *your Secretary* writes to me at *Hutton, near Penrith,* in *Cumberland,* it will come safe."

. . . .

[*Id.*] *Petition of Mary Butler, of Workington, co. Cumberland, widow of Ric. B., of Rawcliffe.*

"Sheweth, that a summons was served upon her, 3rd November, 1718, at Workington, to attend on the 13th of same month at Essex House, London, 240 miles distant: prays not to appear before 5th December, because of the shortness of the notice, and by reason of the great distance she and her witnesses live from one another and from London." The Commissioners fixed the 8th December for her appearance before them.

. . . .

[B. 144.] 12th July, 1718. *Petition of Thomas Foster, of Barnardcastle, co. Durham, to Commissioners of,* &c.

"Sheweth, that Petitioner intermarried with Catherine Butler, who has a claim now depending . . . touching her fortune . . . chargeable upon the estate late belonging to Richard Butler, of Rawcliffe, who was attainted of high treason . . . and that her fortune, with some arrears of interest which Ric. B. was obliged to pay, is still due and owing to her and petitioner . . . claims to have his case heard this day."

. . . .

One, Thomas Backhouse, also presented a petition claiming the estate of Ric. Butler.

. . . .

[*Id.*] Memorial of JAMES BUTLER, an infant, æt. 14, eldest son of Richard B., late of Scorton, co. Lanc., gent., dec., who was 2nd son of Richard B., of Rawcliffe, Esq., dec. "Sheweth, that his grandfather, Richard B., was tenant for life, and that Henry B. (yet living), as his eldest son, was entitled to the remainder in fee tail of the several manors of Out-Rawcliffe : Refers to marriage articles dated 13th December, 1683, of Henry B. and Magdalen, da. of John Girlington, Esq. Sheweth, that Henry B. had issue Richard, his eldest son (who attained his majority and d. s. p. in 1716), and Nicholas, his 2nd son, who died a minor and unmarried, and that Memorialist is not only entitled as next heir in tail to the estates, but is also a Protestant, the others who preceded in the limitations being Papists : prays, therefore, to enter his claim to the estates."

. . . .

[*Id.*] The petition of JOHN MANDEVILLE to Com$^{rs.}$
"Sheweth, that Francis Butler, late of the City of London, gent., dec., who was in his lifetime a Papist, by his will devised several lands, &c., to [his sister] Mary B., a Papist and Abbess of a convent in Flanders, in prejudice to your Petitioner (who is next male relation), on account of your petitioner being a Protestant." Petitioner, in 1718, "made a discovery" to the Com$^{rs.}$ of these premises as being "left to superstitious uses . . ." Prays them to prosecute s$^{d.}$ discovery . . . and grant him his reward.

[W. 12.] WILLIAM WALMESLEY, Esq. of Lower Hall, Samlesbury, under his will dated 15th September, 1712, and proved by Dorothy, his widow, 3rd January, 1712-13, gave legacies to his cousin Elizabeth, da. of Richard Walmesley, of Preston, to his "present wife's sister" Margaret Dandy, and her sister Jane Marsden : to his good friend and agent Mr.

William Hayhurst, of Preston, and his sister, Anne Hodginson [Hodgkinson ?], as also to her da. Helen Eaves.

. . . .

[W. 10.] Deposition of one who states, 20th November, 1716, that 10 years ago he rented an estate called Longlane Head, in Clayton, co. Lanc., of Ric. Walmesley, of Preston, whose son Thomas, outlawed for high treason, married a da. of —— Colegrave, of Bloomsbury Square, London.

[W. 54.] THE WORTHINGTONS OF BLAINSCOE.

23rd October, 1716. "JANE, wife of RICHARD WORTHINGTON, of Blainscoe, co. Lanc., Esq. . . . saith that she has been married . . . 11 or 12 years, and found her husband encumbered with a mortgage for £900, which was assigned to Jeoffrey Prescot, of Preston, and Mr. John Heskin, of Wrightington, in trust for Mr. John Gillibrand, of Chorley, and that the mortgagees remitted to him a great part of the interest, but Mr. Gillibrand persuaded her husband to advance £150, and take it up from him for one or more of the said Worthington's children by a former wife . . . to place one of them, a daughter, in a Religious House or Nunnery at Louvain.

"£700 of the original mortgage was for maintaining certain Popish priests; and though the mortgage was some seven years since in pretence assigned to one Thomas Payne, a goldsmith in London, yet the interest was applyed to the s$^{d.}$ priests. . . . £400 of the original mortgage was a gift from her husband's uncle, one Richard Worthington, for the maintenance of a scholar in the Popish seminary . . . and several such scholars were maintained thereby.

. . . .

[*Id.*] 7th March, 1716. "Nathaniel Pearse and John Mathews, goldsmiths in Lombard Street . . . depose that at the request of Gerard Saltmarsh, Thomas Yaxley, John Browne, and John Gillibrand, they, about 2nd February, 1713, assigned a mortgage on the estate of Richard Worthington, to Jeoffrey Prescot and Thomas Heskin, but that they never received any money from any person on account of such assignment. . . . Deponents say this mortgage came into their hands as executors to Mr. Payne, late of [Lombard Street] London, goldsmith, who was trustee for one Mr. Job Allibone, deceased."

[B. 70 and B. 74.] Two *MSS.*, being the "Register of the appointment of the various officers employed in the administration of the Forfeited Estates," together with their yearly salaries. Each of the seven Commissioners received £1000 a-year, the salary of the minor officers varying from £300 to as low as £40 per annum, one and all having any expenses defrayed.

The following items of expenditure are from Chambers Slaughter's accounts:

A gratuity for his services to Thomas Fletcher, Esq.,	£21	10	0
A gratuity for his services to Rev. Mr. Hitchmough, 19th June, 1717 „ „ „	5	7	6
	5	0	0
20th April, 1718, to Mr. Serj^t Pengelly, a retaining fee,	10	10	0
15th July, 1718, to Thomas Fletcher, Esq., .	27	12	6
29th July, 1718, to Mr. Hitchmough, .	10	0	0
22nd October, 1718, to John Cosens, for work done per himself and his son,	42	0	0
16th January, 1718-19, to the same in full for himself and his son for abstracting the Registry,	21	0	0
28th January, 1718-19, William Moore, Esq., Counsel's fees,	10	10	0

The entries relative to *John Cosin* are of interest, "the abstracting of the Registry" being evidently the "work done," which in 1745, appeared as "Names of the Roman Catholics, Nonjurors," &c. James Cosin is wrong in describing his father as "Secretary to the Hon. Commissioners". The Secretary was Arthur Branthwait, Esq., whose appointment dates from 24th June, 1716, "at a salary of £300 per annum". The name of John Cosin nowhere occurs among those of the officers appointed; he was in all probability merely clerk or transcriber to Chambers Slaughter, the Accountant General, and indeed is so described *on the title page of the original edition.*

[T. 26.] THORNTON PAPERS.

The Petition of ANNE, widow of NICHOLAS THORNTON, of Netherwitton, co. Northumb.

"Sheweth, that she having entered her claim upon the estate, late of John Thornton, her son, for her dower appointed to be heard to-morrow, and having entrusted her case to Mr. Errington, of Gray's Inn . . . who being unexpectedly obliged to go into the country about affairs of his own, and having in his custody several papers of hers without which she cannot instruct her counsell, prays to have her case adjourned."

. . . .

[*Id.*] Her son JOHN, also prays the Commissioners to "postpone the day for hearing his claim on behalf of his wife," on the ground that he had to go into Northumberland to gather up his writings, which were in several places dispersed, and which he had with great difficulty found and brought to London, the abstract of them having still to be made.

. . . .

[B. 60 and T. 26.] Lastly, MARGARET RAMSAY, of Stanton, in the p. of Horsley, co. Northumb., deposeth, 23rd November, 1716, that she has in her custody two beds, one of green cloth and the other of fine lemmon-coloured camblett, an easy chair, a sett of chairs to each bed, a black glass and table, another very good glass, an easy chair of patchwork, several cutts in frames, another large looking-glass cut in the frame, and a tea-table, all which goods she believes were late the goods of Mr. Thornton, and prays to have a fourth part for that discovery. A couple of years later, hearing that these goods had been sold by the Commissioners for £27 15s., she again clamours, 13th March, 1718, for her fourth part of the spoil. Very likely she was some servant or dependant of Mr. Thornton's.

[R. 24.] RIDDELL PAPERS.

"CHARLES TANCRED, of Covent Garden, draper, sworn this 18th May, 1721, saith that he knew Dr. Riddell, dec., and was one of his executors, but refused to take execution: hath heard the will read, but hath no copy thereof: believes he died worth £1300, and that he left a son who is since dead: does not know where George Riddell lives, but that he is reputed a monk, and was by the will to have the residue after some legacies, but whether it was to be applied to any pious uses, deponent doth not know and hath not heard."

. . . .

[*Id.*] "The Petition of EDWARD RIDDELL, Esq., to the Commiss_{rs}. Sheweth, that a summons to attend them on 2nd December next at Essex house, London, relative to a Mortgage made by his father Thomas Riddell to Francis, 1st lord Derwentwater, was served on him a few days ago at his house, 230 miles from London, but by reason of his ill health, the great distance from London, the unfit season for travelling, and the short notice, he cannot possibly be present, and prays to have his attendance postponed for six weeks."

. . . .

[R. 23.] *Report of William Moore relative to Dr. Thomas Riddell, 28th April, 1720.*

"The Master of References (*i.e.*, WILL. MOORE) thinks it his duty to lay before the Board that he hath been informed by a person, *who for some reasons desires his name may be at present concealed (tho' he hopes hereafter to have the benefit of his discovery)*, that under indenture dated 25th April, 1693, Thomas Riddell, of Swinburne Castle, and Edward, his eldest son, conveyed divers manors . . . of considerable value to Jasper Hall and Thomas Beadnel . . . that the marriage settlement of Edward Riddell with Dorothy, da. of Robert Dalton, Esq., bears same date, &c., and that the issue by this marriage was Thomas R., eldest son, who stands attainted of high treason. . . ." Gives details concerning the Mortgage of £4000 of Lord Derwentwater upon the Riddell estate, &c.

[S. 111.] SWINBURNE PAPERS.

"The Petition of Dame MARY SWINBURNE on behalf of her son Sir John S., a minor.

"Sheweth, that she hath been informed that the estate late of Edward S., Esq., dec., is to be sold for the use of the Public, and that certain lands called the Deanhams are included in the sale, which lands are not his, but belong to her son and his heirs."

. . . .

[S. 110.] "The Petition of Sir JOHN SWINBURNE and of

EDWARD WARD, of Morpeth, co. Northumb., gent., his solicitor to Com^rs.

"Sheweth, that your Petitioner being at the time of the late Rebellion and for three years afterwards a minor and beyond the seas, and being at his return from his travels abroad informed that your Honours had caused the estate of Old and New Deanham, co. Northumb., to be seized and sold as the estate of your Petitioner's uncle Edward Swinburne, and being advised that your petitioner has a legal title to those estates, he, acting by counsel's advice, brought ejectments for the said premises. Pet^r. tried his cause at last Northumberland assizes, but not having made his claim according to Act of Parliament before your Honours, was non-suited. . . .

"Edward Ward, the other petitioner, hopes he has not incurred the displeasure of the Commissioners by acting as a solicitor on behalf of his client Sir John Swinburne, having for many years been concerned for the said Sir John's family.

"Both pray to be excused attending on 15th November before the Commissioners on account of the expense, troubles, and charges Sir John S. has been at."

[S. 30.] SHERBURNE PAPERS.

"11th December, 1716. THOMAS RISHTON, of Green Gore, co. Lanc., gent., saith that Ric. Shirburn, late of Preston, co. Lanc., gent., outlawed for high treason, was seized of an estate called Bayley Hall, in the hamlet of Bayley and p. of Mitton, and that the said Ric. Shirburn made his escape from Preston after the battle there, and, it is pretended, conveyed his estate after his escape to one William Cromblehome, to prevent its forfeiture . . . and that an estate called Stidd, in the town of Dutton and parish of Ribchester, belongs to John, younger brother of Ric. Sherburne . . . and prays the benefit allowed by Act of Parliament for his discovery.

. . . .

[*Id.*] *The information of Nathan Marsh, of Preston, co. Lanc., flax-dresser.* 1st January, 1715-16.

Informant saith that, on Thursday evening, 10th November last, he being at the house of one, John Wareing, at Bayley, in said co., John Wareing, together with William Scott, came home to John Wareing's house and lighted off their horses, and when they came into ye house, J. W. said to this purpose, "Damn yee, who is he that says against King James; if I knew that there was, I would sacrifice ym· . . . Deponent further saith that he was present at a place called Dutton Lee, co. Lanc., about Michaelmas last, when the said John Wareing drunke the Pretender's health, by the name and title of King James the third of England and eighth of Scotland, and . . . on Friday evening, 11th November last, he heard that a great company of the rebels from Preston were gone to Stonyhurst, ye seate of Sir Nicholas Sherburne, to fetch him into ye Rebells at Preston, and otherwise to bring away his horses and arms, and the next morning . . . this Informant being nigh a house called Tinckler-feild House, near Stonyhurst, saw 17 or 18 persons on horseback, with each a gunn, and . . . that John Wareing told him the said company had brought away eight guns with them from Sir Nic. Sherburne's, and a sackend full of pistols. Informant saw 7 or 8 guns and a blunderbuss which these persons had (who were said to have been at Stonyhurst), and four coach horses or mares which they ridd upon, and which belonged to Sir Nic. Sherburne.

. . . .

JOHN MASON, of the p. of St. Sepulchre, City of London, mason, saith: "That, he being employed in Sir Nic. Sherburne's of Stonyhurst business for many years . . . happened to be at Stonyhurst on Thursday evening, 10th November, when William Scott and John Wareing came thither, Scott being armed with a gunn and a bayonet fixed on the end of it, who, seeing informant in the kitchen, went away, and he saw them no more that night. Next morning Scott came to this informant, held a hanger over him, and asked him who he was for, to which Informant answered he was for the King and the Church, and, in a little time afterwards, went away . . . and about 7 or 8 o'clock that evening came again and runn at the gates, whereupon, informant went to Mr. Kempe, Sir Nic. Sherburne's steward, and acquainted him of it, who ordered informant to open the gates, which he did, and Mr. Kempe having discoursed with him a little, he went away. A quarter of an hour afterwards, one Mr. John Talbot and two other gentlemen with him . . . came to the gates and rung . . . and Mr. Kempe ordered them to be let in, and brought them to the foot of the dining-room stairs, where they went up. . . . In a quarter of an hour afterwards, William Scott and 20 other persons, all armed with swords and guns, came to ye gates and rung . . . and Mr. Kempe went with informant to ye gates and ordered them to be opened, whereupon William Scott ledd them all up into the hall, where they laid bye their arms, and Scott called for meat and drinke for them. After supper was over, Scott came to informant to borrow a lead pann and some lead, which this informant refused to let him have; he went to Mr. Kempe, who came shortly afterwards and ordered informant to let him have both the pann and some lead, which he did, the lead weighing about 20 *lb.* What use Scott made of the pann and lead, informant knows not, but believes it was to make bullets. A little time afterwards, informant went to bedd, and about 7 o'clock next morning saw Mr. John Talbot and the two gentlemen that came with him with William Scott and the others, all mounted on horseback and armed, going away, and that they took with them four of Sir Nic. Sherburne's coach horses, which were delivered them by his servants."

Jurat. apud, Liverpool, *no date*, but probably September, 1716, the date of another deposition on the same sheet.

. . . .

[*Id.*] The information of Thomas Watson, constable, of Aighton, Bayley, and Chaidgley, and James Eastham, of the said town, taylor, taken on oath before Sir Henry Hoghton, 9th January, 1715-16. Thomas Watson saith that he having a warrant from Sir Henry Hoghton and Thomas Molyneux, Esq., dated 21st December last, to apprehend and seize John Wareing and William Scott, who was formerly a servant to Sir Nic. Sherburne . . . and having reason to suspect that William Scott was then at Stonyhurst . . . he had got near 20 men of his township to search for ye said rebels, and on Tuesday, 27th December last, Informant with his company went about 8 o'clock in the evening to the Stonyhurst to search for Scott, but was refused entrance into the house by Mr. George Kempe, steward to Sir Nic. Sherburne. Informant told Mr. Kempe he had a warrant to search the house, on which Mr. Kempe went away into the house and staid about a quarter of an hour (as this informant apprehends to acquaint his master), and at his return again refused him entrance. Informant further saith that the house is very strong, having a greate paire of iron gates to the front, and a paire of wooden gates on the back of . . . [*MS. defective*] . . . iron gates. James Eastham says he was charged by the constable to go with him to his assistance, and that he went with him to the Stonyhurst, and that Mr. Kempe refused him entrance when he demanded it in the King's name.

. . . .

[*Id.*] 9th January, 1715-16. Robert Barrett, of Aighton, Bayley, and Chaidgley, taylor, saith that on Thursday, 17th November, one Richard Sheppard, *alias* Gudgeon, a post-boy for Sir Nic. Sherburne, came to informant's master's house, and informant asked Sheppard how many Bullets was cast at y_e Stonyhurst . . . for he said he had heard there was a bushell cast there for the service of the rebels. . . . Whereupon Sheppard told informant there was not so many, for Mr. Mason would but give them one pann full of lead to make into Bullets . . . and that there was above 30 of y^e Rebells at Stonyhurst, the Friday at night before the action at Preston.

[C. 88.] *The petition of William Halliwell, gent., to the Commissioners.*

" Sheweth, that your petitioner hath, together with Christopher Graddell, entered their claims for the lands called Rounhead, in co. Lanc., which is included in their trust deed, your Petit$^r.$ having been a considerable time in town with one of the witnesses at the great charge of the trust estate, and cannot stay much longer without great prejudice and inconveniency. Prays for a day to be appointed for the hearing of his claim."

[C. 89.] *Petition of Edward Shaftoe to the Commissioners.*

" Sheweth that your Petitioner hath maide itt his outmost indeavours to serve the Government in giving y$^r.$ Honers severell informations : the last given is a mortgadge belonging to my Lord Derwentwater, upon the manner or Lordshipe of Swinburne Casstell, in y^e co. of Northumby, by which I have gained the displeassure and mallice of all my ffriends and

Relations, who hath no pity or compashtion on my deplorable sircumstances, compells me to addres your Honers for som releafe, for being here attending your Honeres determanation neare six yeares, I am reduced to great want now in my olde Adge, being in August next 75 yeares. I humbly beseech your Honers to consider my deplorable case and assist me in some messure y[t.] I may have som Releafe."

. . . .

This Edward Shaftoe, who seems to have incurred the indignation and contempt of his Catholic relatives, which he justly merited, was probably one of the Shaftoes, of Bavington, although MS. S. 21 describes him as, "of y[e] parish of St. Catherine, near y[e] Tower, London". MS. S. 20 pictures him as clamorous for his "reward" as the *first* "informer" relative to the estate of John Shaftoe, of Bavington, which however the Commissioners denied, and a little later (S. 21) he offers to rent of the Commissioners the mansion house and lands of William Shaftoe, in Little Bavington, provided he can have immediate possession "before the house and gardens run away further to ruin". The same MS. also gives 24th June, 1695, as the date of the marriage settlement of William Shaftoe with Eliz. Riddell. He was the son of John Shaftoe, of Little Bavington, by Frances, his wife, Edward and John being also named as the younger sons of the said John Shaftoe. One son, John, was the issue of the marriage.

[F. 33.] "*Further House*" *given to superstitious uses.*

"WILLIAM MOSS, of Skirmersdale, in par. of Ormskirk, co. Lanc., yeoman, saith that William Moss, of the same, *dec.*, was about 40 years ago seized of a house and seven acres, called 'Further House,' in Skirmersdale, and devised it to his wife, and for Henry Orrel to sell the same. It was sold, accordingly, to Richard Moss, brother of the said William, who was a Papist.

"Richard, in his lifetime made a feoffment in 1703-4 to Alexander Blundell and James Hunter, a Papist of Melling-cum-Conscough, to the use of Richard, John, and James Aspinwall, all bred up in the Popish Religion. John is now in some Popish seminary abroad, and Richard, the eldest son, was, in ye Rebellion, taken at Preston, sent prisoner to Chester, and escaped out of the Castle. [17th October, 1716.]"

[E. 4.] ECCLESTON PAPERS.

The petition of THOMAS ECCLESTON, of Eccleston, co. Lanc., Esq. [to Com^rs.], sheweth, "that the Manor of Eccleston and other your Pet^rs. estate, did, on the death of his father, Henry Eccleston, Esq., descend to your petitioner, his eldest son and heir by right of blood, and in course of hereditary descent, according to the established laws of this kingdome.

"That your Pet^r. entered thereon on his father's death, and subject to the jointure of Eleanor E., his mother, has quietly enjoyed the same, without any interruption, for 53 years.

"That about January last, your Honours were pleased, without any previous summons given or any cause known to your Petitioner, to direct . . . the Sheriff of Lancaster to take possession of your petitioner's estate, who, in an armed and violent manner, turned your Pet^rs. mother, who is about fourscore years old, out of Eccleston Hall, where she had peaceably dwelt above 60 years.

"That your Pet^r., knowing no cause of seizure, he being no ways concerned in the late rebellion, nor his estate anywise given to superstitious uses, ordered search to be made in his Majesty's Court of Exchequer to see if any record there could warrant these proceedings, and, on search, an inquisition was there found, taken above 20 years since by the management of one Baker, wherein your Petitioner's and above 20 other gentlemen's estates were found given to superstitious uses.

"That your Pet^r. . . . applyed to his Majesty's Court of Exchequer to have leave to traverse the said Inquisition, which was granted . . . and the Court declared its sense of the hardship of your Petitioner's case and ordered your Petitioner should retain the possession of his estate.

"That your Honour's officers, notwithstanding this order, keep possession of your Petitioner's estate and receive the profits thereof, whereby his aged mother is reduced to want, being without any fault turned out of her habitation, and reduced to the utmost extremity, a Protestant school deprived of 40 marks a-year settled on it for teaching poor Protestant children, his house falling to ruin and other great damages, and your Petitioner forced to carry on a cause in the exchequer and to maintain himself on credit without any reliefe from his estate.

"Your Pet^{r.} therefore most humbly prays that your Honours will take the hardship of his case into your consideration, and that your Honours will be pleased to appoint a day that he may be heard by his counsell in order to be relieved in the premises:

"And your Pet^{r.} shall, &c.,
"DAN. DANDY, Attorney for the Pet^{r.}"

A note in another handwriting adds: "Not p^{d.} for. Let Mr. E. attend."

. . . .

[*Id.*] WILLIAM LANCASTER, of Eccleston Hall, deposeth—31st October, 1716—"that for the last two or three years he has been employed by Mrs. Eccleston to collect the rents belonging to Eccleston Hall, and that the tenour of his receipts for the same usually ran sometimes in the name and for the use of Mr. Thomas Eccleston, and at other times for rent due to Eccleston. That he pays the rents to the said Mrs. Eccleston, mother of Thomas E., who now lives there, but never took any receipt of her for the same: that the leases of the estate are signed T. E., but does not know where Thos. E. lives, but saw him at the hall about 2 years ago: that he staid there about three days, but knows not from whence he came or whither he went: that he never saw him before or since: has heard that the said Thomas E. has been at Rome."

. . . .

[*Id.*] *The Com^{rs.} to the Rt. Hon. Robert Walpole.*

A certificate shewing "that upon enquiry they found that THOMAS ECCLESTON of Eccleston, co. Lanc., was seized in fee of an estate at Eccleston to the yearly value of £352, and that being so seized, he about 10th October, 1700, became a Jesuit, and was by such profession and the constitution of the order of Jesuits rendered incapable of holding any messuages, &c. . . . to his own use, but to . . . the use and benefit of the Religious House, College, or Society of Jesuits to which he belonged.

By reason whereof we have found that the said messuages, &c., have been given by operation of law to Popish or superstitious uses. And we hereby certify that Ric. Hitchmough, late of Preston, co. Lanc., but now of Whenby, co. York, clerk, was the discoverer thereof. [20 July, 1723.]"

[H. 37.] *Estate of Albert Hodgson.*
Thomas Fletcher in his "observations on the claims made on the estate of Albert Hodgson," says of Job Alibond (one of the claimants), that he was Procurator-general to the Secular College of English Priests at Douay, and that Thomas Roydon, a priest, received interest of money for the use of the college, and further, that Nevil Ridley, Esq., is a common trustee for most superstitious uses in England.

[I. 13.] RICHARD JENKINSON, of Wyersdale, co. Lanc., yeoman, under his will, dated 15th September, 1696, and proved 6th March, 1700, left to his son Thomas Jenkinson "all his estate at Boulton, which came to him by his father". He names also his wife Alice; his other sons John, Richard, and Christopher Jenkinson; his four das. Mary, Jane, and Eliz. J., and Alice Rickmon, and his uncle John J.

[I. 16.] *Will of Jane Johnson, extract. e Registro Episcopali Cestriæ*, dated 16th March, 1702.
"I, JANE JOHNSON, of the Moorside, within Crosby Magna, co. Lanc., widow . . . desire burial in the parish church of Sephton. . . . Names the following relatives: ' My brother Edward Molyneux, sister Margaret Molyneux, 4 nephews, Edward Molyneux, of Formby, with Dorothy his wife, Richard Molyneux, of Alt Grange, Lawrence Breers, and Roger Breers: 5 nieces, Catherine and Eliz. Breers, Anne Golden, Anne, wife of Gilbert Norris, of Liverpool, and Margaret Smith: cousin Bridget Mercer, of West Derby; also Mr. Robert Breers, of Walton Hall, and William, Mary, and Margaret, the children of Lionel Gore, formerly of Ince Blundell." She concludes . . .
"I make my two trusty friends, Mr. John Golden, of Winwick, and William Tarlton, of Crosby Magna, my executors, hoping they will see my will justly performed. . . . *To them also I leave the residue of my estate, to be disposed of as I shall leave orders by a*

schedule annexed to this my ... Whittle and Margt. Smith. ...

. . . . . .

[I. 17.] ALEXANDER HESKE... that Edward, son of Edward M... veyed by the executors of Mrs. ... father in order to be bred a priest ... as yet prevented therein by warran... of deponent, who is a Justice of the ... caster, and further, that the said Edwa... son to deponent. . . . [1st November, 1...

. . . .

[*Id.*] Chambers Slaughter writes fro... Com^{n.} 15th January, 1716.

". . . I have been discoursing, Mr. Hitc... explanation of goods and money in the hands... of Mrs. Jane Johnson. They went so long sinc... 1702 to prove the will, but because of a sch... they were cited to make oath of ye particular... tained, which they refused, so only administered ... received all. A procter of the Court sent this ... inventory [of furniture, &c.] to one Hayward, by whos... Mr. Hitchmough got it, and assures me further that ... undeniable evidence that the amount of the interest ... schedule is applyed to ye maintenance of ye Popish s... clergy, and remains in these trustees' hands. I enclose y... original that you may make the proper use of it. . . . Justices are very active in convicting the Recusants : the ... shewed me last night a list of above 600, Mr. Clifton bein... first. Sir Nicholas Sherburne might be easily convicted by... Kempe's evidence who was his steward, very strong evide... being now found against this Kempe that would make him h... or meritt. . . . But *nobody will prosecute at their own charges*, the... fore, if the Government does not use some method in that respec... all prosecutions, though the facts be never so plain, must drop. ...

[K. 4.] Papers concerning NICHOLAS KENNETT, of Coxhoe, co. Durham. . . . Mr. Day's information about an estate in cos. York and Durham, given to superstitious uses.

"Rachelfe, an estate worth £800 or £900 per annum, within 9 or 10 miles of York, in Bulmer Hundred, is said to belong to two sisters as co-heiresses, both Roman Catholics, but what their name is none of the tenants can tell, nor where they live. A steward from London comes once or twice a-year to receive ye rents. . . . 'Tis thought ye two sisters are professed Nunns in some Religious House beyond sea.

"Eliz. Kennett, da. to ye late Cuthbert Kennett, and sole heiress of ye said Cuthbert, has an estate at Cocksell [Coxhoe?], in ye bishopric of Durham, of £800 per annum. She has been in a Religious house this 18 years beyond sea. The estate is managed by her uncle Nicholas Kennett. She is not outlawed.

. . . .

"Mary, widow of Nicholas Kennett, of Coxhoe, petitions the Commissioners on behalf of herself and other claimants on the Coxhoe estate, and prays for a delay in the time for hearing their claim.

[K. 1 and 2.] KELLET PAPERS.

"8th November, 1716.

"CHARLES MORETON, of Bolton, co. Lanc., deposes that Robert Kellet married Mary Osbaldeston. Rob. K., outlawed for late rebellion and since dead, is said to have left a leasehold estate in Cuerdale, and is brother-in-law to Edward Osbaldeston. Eliz. Kellet, widow, lives with Edward Osbaldeston, and is mother to Rob. K., the forfeiting person."

[L. 41.] *Papers relating to the estate of John Leyburne.*

Mr. FOOTE, one of the Commissioners, suggests the examination of the marriage settlement of John Leyburne with Lucy, da. of Thomas Dalston, of Hornby Hall, co. Westmoreland. Thomas Fletcher also writes from Carlisle, 15th September, 1718, to Mr. Treby, another of the Commissioners:

"Inclosed I send you some papers relating to some discoveries I have made. . . . I went into Yorkshire and there found out two famous Popish schools, endowed with lands to ye value of £200 per annum and upwards: one goes by the name of Osmotherley and lyes in the North Riding, the other is called Egden [Egton] and lies by the sea-shore, near Whitby.

I could not gett into y* particular of those affairs att that time, so deferred my journey till now. I had also . . . information given me of some lands in Furnesse, in Lancashire, which I was going to see, but was unhappily prevented by a Trick putt upon me by Mr. Curwen and the Papists, the truth of which I shall plainly lye before you. Mr. Curwen is in great fear of being obliged to appear before your Honours this winter in London about y* claims he has entered before you, and he has applyed himself to several great men to get him excused, and he has said to severall (as I shall prove) that if I was to appear again before y^r Honours and went on with y^r business, he was ruined, and all the rest of the Papists likewise. Upon this, knowing me to owe several sums of money, and not having as yet settled my affairs, nor gott my money out of Chancery, Mr. Curwen himself prevailed with one of my creditors to sue me, and snapt me just as I was going upon your business, as I hinted before. The person who sues me has other security, and was very well satisfied, but was prevailed upon as I told you before. Mr. Relfe was the person concerned against me, and he and Mr. Curwen actually promised 50 guineas' reward [to the one] who took me prisoner, so that upon the whole I am now made a sacrifice to y* Rage of a party. I would not have you, Sir . . . believe that I would wrong any person from their just debts, but I would willingly have time to breathe and settle my concerns. . . . I beg the favour you would send to me requiring my attendance before you, and also such precept to the Sheriffe of this county as you shall think proper."

Reminding the Commissioners of their power to do so, he adds: " If I am honoured so far . . . I flatter myself the public will reap advantage by it . . . and the rest of my life shall be devoted to show myself grateful for so great a favour. . . . I humbly ask pardon for this great presumption, *which I had not been guilty of but for ye necessity of my affairs at this juncture.*"

[Thomas Fletcher probably alludes to the suit of the sisters of Sir Henry Fletcher for the recovery of the Hutton estates.]

Three days later he still more urgently begs "to be sent for to appear before the Commissioners on account of y* misfortune I now lye under, purely occasioned by y* spight and malice the

Papists have taken against me ". He encloses a copy of the will of " Thomas Dalston, a Papist, who dyed about August, 1716," whose da. *Lucy* (wrongly named *Dorothy* by Fletcher) married John, the son of George Leyburne ". Fletcher also adds that "when [John] Leyburne was discharged out of the Marshalsea by the Act of Indempnity, he came forthwith to Hornby and resided there, and acted as owner of the place, but was advised to leave it and reside at some other place for [fear of] giving umbrage to the Commissioners ".

. . . .

[*Id.*] JOHN LEYBURNE and his wife LUCY petition the Commissioners on behalf of her claim to Nateby Hall for life that their claim may be heard at *Preston*, "they being so reduced in their circumstances that they are not in any capacity either to attend themselves or be at the charge of bringing witnesses to any place more remote ".

[C. 142.] " The most humble petition of JOHN CROOKE, of Broughton, co. Lanc., husb., now a prisoner in Preston . . . on y{r.} Honours' committment: sheweth,

"That when y{r.} Petitioner was under examination before y{r.} Honours on Wednesday, 2nd July, 1718, touching superstitious uses, hee was under some surprise, being a person of meane capacity and understanding in such cases, and not apprehending the questions then asked him, and is now under a great concern for his confinement, and the expense and inconvenience that may attend him and his poor wife and 6 children therein: prays to be re-examined".

This petition was evidently granted, for on 17th July, 1718, he deposed that he "had heard George Crook, a reputed Romish priest, say prayers after the Romish way".

. . . .

This George Crook [the priest], of Broughton in Amounderness, co. Lanc., gent., in his will, dated 7th December, 1705, names his kinsman John Crooke, and his cousins James Catterall, Alice Parkinson, and her son and da. John and Eliz. Parkinson.

[M. 14.] MOLYNEUX PAPERS.

21st July, 1718.

THOMAS GOLDEN, of Hardshaw Hall, saith that "he is sole

executor of his father John Golden, who was one of the executors of Mrs. Jane Johnson, who left £300 for the education of two boys, who were sent to school, and that one of them, Edward Smith, is a ship carpenter at Liverpoole, the other was Edward, son of Edward Molyneux".

To this paper are attached three receipts given to the executors of Mrs. Johnson by Edward Molyneux and Margaret Wodson [Widdowson] "for the scooling, use, and education" of their respective sons Edward Molyneux and Richard Smith.

[S. 2.] HENRY WISWALL to Chambers Slaughter, Esq.
"Ormskirk, 19th July, 1717.

"Sir,—Ere this reaches hope you have had a kind welcome with your lady and family, and a pleasant journey to 'em by reason of such brave settled weather as't has been ever since you left us. Yesterday Mr. Tyrer was pulling down an old house in the lordship of Scarisbrick, a tenement the late estate of Mr. Scarisbrick, and in the wall was found £40 in brave old money. It's kept as secret as possible, yet a person that saw it came and told me. I take it to be Treasure Trove, and if it does not fall under the cognizance of your Commissioners, it must belong to the King, so pray advise about it. . . ."

This letter called forth a very speedy reply, which see *Eng. Cath. Nonj.*, p. 364.

[T. 55.] TOWNELEY PAPERS.

Letter from RICHARD TOWNELEY, dated Rochdale, 12th February, 1716, to Mr. Ric. Starky, at his Chambers in Furnival's Inn, Holborn:

"Sir,—Yours rec^d, and must beg youl not fail going as soon as you receive this to the Commissioners and acquaint them that Thomas Hilton come this day alonge with an atorney and two bailiffs and tooke forcible possession. I desire they will give me orders per the first what I shall do, for the threaten to sell the small goods I have procured for the poor children, and throw them out of doors within a few days. D^r· S^r·, I beg youl not fail me in this by the very first, and youl for ever oblige your humble servant,

"RICHARD TOWNELEY."

[*Id.*] RIC. TOWNELEY in his petition to the Commissioners says that his "wife, the Hon. Mary T., did not have her summons to appear before them on 1st May until 16th April: that she is now at York, and is not in a condition to undertake so long a journey without prejudice to her health and danger of her life. . . ."

This petition was received 19th April, 1718, but the hearing of the claim was only postponed for twelve days.

[T. 32.] Letter from JOHN AYNSLEY, of Hexham, to Mr. Charles Sanderson. [31st December, 1716.]

". . . I am sure what you have said for me is true. I always hated the Popish Principles and all the adherents of the Pretender. I have dayly prayed for a defeat of all their devices against our holy religion and constitution, and was always thoroughly convinced if that party succeeded I and my family and all true Protestants were utterly ruined and undone. And as you give me reason to believe, I stand cleare with these gentlemen from being deemed an enemy to my king and country. . . ."

This Mr. Aynsley was solicitor to Mr. Thornton, of Netherwitton, whom he names in this letter as " my very good client ".

[G. 22.] " WILLIAM BRING [Brining], of the par. of Woodplumpton, co. Lanc., labourer, saith that within that parish there is a Popishe chappell with a small piece of land belonging to it, called Kendal's chappel. The owner of it calls himself at this time John Kendal, but his true name is John Baines, which this informant well knows, ye said Baines (now Kendal) being born and bred up to ye state of a man within the parish aforesaid. He further saith that the said Baines is hid, being a Popish priest as he believes, and doubts not to prove, himself and son having at different times heard him preach, and says one Anne Gregson lives at a little house in ye end of ye said chappel.

" Further, that Baines, *alias* Kendal, did about 3 years ago purchase of William Haddock, Esq., in the name of James Gregson, brother of the said Anne, an outhousing with six acres of land or thereabouts in Cotham, within Preston parish, and that John Gregson their father now dwells in the premises, James Gregson being now outlawed for high treason.

". . . Further . . . that within the parish of Woodplumpton, or the next adjoining parish, is another Popish chapel called Crowhoe, which is a very goodly house endowed with about 20 acres of land as he guesses. The priest who did lately officiate therein is called John Swarbrick, now hid likewise, and that one Mrs. Craichley now or very lately dwelled therein. [3rd September, 1716.]"

INDEX.

NOTE.—*References to the same name do not necessarily indicate the same person. The word "family" has been sometimes employed for the sake of brevity, and merely implies that several persons bearing the same surname occur on the given page.*

ACTON family, 74
  ,, William, 21, 74
Adams, Christopher, 9
  ,, Mary, 39
Adys, Bernard, 20, 49
  ,, Edmund, iv, 20
  ,, Martha, 49
Allaway, Mary, 59
Allibone, Job, 141, 151
Almond, James, 89
Anderton, Francis, 83, 84
  ,, James, 83
  ,, Lady Margaret, 83, 84
  ,, Mary, 84
  ,, Sir Francis, 83, 97, 121
  ,, Sir Laurence, 83, 84
Armstrong, Elizabeth, 38
  ,, John, 120
Arran, Charles, Lord, 56
Arras, Bishop of, vii, 131-133
Arton family, 10
Arundel, Anne, Lady, 56
  ,, Philip, Lord, 56
Arundell, Frances, 8, 12
  ,, Henry, Lord, 73
  ,, Hon. Henry, 37, 72
  ,, Hon. Thomas, 37
  ,, John, 12
  ,, Mary, 8, 33
  ,, Richard, 8
Ashmall, Robert, 23
Ashton, Elizabeth, 31
  ,, Thomas, 31

Askins, Mary, 34
Aspinwall, James, 148
  ,, John, 148
  ,, Richard, 148
Aston, —— (Trentham), 72
  ,, family, 22
  ,, Margaret, 23
  ,, Walter, Lord, iv, 22, 23
Atmore, Magdalen, 70
Atton, Mrs. (Pigott), 17
Atwood, Audrey, 52
  ,, Bridget, 74
  ,, Christopher, xv, 74
  ,, George, 109, 110, 113
  ,, Mary, 74
  ,, Robert, 52
  ,, Sarah, 74
  ,, Thomas, 74
  ,, Ursula, 74
  ,, William, 74, 110
  ,, Winifrid, 111
Auben, Frances, 52
Aubrey, Sophia, 76
  ,, Thomas, 76
Audeley, Mary, 71
Avelin, Anne, 68
  ,, Elizabeth, 68
  ,, James, 68
Ayleworth, Elizabeth, 42
  ,, Hannah, 42
  ,, John, 42
Aylmer, William, 94
Aylward, Anastatia J., 4, 8

Aylward, Helene, 4
Aynsley, John, 157

BACKHOUSE, Thomas, 139
Bagnal, Lady, 68
Baines, John, 157
„ William, xi, 97
Baker, ——, 42, 149
„ Henry, 42
Baladine, Teresa, 38
Baldwin, Edward, 72
„ Elizabeth, 72
„ Mary, 72
Baltimore, *see* Calvert
Banks, Joseph, 118, 119
Barker, Ann, 79
„ John, 22, 79
„ Mary, 22
Barlow, Lady, 44
„ Mr., 122
Barnwell, Mary, 50
Barrett, Robert, 147
Barrimore, James, Lord, 127
Bartlett, Anne, 38, 75
„ Basil, 38, 75
„ Bridget, 75
„ Mrs., 18
„ Rowland, 75
Baskerville, ——, 58
„ Edward, 21
„ family, 70
„ James, 51, 70
„ Mary, 21, 51
„ Mrs. (Adys), 20
„ Mr., 112
Bates, ——, 128
Batson, John, 5
Battersby, Tobias, 81
Baughan, Elizabeth, 72
„ John, 72
Bawcock, Elizabeth, 22
„ Mary, 22
Bawd, Hieronyma, 42, 44
„ William, 42
Beadnell, Thomas, 143
Beard, Henrietta, Lady, iv, 13, 16, 17
„ John, iv, 16
Becke, Thomas, 117
Bedingfield, Dorothy, 76, 77

Bedingfield, Edward, 83
„ Frances, 76
„ Henry, 64
„ Mary, 64
„ Mr., 108
„ Sir Henry, 25, 83
Belchier, Jane, 43
„ Thomas, 42, 43
„ Ursula, 43
Bellasis family, 80
Bennett, William, 100
Benoist, Elizabeth, 41
Berington, Edward, xv
„ family, 21, 52
„ John, 1, 21, 121
„ Thomas, 52
„ William, 52, 74
Berkeley, John, 75
„ Judith, 75
„ Mary, 73, 75
Berriman, Mr., 112
Berry, Catherine, 42
„ Robert, 42
Bertie, Hon. Charles, 7
Betham, ——, 17
„ Frances, 2
„ John, 2
„ Mary, 2, 17, 71
„ Richard, 71
„ Thomas, 2
Beveridge, Catherine, 11
„ George, xv, 11
„ Gertrude, 11
Bickliffe, Alice, 27
„ family, 27
Biddulph, Eliz. (Lady Dormer), 5
„ family, 62, 68
„ Francis, 5, 62, 68
„ John, 62, 68
„ Richard, 5, 62, 68
Bigg, Dorothy, 4
„ Lucy, 4
Biggs, Thomas, 58
Bill, John, 9
„ Robert, 9
Billing family, 3
„ Robert, 3
Binge, Mary, 17
Bingley, Hannah, 77

Bird family, 41
„ Francis, xv, 41
Bishop, Elizabeth, 12
„ family, 20
„ Frances, 20, 75
„ Francis, 33
„ George, 33
„ Richard, 20, 75
Blackmore, Thomas, 53
Blacoe, James, 96
Blake, Charles, 38
„ family, 38
„ James, 23
Bland, John, 134
Blevin, Helena, 50
Blofield, Thomas, 27
Blood, —— (Trentham), 72
Bloore, Elizabeth, 19
„ Richard, 19
Blount, Catherine, 76
„ family, 3, 50
„ George, 76
„ Michael, 50
„ William, 3
Blundell, Alexander, 148
„ family, 84
„ Frances, 27, 84
„ Mary, 48
„ Mr., 105
„ Nicholas, 27
Bodenham, Catherine, 22
„ Charles, 15, 21, 22, 43, 51
„ family, 22
„ Mary, 22
Bolney, Elizabeth, 60
„ George, 60
„ James, 60
Bond family, 35, 41, 65
„ Henry Jermyn, 35, 65
„ Mary, 35, 64
„ Sir Henry, 41
„ Thomas, 35
„ William, 31
Bostock, Anne, 52, 66
„ Catherine, 47, 52
„ Elizabeth, 52
„ family, 52
„ Henry, 20, 47, 52
„ John, 52, 66

Bostock, Mary, 47, 52
„ Nathaniel, 47, 52, 66
„ Richard, iv, 20, 47
Boswell, Mrs. (Morley), 29
Boswicke, Edward, 98
Boucher, Margaret, 113
Bourne, Philippa, 58
Bowen, Mrs. (Pigott), 17
Bowes, Alice, 130
„ Johanna, 37
„ Lucy, 130
„ Margaret, 130
„ Mary, 130
„ Stanislaus, xv, 37
Box, Mary, 76
„ Philip, 76
Brand, Christian, 1
„ Margaret, 1
„ Mary, 1
„ Peter, xv, 1
„ Petronilla, 1
„ Susan, 1
„ Winifred, 1
Brandon family, 10
„ Richard, 19
„ Thomas, 10, 19
Brand-Trevor (Dacre), Anne, 56
Branthwait, Arthur, 141
Breers, Bridget, 136
„ Catherine, 121, 151
„ family, 136, 151
„ Laurence, 121, 151
„ Robert, 136, 151
Brent, Catherine, 10, 18
„ Elizabeth, 18
„ Frances, 3
„ Margaret, 17, 18, 81
„ Mary, 18
„ Robert, 3
Brett, Mr., 112
„ Thomas, xiii
Briggs, Elizabeth, 27
Brinkhurst, Catherine, 50
„ John, 50
Brining, William, 105, 106, 157
Brockholes, John, 97
„ Thomas, 95, 121
Bromley, Amy, 16
„ John, 16

Brooke, Francis, vi, 106, 113
Brooks, Esq., 127
Brown, Edward, 25
„ Francis, 25
„ Laurence, 25
Browne, Anne, 35
„ Daniel, 34
„ family, 34, 66, 69
„ Honora, 66
„ John, 34, 140
„ Mr., 10
„ Mark, 66, 69
„ "Misses," 13
„ Rev. Charles, 15
„ Thomas, 30, 88, 89
Brownlow, Elizabeth, 39
„ Sir John, 39
„ William, 39
Brudenell, Caroline, 48
„ Hon. James, 48
„ Mrs., 127
Bruning, Anne, 61
„ family, 60, 61
„ Richard, 60
Bryant, Mary, 64
Buckley, Judith, 31
Burdet, Edward, 11
Burgh, Fych, 20
Burnham, Dorcas, 6
„ Richard, 6
„ Robert, 6
Burton, Catherine, 40
„ Robert, 40
Busby, Charles, 17, 71
„ Constantia, 17, 71
„ Dorothy, 9
„ Hannah, 17, 71
„ John, 17, 71
„ Mary, 71
„ Thomas, 28, 112
Butler, Catherine, 138
„ Elizabeth, 77
„ Frances, 37
„ Francis, 139
„ Henry, x, 136, 139
„ James, 139
„ Nicholas, 139
„ Magdalen, 139
„ Mary, 137, 138, 139

Butler, Richard, vi, 136-139
Byfield, Catherine, 61
„ John, 61

CADOGAN, Henry, 42
„ Roger, 42
Calvert, Anne, 31
„ Charles (Lord Baltimore), xv
„ family, 38
„ Margaret (Lady Baltimore), 38
„ Mary Ann, 33
Cam, Morris, 29
„ Winifred, 29
Cann, Edward, 57
Canning, Ann, 51, 71
„ Appollonia, 71
„ family, 17, 71
„ Francis, 17, 51, 71
„ Richard, 17, 71, 111
„ Thomas, 63
Cantril, Bruno, 132
Carew, Henry, 73
„ Mary, 73
Carington, Constantia, 14
„ Francis, 72
„ Mary, 72
„ Mary-Teresa, 72
Carne family, 57
„ Francis, 57
„ Mary, 57
Carns, Catherine, 36
Carr, Thomas, 95
Carroll, Charles, 96
Carter, Catherine, 11
„ George, 132
„ Thomas, 120
Cary, Edward, 11
„ family, 43
„ George, 11, 15
Caryl, Catherine, 17
„ Edward, 17
„ Elizabeth, 17
„ Philip, 68
Cassey, Anne, 18, 75
„ Mary, 18
Casy, ——, 63
Castlehaven, Eliz., Lady, 37, 45
Catanach family, 27

INDEX.

Catherine, Queen, 11
Cattaway, Alice, 59
  ,,   Elizabeth, 59
  ,,   Margaret, 59
Catterall, James, 155
Cawthorn, Mr., 137
Chaddock, Mr., 85
Chadwick, Mary, 4
Chafin, George, 12
  ,,   Rachel, 13
Challence, Mr. (alias of Bp. Challoner), 23
Challiner, Elizabeth, 46
Challoner, Bp. Richard, 18, 23, 81
Champion, Anne, 73
  ,,   family, 73
  ,,   Joan, 73
  ,,   Mary, 73
  ,,   Thomas, 73
Chapman, Frances, 15
Charles II., 10, 78
Charleton, Edward, 22
  ,,   William, x, 22, 115
Charnley, Peter, 100
Cheseldine, Sarah, 34
Chevalier de S. George, x
Chewton, Lord, 16
Chichester, Catharine, 7
  ,,   Mary, 7
  ,,   Prudence, 43
Cholmley, Catherine, 69
  ,,   Thomas, 69
Christmas, Mary, 80
Clapcoate, Dorothy, 6, 59
  ,,   Elizabeth, 59
  ,,   family, 59
  ,,   Mary, 59
  ,,   Richard, 59
  ,,   Winifred, 6, 59
Clarke, Thomas, 94
Clarkson, Christopher, 84
Clavering family, 80
  ,,   John, 49
  ,,   Mary, 49, 80
  ,,   Ralph, 49, 80
Clayton, Elizabeth, 52
  ,,   family, 52
  ,,   Isabella, 28
  ,,   Ralph, 52, 81

Clayton, Richard, 3, 28
Clement X., Pope, 63
Clifford, Alethea, 53
  ,,   Anne, Lady, 11
  ,,   Hugh, Lord, 11
Clifton, Charles, 4
  ,,   family, 45, 87, 100
  ,,   Francis, 4, 22
  ,,   George, 45, 87, 101
  ,,   "Master," 100
  ,,   Sir Gervase, 45
  ,,   Thomas, 87, 89, 100, 152
Clough, Ann, 52
  ,,   Elizabeth, 52
  ,,   Richard, 13
Cockayne, Hon. Eliz., 77
  ,,   Hon. Mary, 77
Coffin, Bridget, 15
  ,,   Charles, 4, 71
  ,,   Francis, 4
  ,,   Martha, 15
  ,,   Mary, 15
Cole, Christian, 117
Colegrave, ——, 140
  ,,   Barbara, 14
  ,,   family, 14
  ,,   Frances, 14
  ,,   Mary, 14
  ,,   William, 14
Coleman, Thomas, 58
Collett family, 4
  ,,   Mary, 4
Collingwood, Anne, 81
  ,,   Catherine, 101
  ,,   Charles, 101, 102
  ,,   George, 101, 102
  ,,   John, 81
  ,,   Robert, 101, 102
  ,,   William, 101
Collins, Christopher, 24
  ,,   family, 24
Colstock, Anne, 61
Colstone, Dame Anne, 47
Combe, Dr. Edward, Rev., 74
Compton, Anne, 33
  ,,   Dorothy, 33
  ,,   Edward, 33
  ,,   Margaret, 33
  ,,   Richard, 39

Coney, John, 115
Conquest, Benedict, xv, 1, 63
  ,, Charles, 18
  ,, Elizabeth, 1, 18, 71
  ,, family, 1, 44, 113
  ,, Mary, 1
Constable, Cuthbert [see Tunstall]
Constable, Sir Marmaduke, 78
Conyers, Dame Margaret, 65
  ,, Harriet, 65
Cook, Shadrach, xvi
Cooke, Catherine, 23
  ,, John, 23
Cooper, Dorothy, 10
  ,, William, 9, 10
Cope, Thomas, 9
Coppinger, Esq., 20
Corbett, Richard, 53
Cornwall family, 21, 70
  ,, John, 21, 70
Cornwallis, Cæcilia, xiv
  ,, Mary, 25
Cosin, John, xii-xvi, 3, 19, 26, 29, 35, 141
  ,, James, 141
Cottam, Mary, 123
Cottington, Catherine, 58, 73
  ,, Francis, 58, 73
  ,, John, 58
Cotton family, 87
  ,, Maria Teresa, 52
  ,, Richard, 83, 84
Couche, Anne, 8
  ,, family, 8
  ,, Richard, 8
Cown, Mary, 44
  ,, Robert, 44
Cox, Alicia, 50
  ,, Gabriel, 50
  ,, Samuel, 50
Coxon, Elizabeth, 32
  ,, Mary, 32
  ,, William, 32
Coyney, John, 75
Craichley, Mrs., 158
Crane, Mary, 35
Crawford, Anne, 28
  ,, John, 28
Craythorne, Hon. Elizabeth, 77

Cromblehome, William, 144
Crook, George, 155
  ,, John, viii, 155
Crouch, Elizabeth, 4
  ,, Stonor, 4
Croucher, Ann, 69
  ,, Francis, 67
  ,, Ralph, 67
Croxall, Philippa, 44
  ,, Rev. Dr., 44
Cruse, Gaynor, 73
Cuffaud, Henry, 39
Culcheth family, 26
  ,, John, 17, 26
  ,, Mary, 17, 26
  ,, Roger, 26
  ,, Thomas, 17, 26
Curwen, Henry, 79, 137, 154
  ,, Magdalen, 79
Curzon, Henry, xv
  ,, Peter, 50
  ,, Sir Francis, 50
  ,, Winifred, 50
Cutler family, 77, 78
  ,, Grace, 78
  ,, Henry, 77, 78
  ,, Magdalen, 78
  ,, Sir Thomas, 78

DACRE, Lord, 56
Dacres, Elizabeth, 48
Dally, Jane, 39
  ,, Mary, 39
Dalston, Dorothy, 155
  ,, Lucy, 153, 155
  ,, Thomas, 153, 155
Dalton, Dorothy, 143
  ,, Elizabeth, 77
  ,, John, 97
  ,, Robert, 77, 143
Danby, Mr., 81
Dancastle family, 4, 15
  ,, John, 4, 8, 15, 51
  ,, Thomas, 4, 15
Dandy, Daniel, 150
  ,, Dorothy, 120, 139
  ,, Ellen, 121
  ,, Jane, 121, 139
  ,, John, 121

INDEX. 165

Dandy, Margaret, 121, 139
Daniel, Barbara, 16
Darbyshire family, 25
  „   John, 25
Darell family, 25
  „   John, 25
Davers, Sir Robert, 35
Davies, Thomas, 43
  „ Winifred, 43
Day, Mr., 152
De Grammont, Count, iv, 56
  „   Countess, iv, 56
  „   Claude-Charlotte, 56
De la Fontaine, Agnes, 36
  „   family, 36
De la Rose, Anne, 61
  „   William, 61
Derwentwater, Anna-Maria, Lady, v, x, 8, 9, 26, 104
  „   family, 64, 102, 104, 117
  „   Francis, Lord, 103, 137, 143
  „   James, Lord, 6, 86, 98, 102, 103, 104, 114, 138, 147
  „   Mary, Lady, 104
Desbrowe, Jane, 59
  „   Samuel, 59
D'Ewes, Mary, 65
  „   Henrietta, 65
  „   Merelina, 65
Devall, Henry, 47
  „ Mary, 47
Dicconson, Edward, 119, 120
  „   Hugh, 119, 120
  „   Roger, 119, 120
  „   William, 119, 120
Digby, Dorothy, 111, 113
  „   John, 111
Dillon, Grace, 57
  „   Mr., 57
Dixwell, Lady, 80
  „   Sir Basil, 80
Dobson, Andrew, 100
Dod, William, 115
Dolman, Robert, 27
Dormer, Charles, Lord, 5
  „   Eliz., Lady, iv, 5, 62
  „   family, 5, 60, 62

Dormer, Frances, 5, 16
  „   John, 5, 60
  „   Mary, 5
  „   Robert, 5, 6
Dorson, Mary, 34
Doughty, Elizabeth, 39
  „   family, 39
  „   Frances, 39
  „   George Brownlow, 39, 50
  „   Mary, 39
  „   Philip, 39
Dover, Lord, 35
Draycot, Philip, 127
Dreisdale, Hugh, 123
Dresser, Thomas, 125
Drew, Frances, 48
  „   Thomas, 48
Dunbar, Dorothy, Lady, iv, 48
  „   Lord, 48
Dunne, Elizabeth, 66

Eales family, 20, 21
  „   John, 20
Eastham, James, 146, 147
Easton, Dorothy, 57
  „   John, 57
Eaves, Helen, 140
Eccleston, Eleanor, 149, 150
  „   Henry, 149
  „   Thomas, viii, 26, 149, 150
Edney, ——, 18
Edwards, Rebecca, 60
Egerton, Mary, 123
Elizabeth, Queen, ix
Ellerker, Elizabeth, 30, 77
  „   family, 77
  „   Hannah, 77
  „   Sarah, 77
  „   Thomas, 30, 77
Elliott family, 17, 71
  „   Humphrey, 17, 71
Ellis, Bp., 107
  „   Elizabeth, 68
  „   family, 68
  „   Jane, 70
  „   John, 68
Elstob, Mr., 137
Elwes, Merelina, 65
  „   Richard, 65

England, Elizabeth, 16
,, Roger, 16
Englefield, Catherine, 5
,, family, 72
,, Henry, 5, 72
Errington, Charles, 49
,, family, 49
,, Frances, 39, 49
,, George, 49
,, Mr., 142
,, Nicholas, 30, 80
Estcourt, Canon, Rev., xvi
Eure, Ann, 15, 30
,, Edward, 15, 30
,, Charlotte, 30, 79
,, family, 30
,, Ralph, 15, 30
Evans, Elizabeth, 105
Eycott family, 19
,, John, 19
,, Thomas, 19
Eyles, Sir John, 129
Eyre, Anne, 52, 66
,, family, 48
,, Henry, 11, 83, 108, 128, 129, 130, 131
,, James, 11
,, John, 11, 47
,, Vincent, 44, 66
Eyston, Charles, iii, 2, 3, 61
,, family, 3
,, Mary, 22
,, Robert, 3
,, Winifred, 2, 3, 61

FAIRBROTHER, Percy, 10
Fairfax, Charles, Lord, 77
,, Helena, 116
,, Mary, 77
Fane, Hon. Jane, 48
Farine, Matthew, 68
Fauconberg, Thomas, Lord, 80, 127
Fenwick, Elizabeth, 49
Feria, Duchess of, 48
Fermor family, 6, 50
,, Henry, 50, 51
,, James, 6, 50, 51
Ferrers, Edward, 71
Ferrers, Teresa, 71

Fetherstonhaugh, W., 100
Fielding, Catherine, 73
,, Sarah, 73
,, Ursula, 73
Finch, Anne, 76
,, Francis, 76
Fincham family, 61
,, John, 61
Fisher, Augustine, 59
,, Bishop, iv, 3
,, Elizabeth, 6
,, family, 59
,, John, 6
Fishwick, Edmund, 105
Fitzgerald, Archdeacon, xvi
,, Rebecca, 74
,, Richard, 74
Fitzhenry, Ann, 66
Fitzherbert, Basil, xv, xvi, 8, 61, 108
,, Constance, 30
,, Jane, 61
,, Thomas, 30, 61
,, William, 9
,, Winifrid, 61
Fitzwilliam, Anne, 29
,, Elizabeth, 29
,, family, 29, 30
,, Frances, 29
,, Jane, 39
,, John, 29
,, William, 29, 44
Flatman, Frances, 36
Fleetwood, Mr., 112
,, Philippa, Lady, 53
Fletcher, Catherine, 130
,, Harry, 130
,, John, 130
,, Marcus, 130
,, Sir Henry, vi, vii, 108, 128-134, 138, 154
,, Thomas, vi., vii.. 93, 128-135, 137, 138, 141, 151-155
Floyd, Mr., 112
,, Robert, 100
Foote, Francis, 116, 124, 153
Ford, Mary, 48
,, Thomas, 89
Fortescue, Charles, 27, 58
,, Dame Mary, 22, 45

Fortescue family, 27, 58
,, John, 70
,, Nicholas, 132
,, Sir Francis, 22, 45
Foster, Catherine, 138
,, General, 98
,, Mary, 79
,, Thomas, 138
Fowler, Dorothy, 63
,, family, 63
,, Walter, iv, 63
,, William, 63
Fox, Frances, 59
Frankland, Hugh, 19
,, William, 13
,, Winifrid, 13
Fraser, Ann, 79
,, John, 112
,, Mary, 39, 79
,, Thomas, 79, 112
Freeman, Robert, 70
Fretwell, Joseph, 10
Fryer, Sir John, 129
Fuller, Mr., 24
Furnace, Elizabeth, 77

GAGE, Delarivière, 65
,, Edmund, 26
,, Elizabeth, 16, 65
,, family, 16, 64, 65
,, John, 16, 64
,, Penelope, 64
,, Sir William, 64, 65, 67
,, Thomas, 16, 64
Galloway, Elizabeth, 76
,, Mary, 76
Gandy, Henry, xvi
Garter, Julia, 48
,, Robert, 48
Gascoigne, Catherine, 80
,, Dame Magdalen, 79
,, Elizabeth, 80
,, Mary, 80
,, Nelly, 80
,, Sir Edward, 79
Gaubrin, M., 119
Gavan, Thomas, 112
Gaydon, Lady, 50
Gazaigne, Elizabeth, 39

Gazaigne, Frances, 39
,, family, 39, 40
,, Mary, 39, 40
Geeres, Mrs. (Winford), 110
Gentil, Ayme, 23
,, Catherine, 23
,, family, 23
,, John, 23
,, Margaret, 23
Gerard, Lady Mary, iv, 63
,, Lady Mary-Clare, 38
,, Sir Thomas, 38
,, Sir William, 90, 126, 128
,, Thomas, 126, 127
Gerrard, Joseph, 121
Gibbons, Mrs., 15, 48
Gibson, Francis, 112
,, George, 120
,, Thomas, 120
,, William, vi, 113, 114
Giffard, Bonaventura, x, 71, 107, 112
,, Frances, 8
,, Mary, 34, 63
,, Sir John, 8
,, Thomas, 63
Gildon, Joseph, 59
Gillibrand, John 84, 140
Gilpin, ——, 128
Girlington, John, 139
,, Magdalen, 139
Goble, Richard, 67
Golden, Anne, 151
,, John, 151, 156
,, Thomas, 124, 155
Golding, Dame Winifred, 73
Goldney, Ann, 58
Gomeldon, Meliora, 25
,, Richard, 25
,, Thomas, 25
Gore family, 151
,, Lionel, 151
,, Mrs., 58
Goring, Lady Dorothy, 54, 68
,, Sir William, 62, 68
Gosling, John, 42
Gower, Hawkins, 24
,, Helen, 62, 75
,, John, 62
,, William, 62, 75

Gowland, Ralph, 103
Graby, Bridgit, 45
,, Jane, 45
Gradwell, Christopher, 136, 147
Gray, Dorcas, 6
,, Joseph, 6
Greathead, Edward, 27
Green, Anne, 57
,, Dorothy, 57
,, Elizabeth, 58
,, Gabriel, 57, 58
,, John, 18, 57
,, Margaret, 57
,, Mary, 18
,, Mrs., 21
,, Thomas, 21, 53, 96
Greenhalgh, Mr., 88
Greensmith, Anthony, 9
,, Ignatius, 9
,, Laurence, 9
Greenwood, Ann, 19, 51, 71
,, Charles, 51, 71
,, family, 18, 19
,, Margaret, 18
,, Mary, 51, 71
,, Thomas, 51
Gregg, Captain, 121
Gregson, Anne, 157
,, James, 157, 158
,, John, 158
,, William, 84
Griffin, Joseph, 21, 70
,, Mary, 21, 70
,, Teresa, 70
,, Winifred, 70
Griffith, ——, 72
,, Anne, 75
,, James, 75, 112
Grimbalston, Alice, 27
,, Elizabeth, 27
,, family, 27
,, John, 26
Grimes, Mrs., 45
Grimstone, Charles, 130, 132
Grove, Dorothy, 63
,, family 63,
,, Rebecca, 74
,, Thomas, 63, 74
Grubb, Dorothy, 19

Gudgeon, Richard, 147
Guest, Mary, 57
Guldeford, Dame Clare, 36
,, Sarah, 36
Gunter family, 41
,, Hester, 22
,, James, 22
,, Robert, 41

HACCHER, Eliz., Lady, 56
Haddock, William, 157
Haggerston, Sir Carnaby, 78
Halcott, Matthew, 48
Hall, Jasper, 143
,, Mr., 113
Halliwell, William, 147
Hammerton, Anne, 31
,, Anthony, 111
,, Catherine, 111, 113
,, family, 111
,, James, 31
,, John, 111, 112
,, Judith, 31
Hammond, ——, 77
,, Gervase, 77
Hancock, Alice, 3
,, Edward, 3
,, William, 3
Hanford, Dorothy, 37, 111
,, Edward, 37, 74
,, Frances, 37, 74
,, Robert, 74
Hankin, Dorothy, 49
,, John, 49
Hanne, Bridget, 66
,, Frances, 12
,, John, 12
Harbord, Grace, 39
,, William, 39
Harcourt, Judith, 47
,, Lucy, 47
,, Vere, 47
Harles, Mr., 75
Harnage, Anne, 81
,, Richard, 81
Harper, Joseph, 21, 76
,, Robert, 21
,, Thomas, 21
Harris, Elizabeth, 69

INDEX. 169

Harris, Margaret, 69
 ,,   Martha, 69
Harrison, John, 85
 ,,   Mary, 91
 ,,   Nicholas, 9
 ,,   Richard, 9
 ,,   William, 90, 91
Harston, Thomas, 10
Hart, John, 96
Hassall, Anne, 55
 ,,   Appollonia, 55
 ,,   family, 55
 ,,   Frances, 55
 ,,   Mary-Magdalen, 55
 ,,   William, 55
Hastings, Anne, 25
 ,,   Christiana, 113
 ,,   Dorothy, 79, 111, 113
 ,,   family, 111
 ,,   Ferdinando, 79, 111, 113
 ,,   George, 25
Hatcher, Grace, 39
 ,,   Thomas, 39
Havers, John, 64
 ,,   Henrietta, 65
 ,,   Mary, 5, 64
 ,,   Thomas, 64, 65
 ,,   William, 64
Hawarden, Edward, 55
Hawett, Mrs., 89
 ,,   Richard, 89
Hawkins, John, 24
 ,,   Thomas, iv, 24
Hayhurst, William, 140
Hayward, ——, 152
Heath, Ann, 64, 66, 69
 ,,   John, 66
 ,,   Richard, 64
Henchknowle, Lord, 80
Heneage family, 30, 31
 ,,   George, 30, 31
 ,,   Thomas, 22, 30, 31
Herbert, Lord Edward, 16
 ,,   family, 21, 42
 ,,   Lady Henrietta, 16
 ,,   Lady Lucy, 68
 ,,   William, 21
 ,,   Winifred, 21, 42
Herron, Dorothy, 130

Hesketh, Alexander, 152
 ,,   Dr., 121
 ,,   Margaret, 121
 ,,   Thomas, 136
Heskin, John, 140
 ,,   Thomas, 140
Heveningham, Bridgit, 45
 ,,   Elizabeth, 45
 ,,   family, 45, 63
Hickin, Anne, vii, 14, 61
 ,,   Mary, 14, 61
 ,,   Thomas, vii, 61, 127-132
Higford, Frances, 19
 ,,   William, 19
Higgins, Caleb, 55
 ,,   Mary, 55
Hilder, Valentine, 35
Hills family, 38
 ,,   John, 38
Hilton, Thomas, 156
Hinderson, Anne, 70
Hine, Elizabeth, 59
 ,,   George, 59
 ,,   Mary, 59
Hinton, Mary, 40
Hitchmough, Richard, vi, 89, 121-126, 141, 151, 152
Hockley, William, 71
Hodgkinson, Anne, 140
Hodgson, Albert, 97, 151
 ,,   Catherine, 10
 ,,   Elizabeth, 10
 ,,   Mary, 10
 ,,   William, 75
Hoffman, Mary, 37
Hoghton, Sir Henry, 88, 92, 93, 138, 146
Holcroft, Henry, 16
Holford, Constantia, 14
 ,,   Peter, 14
Holman, Mary, 48
 ,,   William, 48
Holne, John, 126
 ,,   Richard, 126
Honywood, General, 83
Hood, Ann, 10
Horncastle, family, 79
Hornsby, Percival, 129, 130, 132
Hornyold, Anthony, 74

Hornyold, Bridget, 74
,, family, 74
,, Frances, 74
,, John, 17, 74
,, Ralph, 74
Horton, Joseph, 23
Hoskins, Bridget, 81
,, Elizabeth, 81
Hotham, Sir Charles, 123
Howard, Bernard, 45, 78
,, Charles, 8, 45, 56, 78
,, Elizabeth, 8, 46
,, family, 8, 45
,, Frances, 8, 33
,, Henry, 8, 45, 78, 89
,, Henry-Charles, 8
,, Mary, 8, 25
,, Philip, 8, 45, 78
,, Thomas, 8, 45, 78, 137
,, Winifred, 45, 50
Howes, Mr., 112
,, Mrs. (Digby), 111
Howell, Ann, 75
Howse, Ann, 6
,, Charles, 5, 76
,, family, 76
,, Frances, 5, 76
,, John Temple, 76
Huddleston, Catherine, 22
,, Mary, 22
Hulme, Richard, 122
Humberston, Henry, 112
Hungate family, 77
,, Lady Mary, 77
,, William, 77
Hunloke family, 11
,, Sir Windsor, 11, 30
Hunt, Brace, 75
,, Edward, 75
Hunter, James, 148
Hussey family, 11, 12
,, Giles, iv, 11, 48
,, John, iv, 11, 12, 48, 57
,, Rebecca, 12
Hutten, John, 55
,, Mary-Magdalen, 55
Hyde family, 4, 50, 71
,, Francis, 4, 71
,, Mary, 4, 50, 71

Ince, John, 123, 124
Ingleby, Columbus, 128
,, Sir Charles, xv, 78, 108
,, Thomas, 78
Ingleton, Dr. John, x
Ireland, Charles, 64
,, Elizabeth, 52
,, Thomas, 52

Jackson, Dick, 124
,, Francis, 10
,, Mr., 102
James II., King, 5, 14, 121, 137
,, III., King, xi, 98, 145
,, John, 58
,, Samuel, 58
,, William, 58
Jenison, Mr., 102
Jenkins family, 31
,, Thomas, 31
Jenkinson, Alice, 151
,, family, 151
,, Richard, 151
Jenks, Robert, 36
Jennings, Lucy, 28
,, Mary, 28
Jernegan, Elizabeth, 16
,, family, 46
,, George, 46, 61, 81
,, Lady, 6
,, Lady Margaret, 19
,, Sir Francis, 46
,, Sir John, 19
,, Thomas, 16
Jerningham, Mr., 35
Jessop, Benjamin, 32
John, Anne, 8
Johnson, Barbara, 16
,, Frances, 55
,, Jane, 126, 151, 152, 156
,, Richard, 55
Jones, Aurelius, 40
,, Catherine, 41, 43, 44
,, Elizabeth, 43
,, family, 41, 42
,, George, 43
,, John, 21, 41, 42
,, Mary, 40
,, Matthew, 42

Jones, Thomas, 43
,, Winifred, 43

KELLETT, Elizabeth, 153
,, Mary, 153
,, Robert, 121, 153
Kelly, Elizabeth, 36
,, John, 73
Kemble, Dr., 112
Kemp, Anthony, 67
,, Hon. Barbara, 67
,, Hon. Jane, 67
Kempe, George, 145-147, 152
Kendal, John, 157
Kennett, Cuthbert, 153
,, Elizabeth, 153
,, Mary, 153
,, Nicholas, 152, 153
Kerington, Elizabeth, 16
,, James, 16
Kersey, Mary, 25
Kettle, Richard, 76
Kibbel, Elizabeth, 57
Kilby, Ann, 50
,, Robert, 50
King, ——, 72
,, Appollonia, 55
,, family, 55
,, William, 55, 59
Kingsley, Anne, 25
,, family, 24, 25
,, George, iv, 24
Kinnaird, Lord, 67
Kinnes, Charles, 27
,, Thomas, 27
Kippen, John, 60
Kirby, Henrietta, 79
,, Mr., x
,, Robert, 79
Kitchen, Edward, 84
Knatchball, Mary, 18
Knight family, 27, 28
,, Lucy, 27
,, Margaret 28, 35
,, William, 27
Knipe, Bridget, 73
,, Edward, 32, 73
,, family, 73
,, George, 73

Knipe, John, 12, 73
,, Thomas, 73
Knottisford, Bridget, 70
,, family, 70
,, Teresa, 70
Knowles, Catherine, 113

LACON, Mary, 10
,, Richard, 53, 71
,, Rowland, 53
Lacy family, 12, 52
,, Margaret, 12
Lamb, Seth, xvi
Lambert, Cuthbert, 117
Lamport, C., 113
Lancaster, William, 150
Lane, Elizabeth, 59
,, family, 36, 49
,, Mary, 36
,, William, 36
Langdale, Dorothy, 120
,, family, 57, 62
,, Jordan, 120
,, Joseph, 28
,, Marmaduke, Lord, 62, 64
,, Mary, 28, 58
,, Philip, 120
Langhorne, Catherine, 40
,, Charles, 16
,, Lætitia, 16, 40
,, Richard, 16, 43
Langley, Gilbert, 18
,, Holdenby, 18
,, James, 18
Langworth family, 34
,, Mary, 34
,, Robert, 34
Laurance, Elizabeth, 64
Laurence, Helena, 48
,, Samuel, 48
Lea, Elizabeth, 70
Lee, Margaret, 36, 37
,, Richard, 36, 37
Leeremans, James, 68
,, John, 68
,, Sarah, 67
Leigh, Francis, 97, 98
,, Peter, 97
Le Maitre, Rev. C., 15

Le Noir, Elizabeth, 41
" Simon, 41
Lenoxe, "Aunt," 52
Leonard, Thomas Barrett, 40
Levery, Flora, 70
Levison, Edward, 112
Lewes, Anne, 73, 74
" William, 73, 74
Lewkenor, Anthony, 66, 67
" Edmund, 66
Leyburne, George, 155
" John, 97, 153, 155
" Lucy, 153, 155
Lichfield, George, Earl of, 8
Lindsey, Lady Elizabeth, 6
" ——, 68
Littlehales, Mary, 10
" Samuel, 53
Lloyd, Anne, 67
" John, 73
Lodge, Christopher, 49
" ——, 128
Lomax, John, 62
Longville, Frances, 35
Loup, George, 112
" William, 31
Loraine, William, 115
Lorimer, Michael, 21, 41
Lovell, William, 4
Lowe, Anne, 55
" Arthur, 55
" Charles, 10
" Elizabeth, 52
" family, 10, 55
" John, 16
" Mary, 10, 16, 55
Lunt, John, 10
Luttrell, Mary, 69
Lynch, Peter, 64
Lytcot, Dame Anne, 20
" Elizabeth, 20
" Robert Brent, 18, 20
Lyttleton, Mary, 53

MACKRELL family, 12
" John, 12
Macnamara, Honora, 40
Maire, John, 39, 49, 75
Malbon, Robert, 67

Manby family, 15, 71
" Sir Thomas, 15, 71
Mandeville, Bridget, 73
" George, 73
" John, 73, 139
Manning, Robert, 55
Mannock family, 65
" John, 112
" Lady, 66
" Mary, 39, 64, 65
" Mr., 24
" Sir Francis, 65
" Teresa, 65
" Thomas, 39, 64, 65
Mansergh, John, 134
Markham, Anne, iv, 29
" Edward, 44
" family, 29
" George, 1, 44
" Mary, 1, 35
" Percy, 29, 30, 44, 65
" Thomas, 29, 35
" Ursula (Pole), 29
Marsden, Jane, 121, 139
" James, 121
Marsh, Nathan, 144
Martin, Catherine, 16, 66
" Dorothy, 32
" John, 66
" Margaret, 16
Mary, Queen, 5
Mary, Queen of Scots, iv, 56
Massey, Catherine, 121
" William, 95, 121, 130
Mason, John, 145, 147
Mastin, Catherine, 32
" Robert, 34
" Samuel, 32
" Troth, 31, 32
" William, 34
Matson, "Goody," 24
Matthews, Catherine, 65
" John, 140
Maughan, Jonathan, 94
Maurice, Thomas, 55
Maxwell, Mungo, 68
" Robert, 68
" Sir George, 68
Mayfield, John, 87, 100

Mercer, Bridget, 151
Merry, Ann, 33
,, Elizabeth, 62
Metcalfe, Christopher, 102
,, Peter, 32
,, Thomas, 102
Metham, Catherine, 77
,, Jordan, 77
Micham, Mary Ann, 74
,, Rachel, 74
Michel, Mary, 60
Middlemore, Mrs. (Culcheth), 26
Middleton, Charles, 48
,, Helena, 77
,, Lord John, 48
,, Lady, 48
,, Mary, 77
Migliorucci, Count, 28
,, family, 28
,, Mary, 28, 65
Millington family, 35
,, Jane, 30
,, John, 30, 35
,, William, 35
Milnhouse, Basil, 9
,, Gregory, 9
,, Richard, 10
Minshull, Anne, 76
,, Catherine, iv, 76
,, Mary, 6, 76
,, Richard, 76
,, William, 76
Mitchill, Thomas, 18
Mole, John, 9
Molins, John, 57
,, Mary, 57
Molony, Bishop, 40
,, Daniel, 40
,, Dennis, 40
,, Honora, 40
Molyneux, Ann, 49
,, Bridget, 49
,, Edward, 126, 151, 152, 156
,, Elizabeth, 49
,, family, 127, 151
,, Hon. Richard, 122
,, Hon. Mrs., 36
,, Jane, 151
,, Lady, 48

Molyneux, Robert, 90, 127
,, Thomas, 88, 146
,, William, 127
,, Sir William, viii, 26, 86, 89, 90, 92
Mompesson, Elizabeth, 80
Monington, Anne, 58
,, Edward, 58
,, Thomas, 21
Monson, Edward, 30
,, Elizabeth, 30
,, George, 30
Montague, Barbara, Lady, 13
,, Dowager Duchess of, 88
,, Henry, Lord, 101
,, Viscountess, 64
Moore, Ann, 62
,, Dame Anastatia Jane, 4, 8
,, family, 4
,, Sir Richard, 8
,, William, 4, 85, 88, 90, 91, 95, 141, 143
,, ——, 84
Mooring, Edward, 4
,, Mary, 4
Mordaunt, Barbara, 14
More, Anne, 81
,, Bridget, 81
,, family, 81
,, Zachary S., 81
Moren, Elizabeth, 40
,, family, 40
Moreton, Charles, 153
Morey, Major, 61
,, Mrs. (Hickin), 61
Morgan, George, 43
,, James, 72
,, Kimbarow, 44
Morley family, 29
,, John, 29
,, Marmaduke, 29
Morphew, James, 10
Mosdell family, 7
,, Longueville, 7
Moss, Richard, 148
,, William, 148
Mostyn family, 17
,, Frances, 17, 44
,, Hieronyma, 44

Mostyn, Sir Pyers, 17, 44, 99, 100
  ,, Thomas, 17, 44
NAIRNE, M., x
Napier, ——, 65
Needham, Anne, 42
  ,, Charles, 20, 42, 43
  ,, Elizabeth, 43
  ,, family, 42, 43
  ,, John, 20, 42, 43
  ,, Lucy, 42
  ,, Robert, iv, 20, 21, 42, 43, 44
  ,, Susan, 42, 43
  ,, Ursula, 43
Nevill, Charles, 44
  ,, Cosmas, 44
  ,, Frances, 65
  ,, Henry, 65
  ,, Lady Mary, 28
  ,, Mr., 95
  ,, Thomas, 65
Newport, John, 22
  ,, Mary, 22
Nisdale, Winifred, Lady, 26
Norfolk, Edward, Duke of, 45
  ,, Thomas, Duke of, x, 89
Norris, Anne, 47, 151
  ,, Gilbert, 151
  ,, Jeremy, 46, 47
  ,, Mary, 47
  ,, Teresa, 47
Northampton, Earl of, 33
Northey, Sir Edward, 133
Novills, Mrs. (Fincham), 61

OGLE, William, 117
O'Hara, Anna-Maria, 12
  ,, Charlotte, 12
Oldacre, John, 9
  ,, Thomas, 10
O'Neil, Dame Frances, 49
Ord family, 94
  ,, Lancelot, 94
Orrell, Henry, 148
  ,, Humphrey, 121, 124
Osbaldeston, Edward, 153
  ,, Mary, 153
Osborne, Thomas, 33
Overbury, Thomas, 75

PAIN, Bridget, 72
Palin, Thomas, 21
Palmer, Catherine, 7
  ,, family, 9
Panket, Charles, 95
Panton, Dorothy, 36
  ,, family, 37
Parker, Charles, 15
  ,, Edmund, 31
  ,, Mary, 19
  ,, Martha, 19
  ,, Mr., 6
  ,, Robert, 15
Parkinson, Alice, 155
  ,, Elizabeth, 155
  ,, John, 155
Parry, Thomas, 99, 100
Paston, Catherine, 20, 47
  ,, family, 19, 20
  ,, Frances, 20
  ,, John, 19
Pattison family, 80
  ,, Joseph, 80
Payne, Thomas, 140
Pearse, Nathaniel, 140
Pegg, Charles, 10
  ,, George, 10
Pell, Mary, 47
Pemberton, Hugh, 22
Penderel family, 20
  ,, John, 20
  ,, Richard, xv, 20
  ,, Thomas, xv
Pengelly, Thomas, 102, 103, 141
Pennant, Peter, 99, 100
Penne, Elizabeth, 12
  ,, family, 12
  ,, George, 12
Pennythorn, Mrs. (Knight), 28
  ,, Peter, 27
Penson, Catherine, 51
  ,, family, 51
  ,, Thomas, 51, 61, 62, 132
Peploe, Samuel, 85
Pepper, Richard, xv
Percy, Elizabeth, 37
  ,, William, 37
Perkins family, 1, 2
  ,, Francis, 1

INDEX. 175

Perkins, ——, 3
Petre, Anne, 71, 111
　,, 　Anne, Lady, 13, 26
　,, 　Benjamin, Bp., 23, 39, 71, 81, 104
　,, 　Bridget, 70
　,, 　family, 14
　,, 　Francis, 14, 15
　,, 　George, 70
　,, 　Joseph, 14, 61
　,, 　Lady Mary, 14
　,, 　Laurence, 70
　,, 　Mary, 14, 61, 71
　,, 　William, 14
Peyton, Lady, 80
Phillips, Teresa, 17
Philpot, Edward, 42
　,, 　Hannah, 42
Pickering, Thomas, 5
Piercy, Mr., 112
Pigott, Catherine, 17
　,, 　family, 17
　,, 　Nathaniel, xv, 17, 18, 70, 71, 108
　,, 　Rebecca, 17, 71
Pinkard, George, 43
　,, 　Robert, 43
　,, 　Susan, 43
Plowden, Cotton, 68
　,, 　Dorothy, 68
　,, 　family, 5, 53, 61, 68
　,, 　Frances, 5, 54, 61
　,, 　John Trevanion, 55, 68
　,, 　Mary, 5, 53, 61, 68
　,, 　Penelope, 54
　,, 　William, iv, 5, 53, 54, 55, 68
Plowman, Ambrose, 59
　,, 　family, 59
Plumton, Elizabeth, 80
Pole, Cardinal, iv, 11
　,, 　family, 10
　,, 　Francis, iv, 10
　,, 　John, iv, 10
　,, 　Ursula, 10, 29
Poole, Edward, 121
　,, 　family, 7
　,, 　Francis, v, 7
Porter family, 30
　,, 　Mary, iv, 30

Portland, Duke of, 128
Poston, Elizabeth, 15
Potts, John, 137
　,, 　Peter, 117
Powell, James, 42
Powtrell, Mary, 17
Prescott, Geoffrey, 140
Price, Ursula, 6
Prichard, Catherine, 22
　,, 　family, 42
　,, 　John, 42
Progers, Catherine, 42, 44
　,, 　Edward, 42, 44
　,, 　Elizabeth, 42, 44
　,, 　family, 42, 44
　,, 　Frances, iv, 44
　,, 　Hieronyma, 42, 44
　,, 　William, 44
Prujean, Elizabeth, 35
　,, 　family, 35, 36, 70
　,, 　Francis, iv, 35, 70
　,, 　John, 39
Pulton family, 48
　,, 　Ferdinand, xv, 48
　,, 　Julia, 48
Purcell, Ann, 39, 61
　,, 　Catherine, 53, 61
　,, 　Dr. John, v, 51, 61, 62
　,, 　Elizabeth, 39
　,, 　family, 51, 52
　,, 　Mary, 51
　,, 　Richard, xv, 109, 110, 113
　,, 　Thomas, 51, 52, 53, 62
　,, 　Winifred, 51, 52
Pye, Anne, 21, 42
　,, 　Charles, 42
　,, 　Elizabeth, 75

QUIN, William, 30

RACKETT, Elizabeth, 37
Radcliffe, Anna Maria, Lady, 8, 104
　,, 　Ann, Lady, 64
　,, 　Catherine, Lady, viii, 49, 103
　,, 　Colonel, 102
　,, 　Elizabeth, Lady, viii, 103
　,, 　Hon. Barbara, 67
　,, 　Hon. James Bartholomew, 67

Radcliffe, John, 103, 104
,, Mary, Lady, 102, 103, 132
,, Thomas, 102
Ramsay, Margaret, 142
Randle, Leo, 112
Rayment, Thomas, 1
,, William, 1
Reeve family, 70
,, John, 70
,, Mrs. (Culcheth), 26
Reilly, Anne, 47
Relfe, Mr., 154
Remington, Mary, 63
Reyley, Jane, 27
,, Owen, 27
,, Robert, 27
Reynes, Anne, 81
,, Thomas, 81
Reynolds, John, 49
Reynoldson, Susannah, 76
Rich, Elizabeth, 58
,, Francis, 37
,, Richard, 37
,, Samuel, 58
Richardson, Mary, 88
Richmond, Duchess of, 23
Rickmon, Alice, 151
Riddell, Dorothy, 143
,, Dr., 142
,, Edward, 143
,, Elizabeth, 148
,, George, 142
,, Thomas, 143
Ridley, Nevil, 151
Rigmaiden, Anne, 28
,, Bennet, 19
,, Francis, 28
Risdon, Francis, 50
Rishton, Thomas, 144
Rivers, John, Lord, 127
Roberts, Anne, 66
,, Mr., 66, 99, 100
,, Mrs. (Lewkenor), 66
Robinson, John, 32
,, Mary, 32
Robotham, *see* Rowbotham
Robson, Matthew, 114
Rokeby, James, 46
Rooke, Elizabeth, 6

Rooke, James, 104
,, John, 6
,, Lady Mary, 104
,, Robert, 6
Rookwood, Elizabeth, 16
,, family, 16
,, Thomas, 16
Roper, Anne, 40
,, John, xv
,, Thomas, 112
Rouge, John, 41
,, Mary, 41
Rous, John, 38
,, Mary, 37, 38
,, Sarah, 38
,, Thomas, xv
Rowbotham, Ann, 38
,, Elizabeth, 37
,, Francis, xv, 67
,, John, 38
,, Sarah, 67
Rowe, Elizabeth, 43
,, John, 57
,, Prudence, 43, 57
,, Robert, 43, 57
Rowt, Ann, 69
,, family, 68, 69
,, Mary, 68
,, Richard, 68, 69
Roydon, Thomas, 128, 151
Russell, John, 51
,, Martin, 112
,, Thomas, 112
Rutherford, Magdalen, 78

SADLEIR, Mrs., 22
Sadler, John-Vaughan, 70
Salkeld, Thomas, 137
Sallom, John, 89
Salter, ——, 135
Saltmarsh family, 81
,, Gerard, 81, 140
Salvin, Anne, 81
,, William, 81
Sanders, Amy, 28
,, John, 28
Sanderson, Charles, 157
,, Elizabeth, 8
,, James, 100

INDEX.

Sanderson, John, 100
,, Nicholas, 100
Sands family, 70
Sandys, Joseph, 80
,, Mary, 80
Santini, Mgr., x
Saunders, Elizabeth, 50
,, Walter, 50
,, William, 44
Savage, John, 127
Savery, John, 14
Scarisbrick, Mr., 156
Scarisbrook, Robert, 26
Scott, William, 26, 144, 145, 146
Scudamore family, 21, 22
,, George, 21, 43
,, Henry, 21, 22, 42
,, Lucy, 42
,, Winifred, 21, 42
Seagrave, Margaret, 3
Seaman, Mary, 47
,, Thomas, 47
Sedgwick, William, 101
Shaftoe, Edward, vi, 147, 148
,, Elizabeth, 148
,, family, 148
,, William, 148
Shaw, Edward, 5
,, Mr., 87
Sheldon, Edward, 75
,, family, 75
,, Mary, 15, 75
,, William, 15, 75
Shelton family, 45
Shepherd, William, 90, 91
,, John, 18, 136
Sheppard, Richard, 147
,, William, 105, 106
Sherburne, Catherine, Dame, 26
,, Charles, 47
,, John, 144
,, Richard, 144
,, Sir Nicholas, xi, xii, 26, 86, 95, 105, 145-147, 152
,, ———, 132
Sherlock, Thomas, 9
Sherwood, Anne, 3
,, Edward, 3
Shewell, John, 19

Short, Catherine, 32
,, Francis, 59
,, George, 34
,, Margaret, 59, 60
,, Sarah, 77
,, Thomas, 77
,, William, 59
Shuttleworth family, 33, 34
,, Richard, 33, 89
,, Thomas, 33, 34
Sidall, William, 124
Simeon, Margaret, 13
,, Sir Edward, 63
,, Sir James, 13
Simpson, Edward, 14
,, Elizabeth, 31
,, family, 31
,, Frances, 14
,, George, 31
,, William, 31
Singleton, James, 98
Skelton, Barbara, Lady, 40
Slaney, Frances, 54
Slator, John, 9
Slaughter, Bellingham, 21
,, Chambers, viii, 92, 98, 101, 138, 141, 152, 156
Slauter, Anthony, 18
,, Mary, 18
Smalbone, Charles, xv, 40
,, Elizabeth, 4, 22
,, Margaret, 4, 22, 40
,, Mary, 4
Smalley, ———, 77
Smith, Amy, 28
,, Anne, 32, 52, 57
,, Audrey, 52
,, Bartholomew, 59, 60
,, Catherine, 28, 30
,, Charles, 72
,, Christopher, 32
,, Edmund, 28
,, Edward, 28, 84, 156
,, Elizabeth, 18, 22, 52, 59, 60, 68
,, family, 28, 52, 59, 60
,, Frances, 59, 60
,, Francis, 28, 30, 52
,, Grace, 78

Smith, Helena, 28
,, Isabella, 28, 59, 60
,, John, 7, 22, 34, 57, 75
,, Margaret, 126, 151, 152
,, Mary, 32, 52
,, Richard, 126, 156
,, Susan, 36
,, Thomas, 9, 60
,, William, 32, 52, 60, 72
Smythe family, 13
,, Sir John, 13
Somerset, Charles, 37
,, Frances, 37
,, Henry, 37
Southcott, Catherine, 30, 31
,, Constance, 30
,, Dame Mary, 30
,, Edmund, 31
,, family, 13, 14
,, Sir Edward, 13, 61
,, Thomas, 61
Sparry, Anne, 70
,, Elizabeth, 70
,, Humphrey, 70
,, Magdalen, 70
Spelman, Clement, 46
,, Dorothy, 46
Spicer, Laurence, 3
Spinckes, Nathaniel, xvi
Spurr family, 31
,, Thomas, 31
Spurrier, Thomas, 70
,, William, 70
Stacey, Edward, xvi
Stafford, Anne, 61, 66
,, Claude-Charlotte, Lady, 56
,, family, 56, 61
,, Henry, Lord, iv, 56
,, John, 52, 56, 61, 66
,, Mary, 56, 61
,, Matthias, Lord, 13, 61
,, William, Lord, 61
Stamp, Thomas, xvi
Standish, Alexander, 25
,, Margaret, 25
,, Ralph, 135
Stanford, John, 112
,, Mary, 2
Stanley, Meliora, 25

Stanley, Thomas, 25
Stapleton, Ann, 16
,, Charlotte, 79, 80
,, family, 30, 49, 79, 80
,, Mary, 49, 80
,, Nicholas, 30, 49, 79, 80
,, Philadelphia, 16, 80
,, Sir Miles, 49, 80
Starky, Richard, 156
Stary, Postern, 70
Steare, Anne, 58
,, Humphrey, 58
,, Robert, 58
Steele, Sir Richard, 106
Steevens family, 29
,, John, 28
,, Winifred, 29
St. George, Richard, 111
Stibbs, George, 57
,, John, 57
Stilles, Edmund, 28
Stoddart, Elizabeth, 73
Stone, Thomas, 37
Stonor family, 50
,, Mary, 53
,, Thomas, 50
,, Winifred, 50
Stourton, Charles, 58
,, family, 57
,, Mary, 58
,, Thomas, Lord, 57
,, William, 57, 63
Strickland, Dame Winifred, 72
,, family, 72
,, Mannock, 15
,, Mary, 15
,, Thomas, 15, 72
Strode, Jane, 12
Strother, Edward, 26
Stubbington, Anne, 59
,, Elizabeth, 66
,, John, 59
,, Thomas, 66
Sulman, Mary, 47
,, Thomas, 47
Sulyard, Edward, 66
,, Elizabeth, 64, 66
,, family, 66
,, Penelope, 64

INDEX.

Sussex, Anne, Lady, 40
Sutton, Mr., 112
,, William, 33
Swan, Lady, 80
Swarbrick, John, 158
Swinburne, Edward, 120, 143, 144
,, Lady Mary, 143
,, Matthew, 50
,, Sir John, 50, 143, 144

TAAFTE, John, 121
Talbot, George, 96
,, Gilbert, 26
,, James, 96
,, John, 145, 146
,, Robert, 115
Tancred, Anne, 34, 79
,, Charles, xv, 34, 39, 79, 142
,, Elizabeth, 79
,, family, 79
,, Frances, 39, 79
,, Henrietta, 79
,, John, 22, 79
,, Mary, 22, 34, 79
,, Thomas, 79
Tarlton, William, 151
Tasburgh, Anne, 38
,, Frances, 65
,, Francis, 38, 65
,, George, 60
,, Henry, xv, 38
,, John, 65
,, Lettis, 60
,, Margaret, 65
,, Mary, 65
,, Mary Clare, 38
,, Susannah, 38
Tattershall, Clement, 11
,, Mary, 11
Taunton family, 56, 57
,, Grace, 56, 57
,, John, 56
,, Thomas, 56
Taylor, Elizabeth, 43
,, Martha, 67, 68
,, Mr., 88
,, William, 43
Tempest, Charles, xv
Teynham, Henry, Lord, 40

Thickness, Mrs. (Bostock), 47
Thimelby, Dorothy, 34
,, Mary, 34
Thomas, Catherine, 44
,, Hugh, 44
,, William, 44
Thompson, Catherine, 58
,, Mary, 70
,, William, 55
Thornton, Anne, 141
,, John, 142, 157
,, Nicholas, 141, 142
Thorold, Dorothy, v, 32, 33
,, George, 32
,, Mary, 32
,, Philadelphia, 25, 81
,, Richard, 32
,, Robert, 32
,, William, 32, 33
Throckmorton, Dame Anne, 71
,, Sir Robert, 6, 26, 71
Tiffin, John, 93
Tilden, George, 38
,, Teresa, 38
Timbrell, Mr., 95
Tootell, Elizabeth, 81
,, Jane, 81
,, John, 81
Tourner, Anne, 67
,, Bernard, xv
,, Elizabeth, 64, 69
,, family, 64, 69
,, John, 64, 67, 69
,, Martha, 67
,, Mary, 64, 69
,, Nicholas, 67, 68, 69
Towneley, Hon. Mary, 116, 157
,, Richard, viii, xv, 87, 97, 116, 156, 157
Townshend, Lord, 88, 114
Trafford, John, 97
Trapps, Henry, 81
Traunter, Mary, 21
,, Thomas, 21
Travor, Elizabeth, 72
,, Thomas, 72
Treby, George, 92, 153
Trelawney, Barbara, 34
Trentham, Winifred, 72

Tresham, Lady, 65
Trinder, Anne, 50
,, Charles, 15, 19, 50
,, Eugenia, 15
,, John, 50
,, Teresa, 19
Tuite family, 27
,, Jane, 27
,, Robert, 27
Tuke, Mary, 19
,, Teresa, 19
Tunstall, Cuthbert, 48, 81
,, family, 81
Turberville, Mr., 40
Turner, Edmund, 28
,, Mr., xv
Twell, Catherine, 36
,, Emerentiana, 36
,, Mary, 36
Tyldesley, Bridget, 66
,, Edward, 87, 97
,, family, 66
,, John, 66
Tyrer, Mr., 156

VANE, Anthony, 35
,, Catherine, 130
,, family, 130, 135
,, Henry-Fletcher, 135
,, Lionel, 130
Van Rose, Mary, 55
,, Mr., 55
Vaughan, Elizabeth, 21, 41
,, family, 21
,, John, iv, 21, 41, 70
Vavasour, Peter, 62, 81
,, Thomas, 62
,, Sir Walter, 62
Velson, Mary, 27

WAGSTAFF, Thomas, xvi
Wainwright, Cutler, 78
,, Jane, 78
Wakeman, Benedict, 19
,, Frances, 19
,, Henry, 19
,, Mary, 55
,, William, 19

Waldegrave, Henrietta, Lady, iv, 15, 16, 64
,, Hon. James, 64
,, James, Lord, iv, 15, 16, 56, 57
,, John, 16
,, Philip, 64
Walker, Charles, 22
Wall, William, 94
Walmesley, Anne, 140
,, Dorothy, 120, 139
,, Elizabeth, 139
,, John, 121
,, Mary, 14
,, Richard, 139, 140
,, Thomas, 140
,, William, 100, 120, 139
Walpole, Dymock, 31, 34
,, Edward, 31, 34
,, family, 34
,, John, 31, 34
,, Mary, 31, 34
,, Robert, 150
Warburton, John, 113, 114
Ward, Edward, viii, 144
Wareing, John, 144, 145, 146
Warren family, 31
,, John, 105
,, Simon, 31
Warwick, John, 137
,, Thomas, 132
Waters, Mary, 1
,, William, 6
Watkins, Charles, 41, 121
,, Frances, 41
,, Mary, 41
Watson, Catherine, 37
,, Mary, 36, 37
,, Thomas, 146
,, William, 36, 37
Webb, Anna Maria, 8, 9
,, Anne, 13, 79
,, Barbara, Lady, 13
,, Edward, xv, 3, 5, 37, 41, 72
,, family, 5, 13, 64
,, Sir John, 9, 13, 49, 80, 114
,, Thomas, 13, 79
,, Winifred, 13
Weedon, Anne, 6

Weld, Edward, 13, 63
,, family, 13, 45, 63
,, Humphrey, 13
,, Margaret, 13
Wells, Frances, 39
,, Henry, 39, 48
Westmoreland, Thomas, Earl of, 48
Weston family, 69
,, John, iv, 69
,, Mary, 69
Whaley, Dr. Thomas, 99
Whalley, Mr., 137
Wharton, Charles, 112
Whetnall, Catherine, 11
Whitaker, Mary, 70
White, Mr., 23
Whitehall, Gilbert, 10, 18, 63
Whitehead, Richard, 96
,, Thomas, 88, 96
Whitgreave family, 62
,, Thomas, 62, 127
Whittle, Richard, 152
Whitworth, Penelope, 54
Wickstead, Anne, 58
,, James, 58
Widdowson, Margaret, 126, 156
,, Thomas, 126
Widdrington, Ann, 49, 71
,, Appollonia, 116
,, family, ix, 49, 71, 115, 118
,, Hon. Elizabeth, 49, 116, 119
,, Lady Jane, 118
,, Mary, 49, 116
,, Peregrine, 117
,, Ralph, 115
,, William, Lord, 116, 117, 118, 119
Wierex, Judith, 38
,, Laurence, 38
Wilcox, Henry, 85
Wilkinson, Mary, 31
,, Perpetua, 136
Williams, Elizabeth, 42
,, Walter, 42
Willoughby, Catherine, 69
Wills, General, 86
Willy, Francis, 78

Wilmott, Mr., 99
,, Mrs. (Winford), 110
Wilson, Mr., 23
Windsor, William, 74
Winford, Catherine, vi, 109, 110, 111, 113, 130
,, family, 110, 111
Winne, Mr., 99
Winstanley, Diana, 26
,, William, 25, 26
Wintour, Dame Frances, 65
Wise, Richard, 3
Wiswall, Henry, 124, 125, 156
Witham, Bp., 107, 127
Wogan, William, 3
Wolfall, Mr., 126
Wollascott, Catherine, 2, 4
,, Edward, 2
,, family, 2, 4, 71
,, Mary, 2, 4
,, William, 2, 4, 71
Wood, John, 9
,, Mary, 9
,, Thomas, 9
Woodington, Peter, 13
Woodrow, Samuel, 24
Woolfe, Frances, 37, 65, 69
,, John, 69
,, William, 37, 65, 69
Woolmer, Anne, 47
,, Brace, 75
,, Charles, 73
,, Francis, 73, 75
,, Mary, 73, 75
,, Philadelphia, 70
,, William, 47
Worthington, Jane, 140
,, Mr., 74
,, Richard, 140
Wright, Anthony, 5, 41
,, Constantia (Carington), 14, 72
,, Elizabeth, 77
,, Eugenia, 15
,, family, 15
,, John, 6, 14, 15
,, Laurence, 15
,, Mary, 1, 15
,, Richard, xv, 48
,, Teresa, 65

Wybarne, Charity, 60
„ Elizabeth, 37, 60
„ Henry, 60
„ John, 37, 60
„ Lettis, 60
Wytham, Thomas, 132

XAVIER, St., 113

YALLOP, Dame Dorothy, 46
„ family, 46
„ Sir Robert, 46

Yate, Appollonia, 113
„ family, 3
„ George, 66
„ John, 3, 25, 39
„ Margaret, 25, 39
Yaxley family, 46
„ Henry, 111, 112
„ Thomas, 140
York, Duke of, 78
Young, Charles, 4, 15
„ Helen, 48
„ Thomas, 48, 122

www.ingramcontent.com/pod-product-compliance
Lightning Source LLC
Chambersburg PA
CBHW020923230426
43666CB00008B/1545